Three Marshals of France

LEADERSHIP AFTER TRAUMA

Three Marshals of France

LEADERSHIP AFTER TRAUMA

Anthony Clayton

BRASSEY'S (UK)
(Member of the Maxwell Macmillan Group)
LONDON · WASHINGTON · NEW YORK

First English edition 1992

UK editorial offices: Brassey's, 50 Fetter Lane, London EC4A 1AA
orders: Purnell Distribution Centre, Paulton, Bristol BS18 5LQ

USA editorial offices: Brassey's, 8000 Westpark Drive, First Floor, McLean, Virginia 22102
orders: Macmillan Publishing Company, Front and Brown Streets, Riverside, NJ 08075

Distributed in North America to booksellers and wholesalers by the Macmillan Publishing Company, N.Y., N.Y.

Library of Congress Cataloging in Publication Data
Available

British Library Cataloguing-in-Publication Data
A catalogue record for this book is available from the British Library

ISBN 0-08-040707-2 Hardcover

Printed in Great Britain by B.P.C.C. Wheatons Ltd., Exeter

I hope this book will interest British readers in the achievements of the French Army under three great commanders and thereby, through understanding, make a small contribution to our new Europe.

Contents

Preface

Leadership is an elusive term to define or describe, as we who try to teach it here at Sandhurst know well. With some, powers of leadership are apparent at an early age, with others not until much later in life, in response to an unexpected call. With a gifted minority, the qualities of leadership are inherent, teaching can only fine tune. With others, the ratio is reversed and careful teaching develops a smaller measure of latent ability to an effective level. But there are only a very few who do not benefit from a study of great leaders.

Such a study is the aim of this book. It is not so much concerned with *matériel* or tactics, as with three generals, Juin, de Lattre de Tassigny and Leclerc de Hauteclocque, who knew technically very well how to use what *matériel* they had – which was often not very much. Attention is therefore focussed upon them as men, human beings, in command and under a particular national stress, and on their personal impact upon events. The basic qualities that make for military leadership are largely the same for any nation at any time. The precise mix of those qualities, however, will vary greatly by nation and period, as this study focussing on three Frenchmen after the *débâcle* of 1940 will show.

Any British author is inevitably tempted to seek British comparisons but they are difficult to make; they may just be permitted to appear in a subjective foreword but not in an objective text. Juin has features in common with Field-Marshal Slim, in particular patient steady generalship in unpromising situations, and the ability to inspire both European and non-European troops. De Lattre's towering personality finds no parallel in the history of the British Army; perhaps only the Royal Navy's Edwardian Admiral, 'Jacky' Fisher, can equal de Lattre in an explosive combination of energy, imagination – and controversy. For Leclerc one must go even further back, to

Cromwell, for dedication, religious devotion and simplicity. But such comparisons should not be taken any further as all three possessed so many characteristics peculiarly French.

These French characteristics, set out in the chapters that follow, were one main reason why this book was so enjoyable to write. The second main reason was the help, advice and support of many, French and British, which it is a pleasure to acknowledge.

I owe a special debt of gratitude and appreciation to Madame la Maréchale de Lattre de Tassigny for her kindness in sending copies of the three published volumes of the Marshal's papers to me, ultimately for the library of the Royal Military Academy Sandhurst.

I owe also a particular debt to Major Ralph Goldsmith for continuously feeding and stimulating my interest in the French Army and providing me with useful material and comments.

Others who have also helped me with ideas or material include Mr A C Adam, Mlle S Bernard, Dr M Brett, Colonel M Corriger, General P Duplay, the Marquess of Lansdowne, Mr N de Lee, Major-General D Lloyd Owen, Dr P Harris, Monsieur J P Jauffret, Mme S Loizillon, Colonel Bastart de Villeneuve and Mr A Zervoudakis.

I am also very grateful for the help of the *Établissement Cinematographique et Photographique des Armées* and of the Trustees and staff of the Imperial War Museum for the photographs with which they provided me and are credited to them.

The Random Century Group very kindly allowed me to quote the description of Marshal de Lattre de Tassigny given by George Mallaby in his *From My Level*, published by Hutchinsons.

I am once more grateful to Mr M F Nicklinson for his preparation of the maps and yet again, I am very specially indebted to Miss M Alexander for wrestling with my manuscript as patiently, accurately and helpfully as she has always done with others over the last twenty years.

At Brassey's, Brigadier Bryan Watkins has been a great help and encouragement with his thoughtful editing. Finally my wife and children have had frequently to tolerate what they, in understatement, describe as my vague moods while I have been at work on this book. They have been enormously understanding.

Royal Military Academy Sandhurst   Anthony Clayton
May 1991.

Biographical Notes

Alphonse Juin

1888:	Born at Bône, (now Annaba), Algeria; schooling in Constantine and Algiers.
1910–12:	Saint Cyr.
1912–14:	Lieutenant, *1er Régiment de Tirailleurs Algériens*, Morocco.
1914–15	Western Front with Moroccan troops; 1915–16 Morocco.
1917–18	Western Front with Moroccan troops; 1918 Staff training; 1919 Morocco.
1919–21:	*École Supérieure de Guerre.*
1921–23:	Staff appointment, Tunisia.
1923–25:	Morocco, major pacification campaign.
1925–27:	Paris, as Military Assistant to Marshal Lyantey.
1927–28:	Regimental service, Constantine.
1928:	Marriage to Mlle Cecile Bonnefoy, of Constantine.
1929–33:	Regimental and Staff appointments in Morocco, major pacification campaigns.
1933–35:	Directing Staff, *École Supérieure de Guerre.*
1935–38:	Regimental command and Staff appointments, Algeria and Morocco.
1938–39:	Higher Command Course, Paris.
1939–40:	Command of *15e Division d'Infanterie Motorisée.*
1940–41:	Prisoner of War, released June 1941.
1941–42:	Commander Land Forces, Morocco, later all Land Forces in French North Africa.
1942–43:	Commander French Army *Détachement*, Tunisia Campaign.

1943–44:	Commander *Corps Expéditionnaire Français*, Italian Campaign.
1944–47:	Chief of Defence Staff.
1947–51:	Resident-General, Morocco.
1951:	Inspector-General of the Armed Forces.
1951–56:	Commander-in-Chief NATO Land Forces, Central Europe.
1952:	Marshal of France
1967:	Died in Paris.

Jean de Lattre de Tassigny

1889:	Born at Mouilleron-en-Pareds, Vendée; schooling in Poitiers and Versailles.
1909–11:	Saint Cyr.
1911–12:	Cavalry School, Saumur.
1912–15:	Lieutenant, *12ᵉ Dragons*, Western Front.
1915–12:	Captain, *93ᵉ Régiment d'Infanterie*, Western Front; 1919–21 *49ᵉ Régiment d'Infanterie*
1921–29:	Morocco, major pacification campaigns.
1927–29:	*École Supérieure de Guerre.*
1927:	Marriage to Mlle Simone Calary de la Mazière.
1928:	Birth of son, Bernard.
1929–39:	Regimental Command and Staff appointments in France; Higher Command Course, Paris.
1940:	January–June: Command of *14ᵉ Division d'Infanterie*.
1940 July–1941:	13th Military District.
1941–42:	Commander French troops in Tunisia.
1942:	16th Military District. Arrested following attempt to oppose German entry into Unoccupied France.
1943:	Sentenced to ten years imprisonment: escape; arrival in United Kingdom.
1943 December:	Commander *Armée B*, later the *1ʳᵉ Armée Française*.
1944–45:	Liberation Campaign, France and Germany.
1945–47:	Inspector-General and Chief of Staff of the Army.
1947–48:	Inspector-General of the Army; later Inspector-General of the Armed Forces.
1948–50:	Commander-in-Chief of Land Forces, Western European Union.

1950–52:	High Commissioner for Indochina and Commander-in-Chief, Far East.
1952:	Died in Paris. Posthumously created a Marshal of France.

Philippe Leclerc de Hauteclocque

1902:	Born at Belloy Chateau in Northern France; schooling in Amiens, Abbeville and Versailles.
1922–24:	Saint Cyr.
1924–25:	Cavalry School, Saumur; Lieutenant, *5ᵉ Régiment de Cuirassiers*.
1925:	Marriage to Mlle Thérèse de Gargan.
1926–31:	Morocco, pacification operations and training appointments.
1931–33:	Instructor, Saint Cyr.
1933–36:	Morocco, pacification operations.
1936–38:	Company Commander, Saint Cyr.
1938–39:	*École Supérieure de Guerre.*
1939–40:	Staff Officer, *4ᵉ Division d'Infanterie.*
1940 July:	Arrival in London to join de Gaulle, assuming name Leclerc.
1940 August–November:	Command of Free French Forces, French Equatorial Africa.
1940 December:	Command of Free French Forces, Chad.
1941:	Command of force that occupied Kufra in Libya; 'Serment de Koufra'.
1942:	Command of Free French force that crossed Sahara from Chad to Tripoli.
1942–43:	Commander *Force L* in Tunisia Campaign.
1943–45:	Commander *2ᵉ Division Blindée* in Liberation Campaign, including entry into Paris.
1945–46:	Commander French Forces. Indochina.
1947:	Inspector of Land Forces, French North Africa.
1947:	Died in an aircraft accident, Colomb-Béchar, Algeria.
1952:	Posthumously created a Marshal of France.

List of Maps

List of Plates

1. General Leclerc and General Montgomery, near Tripoli, January 1943
2. Generals de Gaulle, de Monsabert, Juin and de Lattre de Tassigny, Italy, July 1944
3. General Juin, Italy, 1944
4. Generals Alexander, Clark and Juin, Siena, July 1944
5. General Leclerc, Paris, August 1944
6. General Leclerc, Normandy, August 1944
7. General de Lattre de Tassigny and his son Bernard, South of France, August 1944
8. General Leclerc de Hauteclocque, Ho Chi Minh and Jean Sainteny, Hanoi, March 1946
9. General Juin arriving as Resident-General, Morocco, May 1947
10. General de Lattre de Tassigny arriving at Saigon, December 1950
11. General de Lattre de Tassigny with General Salan and Colonel Beaufre planning the defence of Tonkin, December 1950
12. General de Lattre de Tassigny with Colonel Edon inspecting a recently recaptured Tonkin village, April 1951

1

Introduction

A Marshal of France holds a very special honour, quite different from a British Field-Marshal. The title is as much a national honour as a military rank. In the case of the Third and Fourth Republics, that is France from 1870 to 1940 and 1946 to 1958, the French government had the right to confer the title of Marshal on a living general, but this was to be done following a *proposition de resolution* passed by the legislature; in the case of a posthumous award only the legislature had the right to make such an award. It was an understood condition that any general so proposed must have been victorious in a major battle or campaign. Once the title had been conferred, it could never be withdrawn as such a withdrawal would reflect upon the soldiers who participated in the victory; Pétain was sentenced to national indignity but he remained a Marshal. The title, also, extended to the Marshal's wife, who became *'La Maréchale'*. The honour carried immense prestige until the Pétain régime, which temporarily tarnished its image.

This book is concerned with three outstanding, and very different, French commanders on whom a *maréchalat* was conferred by the Fourth Republic; Alphonse Juin, Jean de Lattre de Tassigny, and Philippe Leclerc de Hauteclocque. All three fought with distinction in the Second World War and served on in important commands in the post-war years. Juin lived to enjoy his *maréchalat*, and embarrass successive governments, for fifteen years after the honour was conferred. The award for de Lattre was under discussion while he was dying but was only conferred after his death. Leclerc's baton was awarded some years after his death. In 1984 the Fifth Republic, in circumstances rather different, created Pierre Koenig a Marshal fourteen years after his death. Koenig, excellent soldier though he was, never carried field command responsibilities of a size comparable to those of Juin, de Lattre or Leclerc. He is therefore not included in this work, which is essentially a study of general officer leadership at and above division level by the first three.

It has of course to be admitted that after the trauma of May–June 1940, the French Army ceased to play the lead role in the land warfare of the Second World War. But even by August 1940, the Free French forces of Charles de Gaulle had begun to play useful contributory roles; these were to become very much more significant from November 1942 onwards. Despite their contributory level, these efforts threw up remarkable examples of personal leadership and tactical skill on the battlefield. The Cartesian, French logical approach could also offer valuable input in decision-making at strategic levels, even if the ultimate decisions lay with others. But the contributory role has, unfortunately, obscured in anglophone writing both these substantial achievements and the very particular posttrauma circumstances in which they were attained. Critics who say that the French Army was only committed against beaten or nearbeaten Axis forces are also far removed from the truth – as any study of the Tunisian, Italian or Alsace campaigns will quickly reveal.

Two wide ranging sets of background conditions need to be outlined before proceeding to a study of our three commanders as individuals. First, what makes a good battlefield general? A general has two tasks, by his professional skills to deploy his forces and what equipment he has at his disposal to win, and next by his personality to motivate his soldiers, perhaps under conditions only describable as hellish, to exceed their own expectations of themselves. But, additionally, in the case of French officers, their daily discharge of both these roles has been far more frequently bedevilled by political implications than was the case with British commanders. One eye had to be kept looking over the shoulder, even in the thickest fighting of both the First and the Second World Wars. Success, too, often brought whispered allegations of political ambition, as befell de Lattre in 1945 and Juin in 1954, in neither case justified. A successful French general has to possess the quality of 'robustness' expounded by Lord Wavell to a remarkable degree.

Second, although armies are corporate structures, and much scholarly writing has concerned institutional views put forward by soldiers at various levels, essentially they are composed of citizens of a particular nation in uniform for varying periods of time. The behaviour of military commanders will reflect some of the characteristics of that nation. As military commanders have authority, perhaps charisma and above all guns, these attitudes can both highlight tensions and divisions within their nation and exaggerate features of the national temperament.

The French are a volatile people, their politics can be those of *passion*, as were for example the politics of Gambetta, Clemenceau and de Gaulle. French creative art, literary, musical or representational also frequently carries the same characteristic. An element of *passion* seems at times also to enter into the style of some French military commanders but not all; there is also the dour style of Trochu, Gallieni and Pétain. There are many examples of *passion* in the Revolutionary and Napoleonic wars. But *passion* has proved an element of generalship that British and American commanders have found difficult. One of its major ingredients is a romantic nationalism. The British Army has not had to fight in or around Canterbury or Perth, or mount an assault from the sea in Torbay. There is an especial edge to romantic nationalism in the defence or liberation of one's own country that is not always understood by others. This work will show how three French commanders, working within the framework of alliances in war and in the post-war era, fought tenaciously for French interests within those alliances, especially when on French soil. Frequently, French interests would be put before those perceived by other allies. In pursuit of these, *passion* in all its forms – guile, tact, charm, temper, flattery, sulks and arrogance, would all be played. On some occasions, these French interests actually served the alliance as a whole better, and not always so by accident.

Another important ingredient of *passion* in French command may be Christian beliefs. The Catholic faith dominated Leclerc's life, it played a great part in the life of de Lattre and only a little less in that of Juin. Leclerc saw his command and campaigns as a Crusade and de Lattre's views were not so very different. More profoundly, *passion* may also be fuelled by the tensions between volatile temperament and a profession requiring order and discipline – tensions which are sparked off by political interference or constraint that appears to frustrate. The political climate in which French generals often have to conduct operations has not infrequently reduced them to despair, rage, dissent and insubordination.

A dimension of understanding of this conflict between external order and internal tension may be found in classical French drama – a justifiable comparison, as French commanders often viewed generalship as an art. Martin Turnell, writing of the French

Seventeenth Century dramatists, noted the turmoil in which spiritual authority was at the time plunged and went on to observe

> The only healthy condition is a regulated tug-of-war. The peculiar vitality of French Literature in the Seventeenth Century lies in a very delicate poise between 'reason' and 'passion', in a sense of tension-and-repose which is quite different from the tension of the English writers and which is the result of an ambivalent attitude towards authority. Authority is not accepted passively. It is accepted-and-resisted, and it is this that gives the literature its life, its high degree of emotional vitality combined with a high degree of order.*

If 'generalship in the 1940s' is substituted for 'literature in the seventeenth century', 'generals' for 'writers' and 'generalship' for 'Literature', the remainder of the comparison stands – as much of this work will very vividly illustrate. The débâcle of 1940 was a trauma in the full meaning of the word, and as a reflex the generalship of Leclerc, Juin and de Lattre all included a distinctive emotional vitality and sense of urgency. One visible consequential manifestation of this *passion* then was excitement, a sense of high drama. De Lattre, spotting an able staff officer in a subordinate's headquarters and wishing to transfer him to his own staff, said to the officer *'Vous allez voir, nous allons faire des choses passionantes'*. Another drama-related indicator, seen in young officers and amply clear in both the early careers and war adventures of our three commanders, is an almost reckless courage and disregard of danger and even wounds. The sense of urgency led both Juin and de Lattre when in command to accept a high casualty rate – the price that had to be paid for the recovery of nation and honour.

A less attractive characteristic of *passion*, but one again very marked in all our three future Marshals was explosive temper, sometimes simulated, with, on occasions, the acting taking over, and sometimes real. The *colères* of both de Lattre and Leclerc sometimes seemed so violent as to be uncontrollable and even Juin, of more natural equanimity, could explode with ferocity. At the height of the German Ardennes offensive in the winter of 1944–45, Juin went to see Eisenhower's Chief of Staff, General Bedell Smith, to secure American protection for the newly-liberated Strasbourg. Juin erupted to such a degree that Bedell Smith later told Eisenhower that had Juin been an American he would have 'socked him on the jaw'. Bad temper and occasional sulks were however often not simply blown away by a *coup de charme* but recompensed by gestures of great generosity – again a very French characteristic. Once again, we may return to

---

* Martin Turnell, *The Classical Moment, Studies of Corneille, Racine and Molière* (London, Hamish Hamilton, 1947), p. 15.

Corneille and the dramatic assertion of the will, or even more to Racine, whose characters explode in passion for one reason or another, at times brutally, but at the same time will possess great attributes of tenderness longing to emerge.

Another theatrical attribute of *passion* in command, to be seen in all three of these commanders, was a more mundane basic communication skill. The French Army's soldiers have always been receptive to stirring Orders of the Day and addresses on the field of battle. All three attached great importance to these, Leclerc's *Serment de Koufra* being a particularly noteworthy example. De Lattre gave especial weight also to his own non-verbal communication – until the very last months of his life, he was always fastidious in turnout and deportment. Juin fought his battles wearing, as did Montgomery, a highly distinctive beret as a personal 'trade-mark'; Leclerc was rarely seen without his special walking stick. De Lattre and Leclerc ensured that their formations wore a distinctive formation badge, by which they too identified themselves and represented the formation. As will be seen later, de Lattre carried his remarkable communication skills into the field of training.

These characteristics of *passion* can be seen at work in the sequence of events following the collapse of June 1940. The decisions to be made following the Armistice and de Gaulle's appeal from London were not simple. Officers were thrown into turmoil by the crisis of authority, with the dangerous consequence of their beginning to sit in judgement on their government, a danger to continue until the early 1960s. Perhaps the easiest immediate decisions lay with those, like Juin, in German prisoner of war camps for whom there was no freedom of choice. Others took the view that France's Army, unlike that of Britain, was of conscripts whose obligation lay in defence of the soil of France; if that defence failed, no obligation to fight on elsewhere should be imposed upon them. Others, with a memory of the 1871 Paris Commune freshened by the internal troubles of France in the 1930s and the atrocities of the Communists in the Spanish Civil War, believed that only an Army licensed by the Germans could prevent a Communist seizure of power in France; to them the humiliating licence was preferable to the Communists. A very large number, including notably Juin, held Pétain and Weygand in high personal regard and believed that discipline and obedience were overriding priorities. These saw de Gaulle as a disobedient and possibly dangerous irrelevance, some even argued that de Gaulle was a tool of the British with whom alliance had been a major policy error.

Some, like de Lattre, sensed intuitively the June 1940 mood –
that of a national collective loss of confidence, brought about by
appeasement, then a war supposedly to support a country which in
fact was not supported, which was followed by eight months corrosive
inaction, that period in its turn being followed by a campaign lost
more by bad leadership than inferiority in men or equipment. De
Lattre believed that recovery must come from within and not without,
the nation's youth being the agent and the Vichy Armistice Army a
means, even if not ideal. A remarkable photograph of a silent de
Lattre, taken at an Armistice Army military parade in 1941 survives;
around him are cheerful chatting Vichy officers, de Lattre's expression
unmistakably reflects his own internal tensions, those of a man sens-
ing himself, to use a favourite Racine word, as *éperdu*, distracted,
distraught. Very few saw de Gaulle as a champion of national
honour, but amongst those who did from the start was Leclerc.

These divisions led them and hundreds of other officers in different
directions. Argument was supported by *passion* in the form of dubious
and partisan logic, scapegoating, and a measure of persecution in, to
use a Freudian term, 'the narcissm of small differences'. The differences were indeed not large. All but a very few were patriots. There
were many similarities of view, for example over the future shape of
the Army, the teachings to be offered to youth, and the importance of
the family as a social unit, between Pétainist and Gaullist officers. But
the vendettas so formed were to last for many years. They are clearly
to be seen in Algeria at the time of the abortive generals' coup of 1961.
Generals of the old *Armée d'Afrique*, who from 1940 to 1942 had
served Vichy, generally tended to support or at least sympathise with
the plotters, but those who had served de Gaulle from 1940 or 1941
remained steadfastly loyal to him.

A final feature of *passion* in command was excess '*La passion ne peut
être belle sans excès*' wrote Pascal, clearly indicating that in this context he extended *passion* to all general emotion. Leclerc and, above
all, de Lattre provide many an example of excess. One interesting
expression of this excess was bursting into tears on occasions of
emotion or grief; the French view British reserve on such occasions as
cold, a consequence of Protestantism. Lyautey had openly wept at the
death of an aide de camp, tears which have led some to speculate,
without either substance or profit, on the relationship. De Lattre burst
into tears quite frequently, most notably at the ending of his long
quarrel with Montgomery. Juin wept over the death of a former aide
de camp in Indochina.

A curious other-side-of-the-coin feature of *passion*, one quite foreign to the British Army, was that it could help an officer's career, de Lattre being a very clear example. In the British Army, such behaviour or attitudes would be condemned as 'prima donna' tendencies. National temperament is the prime cause of this difference, but another cause may well be that a more charismatic style is necessary to motivate an all-conscript army than an all-Regular force.

At a less philosophical level, all three commanders, Juin and de Lattre directly, Leclerc at one remove, owed much to the teachings and example of two great French officers of the first decades of this century, Marshals Lyautey and Foch. Lyautey was France's greatest colonial soldier and proconsul, responsible for both the subjugation of Morocco and the establishment of an enlightened and dignified colonial régime in the territory. Before he appeared on the Moroccan stage, however, he had written very influentially on the social role of the Army officer. He saw this role as extending beyond simple tactical command within regiments on exercise or in action to much wider national and social responsibilities for the moral and physical welfare of soldiers, developing them as responsible and creative citizens. When in command of a regiment, Lyautey had concerned himself with the detail of his troopers' food, dining halls and recreation arrangements, and had expected his officers to follow his example and know their men. He had also tried to make training more interesting, moving away from platitudes to a language and style ordinary conscripts would appreciate. In different circumstances, de Lattre and Leclerc, and Juin to a lesser extent, approached their role as military commanders in a similar way.

Foch, the Allied Generalissimo in the last year of the First World War, argued that the will to win was all important. As in 1870, defeat could result from moral causes, as could victory; de Lattre and Leclerc thought likewise. At the operational level, Foch had taught that defence was best achieved, wherever possible, by attack, a lesson clearly evident in de Lattre's 1944–45 Winter campaigning, and acknowledged by him as deriving from Foch. Leclerc thought the same. Both Leclerc and de Lattre followed Foch's closely reasoned, infinitely carefully prepared, studied and researched, practical approach to problem solving, with imagination as a major contributor. If earlier we have noted a Racine dimension to French generalship, here we may note a Cartesian. Juin used the teachings of Foch to persuade and convince, rather than to try to order, in his dealings with the British and Americans in Tunisia and Italy, again specifically acknowledging his debt. His deployments in Italy reflected Foch's teaching that success could sometimes be obtained by enlarging battles to the flanks rather than looking for a breakthrough. All three Marshals followed Foch's precepts on the value of frequent visits to the front and all three embraced his views on the importance of a commander's personality, will and determination. De Lattre and Leclerc specifically admired Foch's passionate Christian faith and patriotism, which contributed both to an optimism not based on conceit and to a warm understanding of people of all levels of society. All three agreed with Foch on the need for a commander occasionally to intervene in the direction of some quite local but key operation.

Morocco taught all three commanders many lessons in warfare and the most important of those for each individual will appear in the chapters that follow. One general but not immediately evident lesson does, however, merit mention here. Any form of colonial warfare taught improvisation; the clearest French example is the genius of Gallieni in the defence of Paris in 1914. The Moroccan experience of the 1920s and 1930s taught lessons of improvisation well learnt by Juin in using whatever he could lay his hands on in Tunisia and Italy, by Leclerc in his improvised and re-improvised logistic transport arrangements, and by de Lattre when faced with problems as varied as equipping the French Forces of the Interior Resistance Groups or preparing a bridge across the Rhine.

Readers may also need to be reminded of the structures of France's ground forces in the lifetimes of these three commanders. The main metropolitan French Army was composed of regiments of conscripts. These served only in France (and after 1945 in Germany) unless they volunteered to serve elsewhere; to compel them to serve elsewhere required special legislation. The *Armée d'Afrique*, a term in general use to describe a formation that in fact had no separate legal status, garrisoned French North Africa, Morocco, Algeria and Tunisia and, in the 1930s, France as well. Some of its regiments were of Europeans, conscripts from the local *colon* population and from France, or, in the case of the *Légion Etrangére*, volunteers from almost anywhere; other regiments were made up of locally recruited or drafted indigenous Maghreb men with substantial French cadres. These cadre personnel could serve all or a part of their lives with the *Armée d'Afrique*. Finally there was also *La Coloniale*, an autonomous military organisation akin in some respects to the United States Marine Corps. *La Coloniale* was formed originally as part of the Navy for the defence of

French naval ports – indeed, its original title, to which the Force returned after the end of Empire, was *Troupes de Marine*. Its main role from the mid-19th Century onwards was the acquisition and later the garrisoning of French colonies other than the three Maghreb territories. *La Coloniale* consisted of infantry and artillery regiments composed of long service French regular volunteers, supplemented on occasions by a few volunteer conscripts from France, and also draftees from the old pre-Revolution French colonies, mainly Caribbean. But *La Coloniale* also controlled and provided all the cadres for the regiments raised in the Colonial Empire, of which the *Tirailleurs Sénégalais* drawn, despite its name, from a number of Black African territories, was by far the most numerous and important.

De Lattre was a metropolitan officer who served one tour of duty in Morocco with the *Armée d'Afrique* for the experience and excitement. He neither served in North Africa prior to 1914 nor again until 1941. Leclerc began his career as an elite metropolitan cavalry officer who also twice served, for the excitement, in Morocco. But the events of 1940 pushed him into the far from fashionable *Coloniale* whose anchor badge he then wore proudly in Chad. Born in Algeria, Juin was an *Armée d'Afrique* officer who, by choice, only served outside North Africa in time of peace while attending courses or on the staff of Lyautey. Other factors of course played their parts but it is only possible fully to understand Juin's refusals to serve in Indochina in this context. Indochina was traditionally a *Coloniale* not an *Armée d'Afrique* commitment and Juin was, in his own words, a 'Soldat d'Afrique'.

Finally – and sadly – the careers of all three ended tragically. Leclerc died early in an aircraft accident, a little later one of his sons was killed in Indochina in a war Leclerc had tried hard to avert. De Lattre had to face the loss of his much loved and only son in Indochina, dying himself of cancer some six months later. Juin lived on, to watch the collapse of French rule in North Africa, the disbandment of the *Armée d'Afrique* regiments in which he had served and which he had led in war, and the return to France from Algeria of over a million of his fellow French *colons* amid terror and destitution.

2

The formative years: General Juin, General de Lattre de Tassigny, Captain de Hauteclocque

The oldest of our three future Marshals, and the one to reach the most senior appointment in the French Army was Marshal Juin. Juin's early years and pre-1939 career were so very unusual, and his formative experiences were to have such significant implications for the future, that they require full specific description.

Alphonse Juin

Alphonse Pierre Juin was almost the last of the traditional *généraux d'Afrique*: he was also a man of very humble origin. The Juin family were originally from the Vendée, where the future Marshal's grandfather was a simple road foreman of the commune of Saint Denis in the canton of Champdeniers; like his famous grandson he was named Alphonse. This Alphonse Juin's son, Victor, was an infantry soldier who served for most of his fifteen years' service in Algeria; at the end of that service he became a gendarme. A little earlier, Victor had married Précieuse Salini, the daughter of another infantry soldier who transferred to the gendarmerie. The Salini family had moved to Algeria from an inland mountain village, Ucciani, in Corsica.

From both his father's and his mother's family, therefore, the young Juin learnt little of Paris or of the cultures and lifestyles of urban France. His cultural background was of the country, of forests, rivers, hills and above all the Algeria that had united the two families. The magnificent scenery of Algeria, mountain grandeur, rivers, rocks and ravines, open plain and rich farmland was for the young Juin his native land, his home from his earliest days. Algeria was also where his father won his *Médaille Militaire*, a success that gave him status above that of an ordinary infantry NCO, and was later to be the spark for ambition in the boy.

Juin was born on 16 December 1888 at Bône (now Annaba) where his father served in the local *brigade* of gendarmerie. He was the only son of his parents; his father evidently spoke and treated him somewhat brusquely. But from the gendarme's tempered, disciplined character the boy derived the strong sense of duty and integrity which, marred by only a few blemishes, characterised his life. His mother gave him both affection and understanding together with much good advice. From the peasant stock of both his parents' families Alphonse inherited vigour and robust health; he became by temperament both adventurous and imaginative. But as a small child he was also irascible and noisy, disturbing his parents' neighbours. This led his mother to leave him with her own parents for long periods, a practice that lasted for the boy's long summer holidays until he was sixteen. Salini, by that time, had left the gendarmerie to become a lighthouse keeper on the remote Cap Rosa. The coastal scenery with the open sea, creeks, beaches, rocks, streams, cork-oak woods and oleanders, the chirping of cicadas and the beating of waves on the shore wove its spell, binding the boy, usually alone, closer to Algeria. Alphonse learnt to sail a boat and to hunt. On one occasion he found himself face to face with one of Algeria's last panthers; he stood still and the panther slipped away. From his grandparents he learnt more of France's military conquest of Algeria and of how the two shores of the Mediterranean were but river banks. Both sides were France, that part lying on the northern bank was called the Metropole. The young Juin also made his first acquaintance with indigenous Algerians, ordinary shepherds.

When Juin was six, his father was posted to Constantine, an ancient Algerian city surrounded by hills and gorges. Here he entered a primary school run on old-fashioned but very efficient lines. His physical strength was also evident in rough and tumble play with young Arab boys, whose language he learnt. From these early days, Juin harboured a sympathy for the underdog; he grouped together other French and Arab boys to protect the Jewish boys, who were being subjected to persecution. His abilities both in science and humanities quickly became clear. In 1902 the young Juin won a bursary to the local *Lycée*, the *Lycée d'Aumale*, where again he was outstandingly successful. At this time he hoped to enter the French Navy via the *École Polytechnique* and, in that hope, he won a further major award to the *Lycée d'Alger* to develop his mathematics. But on account of a quirk of the regulations, Juin found that he would have only one chance to attempt the entry examination, and that after two years instead of the normal three. Although his award helped, he still needed money from his parents, now aged. He therefore decided to shorten and change his course with the aim of entering the French Army Cadet Academy, Saint Cyr. In 1909 he passed the Saint Cyr entrance examination seventh out of some 200 candidates.

At this time, the French Army required a period of service in the ranks before a young man could actually embark upon Saint Cyr's two-year course. For his soldier service Juin chose the *1er Zouaves*, in the hope that the regiment would be sent to Morocco, where France had embarked on the first occupation campaign. The Zouaves in this era enjoyed a reputation as élite infantry, a reputation earned in Algeria and the Crimea and immortalised in van Gogh's famous painting. The Zouaves regiments were made up of conscripts from the *colon* and Jewish population of Algeria supplemented by young French conscripts and, in some cases, volunteers, from the Metropole. Juin's hopes of service in Morocco were not fulfilled, but he gained much useful experience of the life of an ordinary soldier, including some punishing physical training reserved for the regiment's junior leader cadre. He quickly distinguished himself by his resilience, humour, smartness and fitness, becoming first a corporal and then a sergeant all within the year.

Juin entered Saint Cyr in October 1910; his year, *Promotion Fez*, totalled 223, among them were two close friends from Algeria and the *1er Zouaves* – and also a very tall, moody northern Frenchman, Charles de Gaulle. Membership of a *Promotion* constituted a very strong bond with other members. Despite all the dramas of their later relationships, Juin was always *tu* to de Gaulle, while de Lattre and Leclerc remained *vous*. Also at Saint Cyr and, although a year younger in the previous year's *Promotion*, was de Lattre de Tassigny. Metropolitan France was a new world for Juin, but also one in which his enjoyment was limited by his modest family circumstances. He made an early and rather controversial mark by organising a rifle and bayonet defence for the inhabitants of his dormitory against a raiding party of senior cadets, but his remarkable abilities in all fields, military, academic and literary soon shone once again, first in the first year order of merit and first in the final order. It was the son of the humble gendarme from Algeria and not an aristocratic cavalryman from Normandy or Paris that received the honour of carrying Saint-Cyr's Colour on parade.

At the end of the course in August 1912, Juin opted for the *1er Régiment de Tirailleurs Algériens*; de Gaulle, with whom Juin had struck a warm friendship opted for the regiment in which he had served as a soldier, the *33e Infanterie*. That regiment had, in the meantime, acquired a new commanding officer, Philippe Pétain.

The immediate prospect of fighting lay behind Juin's selection, the cult of a war of revenge against Germany to recapture Alsace and Lorraine, or more theoretical studies of a major European conflict, left Juin uninterested. For him service in France meant dreary garrison barrack life built around a tedious annual cycle of conscript training. The *1er RTA* had mounted two *régiments de marche*, combat units, for operations in Morocco. These operations were now very large scale, some 70,000 men, and were seen by some as useful field training for a future war. In addition, there were reports of German support, including provision of weapons to Moroccans opposed to the French.

Morocco was to be the last, but certainly the most important of the young Juin's formative experiences. He was captivated by its ancient monarchy, its mysterious cities, and the beauty of the country, even more dramatic than his native Algeria. Not long after his arrival, Juin was detached to command sub-units of the French Army's first Moroccan soldiers. In Morocco, Juin was also to meet the two lodestars of his military and later political careers, Commandant Poeymirau and the Resident-General in Morocco, General Hubert Lyautey.

Juin's first service under Lyautey was at almost the outset of the Resident-General's proconsulship. In the course of his long period of rule, 1912 to 1916 and 1917 to 1925, the occupation and pacification of all the territory except the Atlas and certain remote areas was undertaken, the sultanate and Moroccan government was brought into the twentieth century, a generally benevolent and efficient French administration was established, and impressive economic development begun. In the dark years of the First World War, when Morocco was denuded of almost all its French officers and troops, Lyautey was to resist Paris pressures to withdraw to the coast, and, often with little more than his own charismatic personality, he thus kept France's pre-1914 gains secured. For a whole generation of officers of the *Armée d'Afrique* Lyautey was a genius. That Paris, on occasions, treated him shabbily only strengthened their loyalties – and their suspicions of Paris.

Of the two *régiments de marche* of the *1ᵉʳ RTA* one was serving in western Morocco and one in the east near the Algerian border. Juin had hoped for the former, but was posted to the latter, two sub-units of which were in a camp at Guercif, on the Moulouya river; with two *Tirailleurs* companies were also a squadron of cavalry, *Spahis Algériens*, a troop of mountain guns and two companies of the *Légion Etrangère*.

A young officer's first tour of duty and first experiences of action are always special. At Guercif, Juin spent a severe winter, initially under canvas – very limited protection against either the snow and sand storms that swept down from the Middle Atlas or sniping from Moroccan tribesmen at night. Later, the garrison completed their own permanent fort buildings and occupied them. But the garrison's role remained largely passive until the spring when contingents advanced westwards, creating new fortified posts in wild desolate country, skirmishing with Moroccan resistance, pacifying the areas around the new posts and protecting camel supply convoys. In the following spring, 1914, Juin asked to be allowed to serve with the western Morocco forces in one of the Moroccan irregular units that were being formed, the immediate antecedents of the famous *Tirailleurs Marocains*. His unit commander was Commandant Poeymirau, and their task was to form the vanguard of a column under Colonel Gouraud advancing from Fez towards the Taza range. This column fought a minor battle with the forces of a Moroccan chieftain on 1 May 1914, described succinctly by Juin as a *'chaude affaire'*. A little later, Gouraud's column linked up with the eastern Moroccan forces under General Baumgarten, completing the initial occupation of Morocco.

Juin was enormously impressed by the operations. He greatly admired Gouraud's skills in manoeuvre, surprise, and the use of concentrated fire power from machine-gun and artillery positions.

He also saw at work the rich variety of men that composed the *Armée d'Afrique, Zouaves, Légion Etrangère*, the French army's regular regiments of *Infanterie Coloniale*, the Maghreb's *Tirailleurs* and *Spahis Algériens* and Black Africa's *Tirailleurs Sénégalais*. Above all he admired the Moroccans, whose skills in the use of ground, toughness in mountain warfare and aggressive spirit matched his own nature. And he served under the ablest of the Army's officers of the time. At a review of troops, vice-regal in its style, Juin was introduced to Lyautey and was fascinated by the Resident-General's personality.

On the field of battle he admired the calm of Gouraud, and at unit level, he served with Dangan, Billotte, Rollet of the *Légion* and his own commander, Poeymirau. Young officers pattern themselves on regimental officers they respect. Of 'Le Poey' Juin later wrote that he especially admired his enthusiasm, devotion to duty and directness, his courage, panache, humour and fund of stories, but above all his warmth of character and concern for the humblest soldier under his command. These were all attributes of Juin in his turn as a commander.

The outbreak of the First World War prevented further operations in Morocco in 1914. But there was to be no respite for soldiers already weary. The month of August saw the arrival of the Moroccans in France. As the Sultan of Morocco was at the time technically not at war with Germany the five units had to be entitled *Brigade de Chasseurs Indigènes À Pied*. On their arrival and after fitting out with the khaki uniforms of *Chasseurs Alpins*, they marched through the streets of French towns and villages, their guttural chant expressing their view of themselves as mercenaries beyond the law, fighting with a mixture of good humour and a nebulous mysticism:

Men Moulay Idriss djina	We come from (Sultan) Moulay Idriss
la rebi taafou alina	May God forgive our sins.

With them was Lieutenant Juin, for whom most of the war was to be a sequence of hard fighting, wounds and command of Moroccans in the front line.

The unit of Poeymirau was in the van when, after several marches and counter-marches, the Brigade first went into battle on 5 September. It was deployed without artillery support among the lucerne and beetroot fields north of the Marne on the right wing of the Army of Paris. The Moroccans fought ferociously and heroically in a war for which they had not been trained. Despite ten days of bombardment and enforced retreat, they were still capable of mounting bayonet counter-attacks. But a force of 5,000 had been reduced to some 800 by 16 September.

Juin was wounded in the left hand on 6 September; he refused to be treated as a casualty and fought on in considerable pain and with his arm in a sling; he was later awarded the Cross of the Legion of Honour for his courage. He remained with his unit in the trenches, after the line was established, until January 1915 when the Moroccans were withdrawn for rest. At the front again in March 1915, the

Moroccans were committed in the bloody French Champagne counter-offensive. In a dawn attack, Juin was again wounded, in the upper part of his right arm, and evacuated for a long period of hospital treatment. But his right arm had been badly damaged and the disability was to last for life. He was given permission to salute with his left arm, a distinctive characteristic for him.

In hospital he encountered Poeymirau, also wounded, who offered him a period of service in Morocco as a form of convalescence. Juin was discharged to convalesce in Morocco in December 1915. Now a Captain, he joined a unit of Moroccans training for France in 1916. While in Morocco, Lyautey personally offered Juin an appointment as his aide de camp, but he only served in this capacity for six months as he wanted to return to the Western Front. This hope was fulfilled later in 1916, Christmas of that year finding him in France commanding a company of *Tirailleurs Marocains*. He had returned in time for the April 1917 offensive of General Nivelle, his unit serving in the Chemin de Dames sector.

The French Army had begun the 1914–18 war with a doctrine of attack, the doctrine claiming that an attack mounted with sufficient élan and motivation would triumph even over superior numbers. A few officers, notably Pétain, had doubts even before 1914; the experience of others reinforced these doubts. Nivelle, however, shared none of them, with the result that his massive offensive proved a catastrophe, gaining virtually no ground, incurring enormous casualties and undermining the morale of the French Army to the point of a wave of mutiny. The Army Commander in the Chemin des Dames sector was General Mangin, one of several French officers with extensive African experience who believed colonial troops made superior attacking units, being more inured to suffering and less imaginative. In the initial attacks, Juin's Moroccans once again hurled themselves against the Germans with reckless courage and when the further attacks were called off they remained steadfast and disciplined.

In February 1918, Juin was nominated for staff training, at the end of which, in October, he was posted to the divisional headquarters of a division that included his former regiment of *Tirailleurs Marocains*. But hardly had he arrived than he was re-posted to the French Army Mission attached to the United States Army, where he was, to his irritation, serving far from the front line at the time of the Armistice.

Throughout the inter-war years, Juin served in North Africa whenever he could, regarding garrison soldiering in France as nothing more than a bureaucracy in uniform; two of his appointments were in operations in Morocco. He returned with his former regiment of *Tirailleurs Marocains* to Morocco early in 1919, hoping for active service in the campaigns that would have to be mounted for the mountain areas as soon as troops were once more available. He was to be disappointed, being first summoned by Lyautey for his headquarters staff, and then abruptly returned to France for two years' further staff training at the *Ecole Supérieure de Guerre*, where he was one of the youngest student officers. It is clear that this inactive life ill-suited Juin. His instructors appreciated his full potential abilities but noted that he tended to be over-confident and at times immature – a not uncommon attitude towards instructors among young captains with four years front-line experience. Juin himself commented that only the artillery instructors had anything new to offer him and that even they kept to rigid methods and ignored any human factor. At the end of the course he was posted for two years practical experience, not to Morocco for which he had asked, but to the French Army's Division headquarters in Tunis.

Juin accepted this disappointment with his usual equanimity, realising that he had an opportunity to complete his knowledge of France's three North African possessions. In Tunisia he carefully studied both the territory's defence requirements, especially those of the south on the Libyan border, and the danger that a Tunisia in the hands of an enemy might present to Algeria. The knowledge of the terrain that Juin acquired was to prove of immense value in the years 1941–43.

At the end of this probationary staff period, Juin turned down an important Paris posting, preferring to accept an invitation from Poeymirau, now a General and tasked by Lyautey to command the forthcoming pacification campaign.

'Le Poey' however died suddenly in late 1923 and Lyautey decided to divide Morocco into two regional commands, for the northern and western and the southern and eastern areas. Juin was appointed to the staff of the north-western region. On his arrival at Fez he found Captain de Lattre full of ambition for the prestigious G3 Operations staff appointment which should have been Juin's, as he was staff trained and de Lattre was not. With amusement, he gave way, accepting the logistics side, a typical gesture and one that in the event provided him with the more useful experience. His task over the next ten months was supply for a chain of small border forts on the Ouercha river line, containing the northern Rif warriors of Spanish Morocco. These were inspired by their leader, Abd al Krim, who had shattered a Spanish Army and driven the Spaniards back to garrisons on the coast. The logistic task was fourfold, lorry supply in good weather, mule trains in bad, road construction and protection against raids and ambushes, a task that Juin supervised personally on horseback and from tent offices.

With the full opening of the Rif campaign in early 1925 and the establishment of the two new operational commands for Fez Nord and Taza respectively, Juin was assigned to the Fez Nord area as chief of staff to the commander, Colonel Noguès, whom he came to admire second only to Poeymirau as a field commander. The months from April to September saw desperate fighting, with Abd al Krim waging a campaign of killings, torture, plunder and rapine. Small French forces strove to secure Fez and contain the advancing Rif insurgents, who gained local support through terror and were also, some believed, supported secretly by German and United States interests. Juin had first to organise a screening force and relieve the scattered outposts and then to use this force as a mobile counter-attack group. On several occasions Juin personally led this group into bloody engagements to secure or relieve a French position or column attacked by insurgents five or six times stronger in numbers, and firing or sweeping down from steep mountain sides. He would lead from the front, with a walking stick and no personal weapon. Juin was in his element, acquiring a well-earned reputation for unremitting hard work, disregard of danger, clear thinking and organisational ability. He was appointed an officer of the Legion of Honour and given advanced promotion to be a Major.

In the meantime Lyautey had been blamed – conveniently but largely unjustly – for French ill-preparedness. The blame and his relief from command of military operations were conveyed to him insultingly by Marshal Pétain. In disgust, Lyautey resigned also from the civil functions of the Resident-General's office and prepared to return to France.

As a Marshal, Lyautey was a member of the *Conseil Supérieur de la Guerre*, an advisory body of Marshals, generals and political figures that met five or six times each year. As a member of the *Conseil* he was entitled to a small military staff of three officers – an agreeable perquisite to ease transition to retirement customary in the French Army. Lyautey sent for Juin, who arrived at the Residency straight from operations, and asked him to command this small staff. It was a remarkable encounter, illustrating the finest features of Juin's character and his concepts of loyalty. He had asked to be posted away from Lyautey's staff in 1916 when Lyautey was at the height of his fame. Now Lyautey was old, out of favour and without influence. The appointment would mean departure from all the fighting and from Morocco to a desk life in Paris carrying no renown. But Juin accepted with a laugh, saying he had never been good at mathematics and was no calculator. He then accompanied the Marshal back to France. Two Royal Navy destroyers escorted the Marshal's ship, but at Marseille itself there was no official welcome whatever.

For Juin, the two years in Paris that followed were more educative than his years at the *École de Guerre*. Lyautey, in need of company, talked fully and freely both about Morocco and a future war in Europe which he saw as inevitable. He refused to attend *Conseil* meetings as at the time Pétain was its Vice President but he followed closely the opinions of Marshal Foch and General Weygand, who influenced the *Conseil* towards a revised perception of the defence of French frontiers, views which favoured fortified zones and mobile counter-attack forces rather than a fortified line. These views accorded with and influenced those of Juin. He saw a little of de Gaulle, but learnt to admire and gain the confidence of Weygand, and he was best man at de Lattre's wedding. In September 1927, Juin was appointed to command a battalion of the *7ᵉ Régiment de Tirailleurs Algériens* at Constantine, an indigenous regiment with a particularly fine reputation. For eighteen months, Juin threw himself into every aspect of regimental life. He also married Cecile Bonnefoy, the daughter of an Army veterinary surgeon who had settled in Algeria as a landowner and business man, and was now a notable figure in Constantine's *colon* upper middle class. They were to have two sons.

Juin's tour in command was curtailed by a request, early in 1929, from Lucien Saint, newly appointed Resident-General in Rabat, that Juin should head his personal military secretariat under Noguès, now Director of Political Affairs. The post was of particular importance. Lyautey's immediate successor, Steeg, had been weak towards the mountain peoples who, in consequence, had resumed marauding (they had even kidnapped Steeg's nephew out on a picnic). Further, looking ahead, it was clear that France's manpower inferiority against Germany would worsen acutely in the 1930s, a result of the First World War and its consequent demographic trough. Troops would not then be available for Morocco; indeed more Maghreb regiments would have to serve in France. Morocco's pacification had to be completed by the end of 1934. Juin made important contributions to the plans for the operations carried out in the early 1930s, essentially similar in style to those of Lyautey twenty years earlier; military occupation of an area followed immediately by the opening up of roads, markets and basic social services. However, to complete the Army's requirement of a full twenty-four month period in command of a battalion, Juin's staff tour had to be interrupted by six months in command of a battalion of the *1er Zouaves*. But, now as a lieutenant-colonel, Juin was back at Rabat for the opening of the major operations in 1932.

These operations were the last and perhaps most important stage in Juin's apprenticeship for his later command. In the Atlas he saw the best French field commanders of the day at work, de Loustal, Catroux and Huré. He himself gained thereby further experience in the art of fighting in mountains, the importance of knowledge of the terrain, the importance of intelligence and the different roles to be played by different units. In particular, he watched with admiration the exploits of the *goums*, the Berber mountain irregulars organised into units some 180-200 strong, 50 mounted, 120 on foot and the balance in a mule support section. The *goumiers* swarmed by night over mountain areas judged impassable and encircled their opponents. The regular units then followed on less difficult ground to exploit by early morning the success achieved by the *goumiers'* infiltrations.

He observed at first hand the use of new technology, the greatly improved efficiency of command following the provision of improved signals equipment, the consequential ability to call down an air strike and the value of especially trained mountain artillery. But at the same time, he also saw the limitations of motor vehicles and the value of old-fashioned mule transport for logistic support in mountain areas with no roads. In the flatter ground of the Saharan fringe, Juin studied the more mobile style of warfare directed by Giraud, massive sweeps and deep penetrations by lorry-borne infantry, light cavalry and armoured cars, again well supported from the air.

Once again, Juin distinguished himself so well that, in October 1933, he received the reward of a Paris appointment that he did not particularly want, as a member of the directing staff of the *École Supérieure de Guerre*. He found the *École*'s whole system and its static line defensive tactical teaching in particular to be ossified, and after a year left to join the *3e Zouaves* at Constantine as second in command, with command to follow early in 1935. This regiment's efficiency had suffered from garrison duties and exercise soldiering. Juin sharply injected a new enthusiasm and, with the aid of a mechanised platoon of machine-gun carriers which he had acquired, new tactical thinking based on movement. He also took a special and sympathetic interest in the regiment's junior officers, developing both their professional abilities and personal self-confidence.

Noguès, his former commander in 1925–26, was appointed French Resident-General in Morocco in 1937. With war clouds gathering, the appointment was made with a view to Noguès becoming Commander-in-Chief of all North Africa in the event of hostilities; preparations for this were to be made. Noguès summoned Juin to head his command's staff in Algiers. This appointment's responsibilities equated with those of a *général de brigade*, Juin was only a colonel. Accordingly, in 1938, Juin attended his last training course, a special course for officers destined for very senior command at the *Centre des Hautes Études Militaires*; Juin found this course stimulating and was very well reported upon. At its conclusion he returned to Algiers and was duly promoted *général de brigade* in December 1938.

At the outbreak of war, Juin was seen to be destined for higher command. He was now fifty-one, a stocky figure of slightly below average height. At this period he still retained his moustache from his subaltern days; there would often be a cigarette at the corner of his mouth. Despite his successes in command and staff work, he retained all the best characteristics of a frontline infantryman. He was at his most relaxed with ordinary soldiers, Maghreb *Tirailleurs* or *Zouaves*, around a camp fire where his rich infectious laugh and fund of soldierly stories were but the surface evidence of a care and consideration for ordinary soldiers, which in turn created strong bonds of loyalty. Though a man of sound commonsense, with a very robust good humour, together with a dislike of ceremony, there could, however, on occasions be explosions of temper when his voice became raucous. He was ambitious, but not to the point of disadvantaging others. His outstanding career and his marriage had both advanced him socially. However, he was still marked a little by his humble origins; and there were times when his normal modesty failed him. He was a Christian, but not like de Hauteclocque, or even de Lattre, passionately so. North Africa was his home, Morocco his passion, the *Armée d'Afrique* his career. Although a devoted follower of Lyautey, he was insufficiently sensitive to appreciate that Lyautey's colonial philosophy was not a static but an evolving one, and that French policy must evolve also. His Maghreb upbringing and attachments prevented him from seeing that Morocco itself was changing – the changes being the results of the general success of French rule. The old divisions between mountain Berber and lowland Arab were beginning to wane, reliance upon the *grands caids* of the High Atlas – a policy forced on Lyautey at the time of military weakness in the First World War – was soon to be counter-productive and a new proto-nationalism was already stirring.

Jean de Lattre de Tassigny

Our next future Marshal, Jean Joseph Marie Gabriel de Lattre de Tassigny, was perhaps the greatest soldier to serve France since the age of Napoleon I. His dynamic command abilities in two very different types of warfare would by themselves ensure him a unique place in his country's history. To these abilities must be added a highly original imagination, an almost legendary reputation for physical courage, a profound moral courage which shone especially in the last tragic months of his life, and the charm (when he chose), panache, and charisma of a remarkable if very complex personality. But the very brilliance of this personality could antagonise and arouse controversy and dislike, particularly when the vain or the ruthlessly authoritarian sides of de Lattre's character were to the fore.

The de Lattre family were minor gentry, originally from the north of France; in the eighteenth century Tassigny, a family estate near Guise, was added to the family name. Jean de Lattre's father, Roger, came from Poitiers but became a *Vendéen* by marriage when in 1885 he married Anne-Marie Hénault, the daughter of the mayor of the village of Mouilleron-en-Pareds, near Fontenay le Comte in the heart of the Vendée. In 1793, Mayor Hénault's grandfather, a staunch republican, had in romantic and dramatic circumstances rescued and married the daughter of a local royalist aristocrat under sentence of death. Attributes of both aristocracy and ordinary countryman were passed on to the following generations, as was the Vendée's paradoxical tradition of individuality, at times to the extreme, combined with strict Catholicism. The couple at first divided their time between Poitiers and Mouilleron, but by 1911 Roger had followed his father-in-law as mayor and was settled permanently as local squire in an attractively solid country house.

It was at Mouilleron – where Clemenceau had been born in 1840 and near to where he retired – that Jean, an only son, was born on 2 February 1889. The main family influences on his early life were his mother, a very intelligent, kind and good natured woman of strong religious beliefs, his father, with his sense of duty and personal standards, his one sister, two years older than himself, and his maternal grandmother, steeped in Vendée lore and history. Some of the almost feminine attributes of de Lattre's character had their origins in these years. Almost as important though was the Vendée country life, and in particular its horses. These gave the young de Lattre his first opportunity to display courage, panache and his exhilaration at full speed in any form. Even as a young boy, he quickly acquired a reputation of dashing – if not always successful – horsemanship. But, as with other wild boys and young men, he was not always easy to control, giving his parents several anxious moments.

De Lattre's first formal education was from the priest and a locally engaged tutor, but at the age of nine he was sent to the strictly disciplined Jesuit College of Saint Joseph at Poitiers. Here, even at this young age, the mix of personal characteristics that was de Lattre produced very varied results, a pattern to continue through all his education. At his best, when interested in a subject, de Lattre was brilliant with exceptional powers of concentration and application, top or near the top of any class. Père Emmanuel Barbier, the principal of the Saint Joseph college until the eviction of Jesuit teachers in 1908, was most influential figure in de Lattre's school days. From him de Lattre absorbed the religious instruction very conscientiously and gained a developing interest in ritual and ceremony, which led him to organise fêtes, concerts and drama with tremendous zest. From Barbier de Lattre also learned to care for other people, particularly the less fortunate. He devoted a week to helping, barefoot, the carrying of the sick at Lourdes and on other occasions went out of his way to care for people in need. Even as a schoolboy, it was noted that de Lattre was always on the look out for new ideas, new mental stimulus; as a young man he drew much inspiration from the Lorraine writer Barrès whose works sought a detached balance between romantic nationalism, inherited and regional traditions, and excessive preoccupation with oneself – all themes much in de Lattre's mind. But at other times he would regard work almost as a joke, a brief period in Brighton to learn English was evidently very far from studious. After Poitiers he went to an equally disciplined college in the Rue Vaugirard in Paris to study for the entrance examination to the Navy, but an illness prevented his sitting the examination and he moved on to the College Sainte Genèvieve, yet another strict Catholic institution, at Versailles to prepare for the Saint Cyr entrance examination. A Rue Vaugirard contemporary described de Lattre at this time as

.. the most lively, expansive and affectionate but also the most violent of us. He was also one of the most pious and convincing. Already very intuitive and endowed with multiple antennae, traits curiously feminine in so virile a man he would show himself jealous of his friends, but his qualms of conscience after one of his outbursts of temper or a sulk endeared him the more to them.

His physical appearance could express both sides of his character. Although of only average height, determination showed in his face and was emphasised by a Roman nose and a piercing gaze. But his face was also mobile, capable of expressing, at times acting out, his mood of the moment.

In 1908 de Lattre passed fourth into Saint Cyr and then joined the *29ᵉ Régiment de Dragons* for the one year period of service as a soldier required at the time. The impression he gained from this barrack-room experience of indifferent and lazy officers, bullying non-commissioned officers, the uninspired dullness of the life of the ordinary soldier, and the absence of human contact across the rank structures were to bear fruit later in his life when he became concerned with training.

The year complete, de Lattre entered Saint Cyr in 1909. But the discipline and routine of Saint Cyr irked the young de Lattre, who was never tolerant of pedestrian minds. He fell out with one of his instructors of whom he had no opinion; this, together with the fact that by virtue of his entry examination success he was assured of an appointment in the cavalry, weakened his motivation. Some of the complexities of his character were criticised – at one moment precise, the next a dreamer, both aloof and familiar, confident and uncertain, caring and brutal, always a great talker but not always deferential to rank. He finally passed out 201st out of 210, and was kept back for a week for some minor peccadillo. With his many artistic and now political contacts and interests some wondered if he would remain in the Army. The Saint Cyr commandant's report on him concluded '*À stimuler et à diriger*'.

But away from Saint Cyr, blessed with splendid physique and a reputation as a first class rider, de Lattre soon regained esteem both at the Cavalry School at Saumur and in his first regiment, the *12ᵉ Régiment de Dragons* at Pont à Mousson. The regiment, so close to the German border, was in a state of constant readiness in a covering role. De Lattre threw himself into training his troop, developing his own ideas and infecting all with his enthusiasm, his methods reflecting the influence upon him of General Lyautey's views, that the role of an officer in society extended far beyond that of command in the field. On two occasions also de Lattre, disguised as a factory engineer, slipped across the frontier and dined in a Metz restaurant full of German officers.

In the first eight weeks of the First World War, de Lattre was twice wounded. On 11 August, while he was leading a *12ᵉ Dragons* patrol he was hit in the knee by a shell splinter, an injury that incapacitated him until early September. The next injury, on 14 September, was nearly fatal. His troop bumped into a German cavalry patrol in open country. De Lattre charged, outpacing his troopers. He killed two Germans with his sword, but received the full force of a German lance in his chest; the lance then broke. His own troopers came to the rescue as he fell vomiting blood. After driving off the Germans his troop sergeant managed to remount de Lattre on his horse and lead him to a farm where, foot on de Lattre's chest, the sergeant pulled out the point of the lance. The next day he was taken on a stretcher into a house in Pont à Mousson. His predicament was grave, Pont à Mousson was in no-man's-land and German patrols were out looking for a wounded French officer. A German soldier was on the point of discovering him when a French cavalry patrol from another regiment arrived and rescued him. He was later taken away at night on a farm wagon, escorted by cavalrymen.

De Lattre did not give himself, in particular his damaged right lung, sufficient time to recover properly; this wound was to cause pain and inconvenience for some time. But on 20 December, de Lattre rejoined his regiment; he received the Legion of Honour and was again wounded, this time lightly in his right leg. By the autumn of 1914, however, it was clear that the war was an infantryman's battle, with the line of trenches stretching from the North Sea to the Swiss frontier. De Lattre after much soul searching responded to the 1915 appeal of General Joffre to cavalry officers and transferred to the infantry, the *93ᵉ Régiment d'Infanterie*. This regiment recruited in his native Vendée. At the time that he joined, December 1915, the regiment was in an exhausted state, but members of it recalled the impact of the arrival of the smartly uniformed young captain from the cavalry who insisted on the highest standards but also upon proper provision of hot meals for his men. De Lattre practised his beliefs on dedicated leadership being always with his men, sharing discomfort and suffering in the trenches. Early in 1916, his abilities quickly being recognised, he became one of the *93ᵉ*'s battalion commanders after periods as second in command and company commander.

De Lattre served with the *93ᵉ* until May 1917. In this period the regiment was committed in most of the heaviest fighting on the Western Front. This fighting included the blood-soaked battlefield of Verdun in the summer of 1916 and in the grim winter of 1916–17, together with the disastrous Aisne offensive of General Nivelle in April 1917. Survivors recalled the cheer and inspiration of his leadership even under the most appalling of conditions. In July 1916 he was gassed, mustard gas creating complications in his already damaged lung and necessitating a further spell in hospital. He was back with the regiment in October but suffered further ill-health from January to the spring when he returned in time for Nivelle's offensive. Here both he and his battalion fought notably well, taking by surprise a German position based on large underground workings.

A few glimpses of his leadership in the trenches merit mention. He was ruthless in the standards he set and his exacting expectations of his subordinate commanders, but he remained also profoundly concerned with the welfare of all ranks. As before, he was a constant visitor at his soldiers' miserable forward positions – mostly shell craters set in seas of freezing mud in which men often actually disappeared. At the time of the mutinies that followed the failure of Nivelle's offensive, de Lattre and the unit chaplain talked to and mixed freely amongst the soldiers; the unit's discipline was maintained. In a concern more easily understandable to a Catholic mind, he was also worried about men killed during attacks. He felt this could not easily be discussed with most soldiers, but directed the unit's chaplain to follow soldiers forward in an attack and pronounce absolution.

In May 1917, de Lattre was ordered to rest, the strain of almost three years front line fighting and the consequences of his wounds, particularly that of the lance in his chest, had exhausted him, leaving him sick and feverish. At the end of 1917, he was discharged from hospital and appointed Intelligence staff officer of the *21e Division*, in which the *93e Régiment* was serving, on the Aisne front. In May 1918, the division, and in particular the *93e*, took most of the weight of a fifteen-division strong German attack. De Lattre's beloved *Vendéens* were decimated, largely because the Army Commander had not heeded warnings of the coming attack and had not thinned out his forward positions. After this carnage, which affected de Lattre deeply, the *21e Division* was withdrawn for rest and reconstitution, but was back in action on the Aisne at the time of the Armistice on 11 November. This staff period broadened de Lattre's experience, in particular as he worked closely with three United States Army divisions in the same sector, as well as maintaining liaison with the British, all now under the unified command of Foch. In this period, also, de Lattre developed a useful capacity for working right through the night.

At the end of the war, de Lattre emerged having been wounded four times but also twice decorated and eight times mentioned in dispatches. He had, however, to pay a price in terms of health, for his lung never fully recovered and he was frequently unwell. The strains of his experience had affected his temperament, so that a tendency to be authoritarian became more marked, and explosions of temper more frequent and spectacular; French writers use the adjective *jupiterien.*

In need of recuperation, de Lattre was sent in February 1919 to a congenial staff appointment at Bordeaux. Part of his duties included the recreation of American troops prior to their re-embarkation, a task which the de Lattre enjoyed, using to the full his talent for theatre. At the end of 1919, he was posted to the *49ᵉ Régiment d'Infanterie* at Bayonne where he returned to his first love, equitation and hunting. Both at Bordeaux and Bayonne the dashing, impeccably dressed, handsome de Lattre was lionised, particularly by attractive women. Some, including the colonel of the *49ᵉ*, criticised de Lattre's squirearchical, larger than life, style, but such was his complex character that to his close friends de Lattre remained always courteous, simple and natural.

By 1921, however, with his health in part restored and the attractions of social peace-time soldiering beginning to pall, de Lattre sought a posting in Morocco, where he was to serve in the pacification campaigns and the Rif war until early 1926. The splendour of Lyautey's vice-regal style and his sense of ceremony and theatre inevitably greatly impressed de Lattre, who was later to use much the same methods. His first important appointment in Morocco however was strictly military, an attachment to the Operations staff of Poeymirau, at the time commander of the Meknès area. 'Le Poey' recognisee de Lattre's talents and had his infantry regimental posting amended. In this first staff attachment year, Poeymirau was deliberately giving de Lattre an opportunity to familiarise himself with Moroccan conditions while he himself set about two sets of operations, firm assertion of French military control of the Upper Moulouya adjoining the border with Algeria for the summer of 1921, and subjugation of the restless Taza area further west in 1923. The operations were on a sizeable scale, twenty battalions, fifteen batteries, twelve squadrons of cavalry, six of aircraft and hundreds of irregular levies.

In 1923, after the Moulouya operation, Lyautey reorganised the

French command, creating a new northern Morocco command at Fez again under General Poeymirau. De Lattre, still only a captain, was formally appointed Chief of the Operations staff. This command was tasked to enter and subjugate the Taza, an operation in the event largely but not entirely successful. Berber resistance, assessed at some 5,000 of the toughest of the different clans, was desperate; this with the difficulties of terrain and heat curtailed the operation before all areas had been entered.

By 1924 a new and very much more serious threat had appeared, the challenge of Abd al Krim, who had smashed the Spanish Army in the Rif and seemed to the French to be preparing a challenge to the whole French position in Morocco. Equally serious, of course, was the sudden death of Poeymirau.

Lyautey's restructuring of his military command into two regions has already been noted earlier in this chapter. De Lattre was once again appointed Chief of the Operations staff, concerned initially with the Ouergha line chain of forts. Lyautey's forces were increased early in 1925 but they did not prevent conflict. When the full Rif war began in April, Abd al Krim's 30,000 strong army overran or forced the evacuation of most of Lyautey's defence line and the whole Taza area was in acute danger of being overrun; withdrawal from the Taza could lead to the loss of Fez or even all Morocco. In one of the most important decisions in his long military career, Lyautey refused to withdraw from the Taza. He returned to a more mobile concept of defence based on simultaneous attack from different directions. Abd al Krim riposted with a westerly thrust that was contained with little difficulty, the insurgent army then turned south and east to cut the Algeria-Morocco railway at Taza. But there Abd al Krim was again stopped by French forces under Colonel (later General) Giraud.

The nature and scale of events then changed dramatically with the departure of Lyautey and the arrival of Pétain. Pétain secured massive reinforcements of the French forces bringing them, by August 1925, to a total of a little over six divisions each of twelve battalions, supplemented by thousands of irregular levies. Pétain also formed a military partnership with the Spaniards. With his massive forces he then began a slow broad front advance which lasted until November. It was resumed again in May 1926 achieving success by July, with minor mopping-up operations stretching on until the winter.

De Lattre played a notable part in most of these events. Despite his total lack of previous Maghreb experience, he very quickly mastered both the geographical and political complexities of Morocco, together with the country's special military problems, tactics, logistics and intelligence. Poeymirau was greatly impressed by him, and after Poeymirau's death and the outbreak of the Rif war, de Lattre, still only a Captain, had been sent forward to Taza as a local chief of staff. He fought to relieve beleaguered posts and personally organised air lifts of supplies. The local commanding colonel, Cambay, was irresolute and de Lattre played a key role in confirming and supporting Lyautey's decision not to evacuate. He visited all the units in the area and imposed his strong personality and determination upon their commanders and even on Colonel Cambay himself. Giraud, commanding a unit in the area at the time, was wont later to remark of this period 'When I was under the orders of Captain de Lattre .....'

On 26 August 1925, a few days before Pétain opened his massive advance, de Lattre was again wounded while on a reconnaissance. This time, a bullet lodged in his knee. The wound slightly impeded his walking for the rest of his life and it also prevented his participation in Pétain's first campaign. Of Pétain he was sharply critical. He saw the excessive use of equipment and manpower in a cumbersome First World War style to be *'ruineux'*, totally unsuited to Morocco, and one that was so slow that it necessitated expensive winter logistic arrangements which could have been avoided. He denounced Pétain's methods as *'matérialiste'*. They ignored training, fieldcraft and mobility and taught the false lesson that numbers of men and weight of artillery barrages won campaigns.

De Lattre gained invaluable experience in Morocco. He observed at first hand the value of the *Armée d'Afrique*, the regiments of Moroccan and Algerian *Tirailleurs* and *Spahis*, and the Moroccan irregular *goums*. He saw the skill and abilities of the devoted French military officers that formed their cadres or were at work as administrators in the remote mountain areas, and he learnt to work with them. Not all were immediately impressed by the immaculately dressed, yellow-gloved, metropolitan officer who arrived to visit them; this changed quickly when their requests and needs were met. He worked closely with three other captains, Juin, Guillaume and de Monsabert, all to be important in the Second World War. In the Western Front trenches, de Lattre had learnt to lead men. In Morocco, he learnt to lead officers, and developed an ambition to do so.

Also, after four years of linear trench warfare in France, de Lattre saw under Poeymirau in particular, a return to campaigns of tactics, movement and applied fire-power by land and from the air. The *Armée d'Afrique* had from the mid-nineteenth century evolved its own doctrine. An area to be subjugated was approached by at least two, sometimes three or more columns moving at some ten miles per day and arriving simultaneously from different directions. In front of each column would be Moroccan irregulars, *goumiers* and *partisans*, *Spahis* cavalry provided flank guards, in the centre of the column would be infantry *Tirailleurs* or *Légion Etrangère*, and artillery, together with command and logistics personnel. Carefully planned and precisely co-ordinated, the final assaults would then be mounted. This approach was to form the basis of de Lattre's tactics in Alsace in 1944–45 and Indochina in 1951.

As in the First World War, de Lattre's personal style was one of immense energy, as often on horseback with units in action as at his staff desk. He would visit artillery, aircraft, signals and logistics units by day and return to staff work in the evening and night. 'JLT' as he was called at this time, became a well-known figure, his visits welcomed by most but dreaded by the inefficient and lazy. In between operations 'JLT' cut his usual dashing figure among Moroccan colonial society. Here he suffered a mishap.

In addition to the wound of August 1925, de Lattre suffered an earlier injury in Morocco. In March 1924, while entering a Fez hotel for a luncheon party, a Moroccan knifed him in the right cheek. He was only saved from a second stabbing by the quick reaction of another officer. The wound was severe, necessitating surgery and for three weeks de Lattre could neither speak, eat nor drink. Not surprisingly, once again the pressures of the campaigns, the heat and the dust, the strain of his wounds old and new, and a severe attack of dysentery all took their toll. He developed a tendency to be over-confident in himself, at times arrogant. He frequently referred to people with whom he had to deal in a *de haut en bas* diminutive form, *'mon petit'* or *'le petit'*. Although always calm in battle, at other times he seemed to impose his exacting standards ever more severely. The outbursts of temper also became more frequent. On some occasions he appeared to lose control of himself; these occasions would later be followed by a *coup de charme* in which he sought to make amends.

De Lattre returned to France in April 1926. Unlike Juin, he saw no further active service until 1939, his career developing as a promising and ambitious metropolitan officer. The next major step had to be the *École de Guerre* for which two preparatory steps were necessary. First his health had to be restored, and next he had, as a requirement for entry to the *École*, to spend a period of time in serving with a battalion at the same time as working for the entrance examinations.

His health was restored by a summer at Mouilleron, riding providing the physical recreation and occasional conversations with Clemenceau, the mental. More important even was his meeting with the attractive Mlle Simonne Calary de la Mazière. The thirty-seven year old de Lattre, now a Commandant, swept the nineteen year old girl off her feet; they were married in March 1927. Although the age gap was considerable, Madame de Lattre was to match her husband perfectly, tolerating his unpredictable and at times difficult character, calming some of its excesses, and providing stability. In February 1928, their only child, Bernard, was born. In later years, Bernard, too, was to have a very special influence on de Lattre.

Engagement and marriage had to be combined with service in the *4ᵉ Régiment d'Infanterie* and intensive academic preparation for the *École de Guerre* in which de Lattre's quick assimilative mind stood him in good stead; he covered work in four months that took most officers two years. His preferred method of learning was dialogue with a friend. He passed the entrance examination in 1927 with outstanding marks and became the *chef de promotion* of his intake, a status strengthened by the warm relationship he developed with the Commandant of the *École*, General Hering. After the two years course, de Lattre passed out second, having greatly impressed his teachers, and he was appointed to the command of a battalion of the *5ᵉ Régiment d'Infanterie* near Paris. This period of command, marked by the setting of high standards, emphasis on interesting training and impressive ceremonial, and concern for ordinary conscripts was another stage in the development of de Lattre's ideas on training. After promotion to Lieutenant-Colonel, de Lattre was posted to a General Staff transport planning desk in 1931, but was soon selected by General Weygand, the Commander-in-Chief Designate in the event of war, to serve on the Operations staff of the *Conseil Supérieur de la Guerre*. This significant posting brought de Lattre into the centre of all national, strategic and military debate, working under one of the ablest staff intellects of the day. He met and often briefed leading French and sometimes British political figures, and met and corresponded with French military attachés in major embassies, notably Moscow. De Lattre saw his role as pressing for the modernisation of the French Army, the acquisition of information about developments in other countries, in particular Germany and Italy, and reporting accurately on French public opinion. In the course of this, he became increasingly alarmed about German rearmament and increasingly sceptical of the outdated French linear defence strategy still favoured by

Pétain. He saw clearly both that a German armoured assault might break through (he even suggested the Meuse as a likely area), and that the 'Maginot mentality' offered little encouragement to possible allies such a Poland or Czechoslovakia, who might be attacked. For this reason, he believed the military capabilities of the Soviet Union should be examined, and French policy targeted to ensure at least benevolent Soviet neutrality in the event of a war with Germany. Weygand agreed, but the political climate in Paris was antipathetic. Although a Franco-Soviet military alliance had been signed, no staff talks resulted.

In frustration at this political climate, de Lattre became involved in an incident that could have finished his career. In February 1934 the scandal of the illegal operations of the financier Stavisky broke, following his suicide in January. The Radical Premier, Chautemps, tried to cover the affair up. The parties of the Right alleged that Stavisky had been murdered to silence him and Chautemps had to resign in a gathering Right-wing anti-Republican backlash. After a complex series of murky events, demonstrations organised by Right-wing groups, with the aim of bringing down the government, erupted in Paris on 6 February. These demonstrations led to rioting, bloodshed and a number of deaths. Daladier, Chautemps' successor, was forced to resign and his Minister of the Interior, Frot, was accused both of shooting Parisians and of masterminding a coup of assorted Right-wingers and fascists. During the sittings of a Commission of Enquiry that followed the event, Frot was specifically accused by Left-wing figures of secret negotiations with Real del Sarte, one of the leaders of *Action Française*, a Right-wing group, through the intermediary of an Army officer. Frot denied this, but Real del Sarte hinted that it was true, and de Lattre's name appeared a few days later in two extreme Right papers. De Lattre had to answer for himself before the Commission. He admitted that he had met Real del Sarte socially twice and had expressed a personal admiration for Frot, but he denied, flatly and emphatically, any political motive other than that of his duty, learning opinions of members of the public on military matters, and informing the public about the military. Real del Sarte repeated his hinting, but the Commission voted, somewhat hurriedly, by nineteen to eleven with two abstentions that the incident be closed. The nineteen were from the political Left. The most likely explanations for these strange events are that the Right-wing newspapers named de Lattre as revenge for his refusal to be a link between the Army and the Right, and the Left were hoping to implicate the Catholic and conservative Weygand and, realising that they had failed, dropped the charge.

De Lattre's enemies hoped the incident would destroy him and Pétain even asked Weygand to post him away. Weygand firmly refused and retained de Lattre until his own retirement in 1935. But it was a difficult period for de Lattre, his wife was very unwell with protracted chest illnesses, requiring residence in clinics and sanatoria. Many of his acquaintances and Right-wing *Vendéen* neighbours shunned him. The incident left him with a profound and lasting distrust of extreme Right politicians. It was in this period he began to take as his personal motto *Ne Pas Subir* – never give up.

After a brief spell on the staff of General Georges, de Lattre was given the command of the *151ᵉ Régiment d'Infanterie* at Metz. It was a notably good regiment but de Lattre set out immediately and sharply to make it even better, developing still further the ideas and practices he had initiated as a battalion commander. Officers and NCOs were de Lattre's first target for attention, company commanders were directed to keep detailed records of their soldiers' personal particulars and aptitudes, and submit systematised regular reports on training and morale. Military training, with night exercises and sudden emergency alarms, was then made more exciting and realistic, though de Lattre complained of the Army's weakness in anti-tank weaponry. Parades, ceremonial and uniforms all had to be impeccable. The life of the conscript soldier was enriched by the creation of an entirely new system in the French Army '*le service social de régiment*' which provided foyers, recreation rooms, cinema, showers and sports facilities. Drab dining halls were decorated with paintings of the Regiment's past battles, former wartime members invited for special occasions. Once again de Lattre's methods aroused resentment and controversy among some, especially in accounts departments. But they greatly impressed Giraud, the Metz garrison commander, who supported the next stage in de Lattre's career, entry to the same one year higher command course as Juin at the *Centre des Hautes Études Militaires*.

De Lattre finished the course, obtaining excellent reports, in July 1938 and was appointed early in 1939 as Chief of Staff to the Military Governor of Strasbourg, whose war role was Commander of the 5th Army. This general was in fact the former Commandant of the *École de Guerre*, Hering, on whom de Lattre had made so good an impression earlier. At the same time, de Lattre, now fifty, was promoted *général de brigade*. Among his colleagues on the staff was Colonel de Gaulle. In the last few months of peace, de Lattre threw himself into the necessary staff and planning work, paying especial attention to morale and psychological conditions. He made it clear, nevertheless, that he thought any German attack would be elsewhere and that too many troops were devoted to this sector. De Lattre's personal life was now happier, for his wife had recovered. Bernard gave him increasingly pleasure and he himself loved Alsace second only to the Vendée. This staff appointment was, however, only a holding one; de Lattre was to receive his much more significant command in January 1940.

Philippe Leclerc de Hauteclocque

Our third future Marshal, born Philippe François Marie, Vicomte de Hauteclocque, came from the pre-Revolution country aristocracy. His direct ancestors had fought in the Fifth Crusade and again in Tunisia in 1270, at Saint Omer in 1340 and at Fontenoy in 1745. The family survived the Revolution, three members serving in Napoleon's Grand Army, with a fourth, of weak health, in its supply train. The youngest of these had a son, Gustave, a noted Egyptologist, who in turn also had three sons. Of these, the eldest and youngest were both officers who served in France's colonial campaigns, but were both to be killed in the First World War. The second son, Comte Adrien de Hauteclocque, therefore, inherited the estate of Belloy Saint Leonard in the Somme Artois.

Adrien de Hauteclocque was a typical member of his class. His interests were in country life, in particular hunting. He was a Royalist and a Catholic but not of excessive zeal; he was well read, particularly in the classics. As a landowner, he had a reputation of being somewhat cavalier but he was acknowledged to be a fair man and at times a very generous one. He served with the cavalry in the First World War, first as a trooper and then as a lieutenant in the same regiment as his eldest son was serving as an officer, and despite the fact that he was over fifty. He was decorated for bravery in 1918. His wife was Marie Thérèse van der Cruisse des Waziers, of an old Lille family. They had six children of which Philippe, born in 1902, was the fifth; the choice of name was in honour of an ancestor killed by Croats in 1635.

Philippe's early family life moulded his character. Life at Belloy was spartan, leaving the young de Hauteclocque with a disregard for inessentials. From his father he learnt concepts of duty and work, from an elder sister's reading aloud he learnt of his nation's military past, and perhaps most important of all, from his mother he absorbed a very strong Catholicism. The mix produced a young man with a total absence of affectation or sense of caste, and with the natural ease and simplicity of the old aristocracy. Observers had, however, also noted both a great strength of character and a characteristic to become very marked when he was a field commander, formidable powers of concentration and critical path analysis.

De Hauteclocque attended a Jesuit boarding school in Amiens, this school had to be evacuated first to Abbeville and then Poitiers in the First World War. He passed his *baccalauréat*, his major subjects being Philosophy and Mathematics, in 1920. After a further period of preparation at the same Sainte Genevieve College at Versailles as de Lattre had attended, de Hauteclocque entered Saint Cyr in the October 1922 *Promotion Metz et Strasbourg*. From Saint Cyr, fifth in the Order of Merit, emerged a young officer of set religious views and daily practice which he saw no need to discuss but which governed every aspect of his life. Every day of his life, when circumstances allowed, he received the Eucharist. He set himself firm principles and high personal standards, all held as absolutes. He liked to concentrate ferociously upon practical problems that could be solved and leave theoretical debate to others, a seemingly narrow-minded and anti-academic practice which led some later (particularly in the winter and spring of 1943–44) to underrate his abilities. For himself, he believed that the gifts granted to him by the Almighty were to be used and developed to the maximum; in war this belief extended to one in which the Almighty had selected him for special responsibilities – though again he only mentioned this to a very few close associates. He tended, particularly in his early years as an officer, to judge others who failed to measure up to his standards somewhat severely. He had a horror of mediocrity in any form, only his Christian convictions restrained him from intolerance. His natural charm and modesty won him many comrades, but he admitted hardly any to a close friendship.

After Saint Cyr, de Hauteclocque was further trained at the Cavalry School at Saumur. At the conclusion of this, he married Thérèse de Gargan in 1925, a marriage from which six children were to be born, over the years – for de Hauteclocque early marriage and a family was a duty both national and Christian. He then joined his regiment, the *5ᵉ Régiment de Cuirassiers* at the time on occupation duty at Treves, in Germany. He found garrison life unsatisfying and as soon as he could applied to serve in Morocco. He was accordingly transferred first to the *8ᵉ Régiment de Spahis Algériens* engaged in minor pacification operations in the Taza area in 1926. In 1927, he was posted as an instructor to the school for the training of Moroccan officers founded by Lyautey, where he served for two years, learning about Morocco whose semi-feudal structure appealed to him, as well as teaching. In this period, too, de Hauteclocque first came under the spell of one of the most romantic figures of the *Armée d'Afrique*, Captain Henry de Lespinasse de Bournazel. This officer of *Spahis* – Maghreb cavalry – was seconded to the command of a *goum*, these units of foot and mounted men, used in the most difficult of the mountain pacification operations, were officered by the pick of the *Armée d'Afrique*. De Bournazel, a giant of a man, led his *goumiers* into action wearing a scarlet *Spahis* tunic and carrying no weapon other than a riding crop.

When in 1929 de Hauteclocque saw the action for which he had so long desired, he too was posted to a *goum* at M'Zizel, in a still largely unpacified area of the High Atlas. Although the years 1929–31 were not ones of major operations, the life of a *goum* officer was exciting, including the pursuit of Ait Hammou raiding bands, small scale engagements that could last for a whole day and include a cavalry charge, sword in hand. Responsibility for these isolated commands of irregulars was the supreme test of a young officer. In one scrap, de Hauteclocque had two horses shot under him and was himself grazed by a bullet which lodged in his tunic, but he nevertheless led his *goum* with great skill against a numerically superior band of Ait Hammou. He left his *goum* with sadness – and a citation for bravery; he would have preferred to remain but was conscious of his responsibilities to his family.

He was appointed to be an instructor at Saint-Cyr, arriving in February 1931. To his annoyance, that year saw the preliminary stages of the final pacification operations in Morocco, which he felt no young officer should miss. Before leaving the protectorate, he had obtained a promise, from a friend, of a posting in the zone of the operations. A telegram advised him to come. De Hauteclocque dashed to Rabat by train, only to find that the appointment had been given to someone else. He took this setback philosophically and returned to Saint Cyr to hunt and to bide his time.

Two years later, in 1933, Saint Cyr's three month summer vacation provided de Hauteclocque with his next opportunity. The final, large-scale pacification operations in Morocco were in progress. De Hauteclocque obtained official permission – and his wife's consent – to go to Morocco to fight and flew to Rabat at his own expense. On his arrival in Morocco, General Giraud wanted to give him command of a *goum*, but his staff decided that to do so might appear as favouritism and instead he was appointed as a liaison officer. So dull and safe an activity did not suit de Hauteclocque who by personal appeal to Giraud secured himself command of a body of irregular *partisans* levies, even wilder than the *goumiers*. He once again distinguished himself by his fearless disregard for his own safety and was recommended for the cross of the Légion d'Honneur. But the Commander-in-Chief in Morocco, General Huré, held that de Hauteclocque had acted very irregularly and deserved punishment; the award was delayed for three years. The cavalry however took a different view, and arranged an early entry for the lieutenant to captain promotion course for him. In this course, de Hauteclocque made it a point of honour to do well, coming fourth, and so gaining his captaincy in December 1934.

De Hauteclocque's two tours of duty in Morocco had however one other lasting and less fortunate result, a legacy of malaria. This left him frequently irritable, and more prone than before to violent and terrifying outbreaks of temper; these '*colères*' were later to become notorious. After them he would generally not apologise but in some other way seek to make amends, saying with a sad smile 'I know that I have an impossible character but if people only knew what efforts, every day, I make to control it'.

He returned to Saint Cyr as commander of a company of cadets, a very prestigious appointment in which he made a great impression on his students. His biographer, General Vézinet, recounts two very telling incidents of this period in de Hauteclocque's life. On one occasion, during an exercise, a motor car frightened de Hauteclocque's horse, which threw him. In the fall he fractured his leg in two places. After being helped to remount, he told off a student who expressed anxiety about him, inspected the company on its return and then entertained some friends to dinner before accepting the need for treatment. The next morning the company was curtly told that its commander had made the mistake of riding on the shoulder of the road and a fall had been the consequence. On another exercise he made, against advice from one of his officers, an embarrassing tactical error. On return to Saint Cyr he assembled his company and said 'When you make a first class blunder, you must not be afraid to admit it. I have just made one in front of you all. Dismount'.

In 1938 de Hauteclocque entered the *École Supérieure de Guerre* for command and staff training. He stood first at the end of the first year order of merit in 1939, his instructors commenting on his intelligence, judgement, originality and sense of ground. His own preferences for study from the past were those commanders that he considered combined spirit with character and acted with speed and decision, even if not always according to the rule book. In those pre-war years, de Hauteclocque also took some passing interest in politics; he was interested in the Right-wing *Action Française*, its royalism and contempt of bourgeois materialism appealing to him. But like many who viewed the Third Republic with disdain, he did not follow all its extreme views and never became actively involved. He had developed into a very dedicated, if at times unconventional, officer – intelligent and shrewd but within a somewhat limited field of vision, at times abrupt, even opinionated and, after his malaria, short tempered. Although he could mix socially with ease and charm when he wished, he tended to isolate himself. He enjoyed classical music and art and architectural history. In outward appearance, de Hauteclocque was a lithe and slightly built man with an unexpectedly deep voice and brilliant blue eyes. But within him there was *passion* suppressed, fires only damped down; de Hauteclocque was a man waiting for a call.

The German invasion of Poland terminated the staff course and de Hauteclocque was posted to the staff of the *4ᵉ Division d'Infanterie*, a formation of recalled reservists.

At the outbreak of the war, therefore, the French Army's three future *grand chefs* were two junior generals, both well known and with notable records, and a cavalry captain, whose name was not particularly known. Under a new name, totally unknown, it was to be the cavalry captain who would first appear on the world stage.

3

From Chad to Berchtesgaden:
General Leclerc

The *4ᵉ Division d'Infanterie* spent a dull 'phoney war'. The last months of 1939 saw the *Division* at the western end of the Maginot Line, its units engaged in minor patrol activity. Although he was on the headquarters staff, de Hauteclocque led some of these patrols personally. In January 1940, the formation was moved to Montreuil, not far from Boulogne, for training.

May–June 1940; Escape; Equatorial Africa

The May 1940 campaign saw the *4ᵉ Division* very quickly destroyed. Ordered to advance into Holland, the *Division* could go no further than the Escaut. From there it was ordered to withdraw towards Maubeuge, as part of the effort to close the gap opened at Sedan. In forest country near Mornal, the formation was then subjected to an eight day battering from German dive bombers, tanks and mechanised infantry. On 28 May, the few remnants of the *Division*, with other remnants in a similar state, had been pushed back westwards to the Lille area. But these exhausted, demoralised and disorganised bodies of men were no longer capable of effective fighting.

De Hauteclocque's hour had come, and the events that follow merit the description of epic. De Hauteclocque obtained leave from his superiors to try to escape and, acquiring a bicycle and a loaf of bread from deserted lorries, he set off. Before long, soldiers from a German column forced him off the roads into hedges and ditches; they fired wildly at him, and a frightened farmer refused him shelter. He spent the night in a barley field soaked by a storm; a German tank opened desultory fire on him soon after he began to move in the

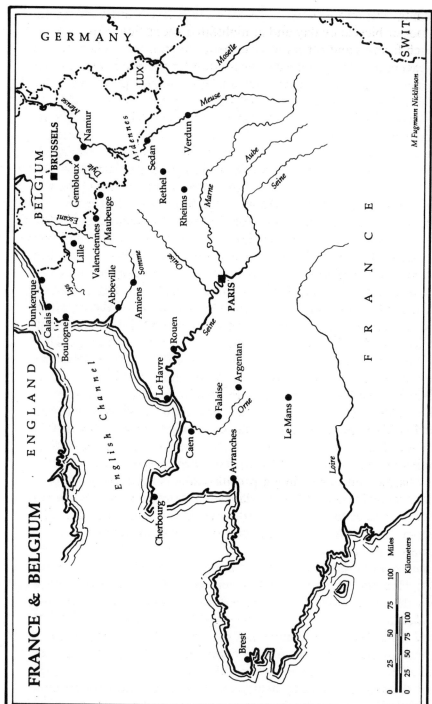

Map 1. France and Belgium

morning. Two more similar days followed, cross-country movement on foot or bicycle by day and at nightfall a succession of refusals by French farmers and others to give shelter to an officer. There were a few exceptions, one provided some food. A farm worker gave him one bicycle, a school boy gave him another and he purloined some civilian clothes. On 31 May, a German checkpoint patrol near Cambrai recognised the scruffy cyclist as a French soldier. De Hauteclocque had accidentally retained a military payslip in his wallet and he was kept under close arrest all night. However, on the next day, he managed to destroy the document while his guard's attention was elsewhere, and he then convinced the patrol commander that he was only a discharged ex-serviceman refugee with six children to look after. Released, and after three further days of evasion and a swim across the Canal du Nord, de Hauteclocque rejoined French forces near Chantilly. On 8 June, after a flying visit to Paris in quest of uniform, he was given command of an armoured combat team.

This team went into action on 10 June and for five days de Hauteclocque led it into battle, on occasions walking out in front of his tanks armed only with a riding crop. Once again, his superiors commented on de Hauteclocque's exceptional bravery and personal qualities. On 15 June, however, he was wounded in the head during a German air attack. Initially refusing anything other than a field dressing, he had to be ordered, at the end of the day, to accept treatment. This entailed a painful journey to a small convent near Avallon where on the next day, the advancing Germans also arrived; de Hauteclocque was again a prisoner. Although weakened by loss of blood and injury, he immediately planned an escape. One of the nuns was charmed into providing a private soldier's uniform.

The following day, 17 June, dawned with a thick mist. Under its cover, de Hauteclocque jumped the convent wall into a nettlebed. He then made his way to the chateau of a kinsman to find German soldiers in the kitchen celebrating the Armistice with champagne. The French private soldier was made welcome. De Hauteclocque when young had had a Czech governess and he struck up a friendship with one of the soldiers who was a Czech. This soldier, out of the corner of his mouth, promised de Hauteclocque a set of civilian clothes. In the night these were quietly laid out and the next day, newly clad and after seizing a girl's bicycle from an astonished German soldier, de Hauteclocque set off again.

He had planned to head south, but the difficulties and the effect of his wound, which at times rendered him nearly blind, led him to change his mind. He headed for Paris where he rested in the rooms of the concierge of a cousin and recovered his strength. On 25 June, he heard de Gaulle broadcast from London; one flaming patriot reached out to another and de Hauteclocque decided to set out for London the following day.

There followed several days of travelling, initially by car but later by bicycle, to the south-west of France. There he bade farewell to his very distressed wife and family who had sought refuge there, at the same time collecting his passport. This had expired but he 'amended' it with the toy printing set of one of his children. The Spanish consul at Bayonne refused a visa, so de Hauteclocque crossed back into Unoccupied France to try again, meeting greater success with the Spanish consul at Perpignan. At midnight on 12 July, de Hauteclocque crossed into Spain, only to be arrested for arriving with funds exceeding the permitted total. He was released pending further enquiries, for which he did not wait. Using his last money – concealed in a sock – he made his way by train to Madrid and then on to Lisbon where he presented himself at the British Embassy. Warmly received, he was put on a ship for Britain two days later.

Before leaving France, he had told his wife that for her protection he would take another name when he arrived in Spain, and that he would let her know his alias by letter. This letter never arrived and only in April 1941 did his wife know of her husband's doings. He 'borrowed' the name Jacques Leclerc from a workman, seeing it as eminently suitable for its plain, ordinary, connotation. He was to use it continuously, with no references to de Hauteclocque at all, until after the end of the war.

In these conditions, then, Captain Leclerc, still exhausted and his head bandaged, arrived in London and reported to de Gaulle, a general known for his particular dislike of the cavalry and in some measure Leclerc's social inferior. Apart from de Gaulle's own personal staff and excepting a number of *Légion Etrangère* and *Coloniale* officers, Leclerc was one of a tiny handful of Free French metropolitan army officers. He was certainly the only cavalryman and one of only a very few aristocrats, a class which was almost uniformly pro-Vichy, to join de Gaulle in the summer of 1940. But the defeat and the French surrender had fuelled his fiery patriotism; he arrived with, in his own words, *'la rage au coeur'*, a *passion* that totally possessed him. There was an immediate meeting of minds, and Leclerc was to remain totally loyal to de Gaulle for the rest of his life.

He had had little time for the Third Republic and from his

perspective as an aristocrat did not see it as having any particular legitimacy. He now viewed Vichy and Pétain in the same cold light; with the national enemy on French soil, any form of compromise was cowardly and treacherous. To fight on was a national, religious and personal imperative that overrode any established military procedures or orders; it must be the way, the truth, the life of a Catholic French officer. The name change is illustrative. De Hauteclocque cannot have believed that his real identity could be concealed for long. 'Leclerc' can be compared perhaps with the adoption of a new simple name by a novitiate entering a religious order. The past life was false and had to be left behind; every energy, every hour must now be devoted to the new cause. Two of de Hauteclocque's ancestors had changed their names, for similar reasons, at the time of the Crusades. De Hauteclocque, or Leclerc as he will henceforth be referred to, entered the Free French camp with the ardour of a Jesuit convert; for him the war was not a fight between professional armies but a crusade.

It is easy to observe that Leclerc had a choice which others, especially those in captivity, did not; he was, also, not in command of or responsible for regimental soldiers. His decision and escape were nevertheless epic in their courage and patriotism. And, not for the last time in his life, Leclerc de Hauteclocque had seen better than most of his superiors when a war should be fought and when it should not.

De Gaulle initially sent Leclerc to a *Légion Etrangère demi-brigade* that was in Britain and had, for the most part, opted for him. The *Légion* refused to have a metropolitan cavalry officer and an angry Leclerc returned to de Gaulle's headquarters.

De Gaulle's situation was unpromising. French North and French West Africa had rallied to Vichy, as had most of the French fleet. Only in French Equatorial Africa was there a spark of resistance. In Chad, Governor Eboué was preparing to declare for de Gaulle, a chance to rally the other Equatorial Africa colonies – Congo, Gabon, Ubangi-Chari and Cameroun – seemed to open up. The governor of Cameroun wavered, inclining always to his most recent visitor or instruction. De Gaulle promoted Leclerc to major and despatched him with his own military secretary Hettier de Boislambert, and René Pleven, a future Prime Minister, to Nigeria. After a somewhat hazardous journey, their flying boat damaging a wing on take off, and a tepid initial reception from the British authorities, a plan of action was prepared. Pleven was to go to Chad to support Eboué, Colonel de Larminat, newly arrived from Syria, was to seize Brazzaville in Congo, while Leclerc, together with de Boislambert, was to land at Douala, in Cameroun. It was intended that they should land with a battalion of *Tirailleurs Sénégalais* that happened to be in the Gold Coast. But the *Tirailleurs* deserted to the Ivory Coast, leaving only their French officers and NCOs, a few of whom agreed to join Leclerc. The British governor of Nigeria, Sir Bernard Bourdillon, lent his support to the plan, two of his ablest officials, M Clifford and G Allen arranging for the necessary ground support. Contacts with sympathisers in Douala were made by Clifford and Allen on a visit. The colony having been a German possession before the First World War a number of French residents were prepared to act to prevent any return of the Germans. Leclerc judged that a major was too junior a rank to command authority and promoted himself to colonel, although he could only find enough material for the rank badges on one shoulder.

Accordingly, during the afternoon of 25 August, Leclerc, de Boislambert and some twenty-five other Frenchmen left Victoria, near the border of Cameroun, in two dug-out canoes arranged for them by Clifford. They had been trained and briefed by Leclerc on a timber estate near the border. But the political situation was as confused as the military. Some of de Gaulle's supporters in Cameroun were losing heart because of the delay in action and Vichy's mixture of threats and blandishments, together with the visit of a Vichy submarine. Allen was in Douala where he had briefed known Gaullists on what to do. On the actual night, Allen's role was to entertain the garrison commander and other notables – and entertain them well.

Outboard motors propelled the canoes for the first part of the journey. After dark, the canoes were paddled to secure surprise. The waters, the choppy estuary of the Wouari River, were difficult and, to add to the difficulties, a storm blew up. Eventually, after paddling through evil smelling creeks and swamps and in their enthusiasm jumping from the canoes prematurely and so becoming soaked, Leclerc and de Boislambert waded ashore, where they joined up with Gaullist supporters in accordance with Allen's arrangements. These transported Leclerc's party to Douala. There some tried to persuade Leclerc to lie up and wait for a few days. Leclerc flatly rejected this and issued a proclamation declaring himself military governor in the name of de Gaulle.

He then arranged for teams to seize the city's key points. This was achieved by 7 am without any incident. The seizure was helped by a company of the local garrison whose commander, Captain Dio, was to become one of Leclerc's most trusted officers. The next day Leclerc despatched the resolute Dio and two companies from the local garrison by train to Yaoundé, the capital of Cameroun. No opposition was offered and the governor finally decided that he was a Gaullist. A little later Leclerc himself arrived to meet the same enthusiastic popular welcome as the coup, once successful, had received in Douala.

Two tasks remained for Leclerc, one political, one military, and both distasteful. The political task was to galvanise Cameroun, hitherto a sleepy colonial backwater, into making a substantial contribution to the war effort. Officials and soldiers who supported Vichy were despatched home via French West Africa, plantation and mine owners were directed to produce the maximum, Frenchmen willing and able were recruited into the Free French Forces, African labour was forced out to work. Leclerc's grip on the colony was ruthless, at times brutal, but African and British observers commented on the absence of any racial bias in his impositions or his personal attitude, very different from that of the French colonial establishment. He had the added difficulties of inexperience, and that some, inevitably, saw him as Captain de Hauteclocque and not Colonel Leclerc; these had to adjust very quickly.

The military task was a brief campaign against Gabon, the one colony of the French Equatorial Africa federation that had opted for Vichy, a campaign that set Frenchmen against Frenchmen. It was also a campaign of great logistical challenge, supplies were exceedingly limited and the terrain very difficult. The Vichy garrison comprised four battalions of *Tirailleurs Sénégalais*, some light artillery, four new American bombers, a sloop and a submarine. The Royal Navy prevented any strengthening, but the British attitude towards the operation was otherwise lukewarm. De Gaulle provided the *13ᵉ Demi-Brigade* of the *Légion Etrangère*, his only non-African regiment, to support the few units of *Tirailleurs Sénégalais* available in Cameroun and Congo, and appointed Leclerc as operational commander.

The operation lasted a month, from 12 October to 12 November. Small columns entered Gabon from Cameroun and Congo, both meeting stiff initial resistance. On 8 November, the *Légion* unit, supported by a *Sénégalais* battalion landed near Libreville. A Free French sloop destroyed its Vichy counterpart, and a British sloop forced the submarine to the surface, thus saving the lives of the crew with the exception of the captain, who opted to go down with his ship and scuttled her. By 12 November, Gabon was in Free French hands.

Some twenty men were killed in the operation which also gave the Free French a number of pro-Vichy captives. These were used by de Gaulle as hostages against any reprisals in France against families of his supporters.

The Bishop of Libreville refused to hold a Mass to give thanks for the victory. Leclerc had him detained and used his own military chaplains for the service. The Bishop's threat to excommunicate him left Leclerc unmoved despite his own strong personal Catholicism. But he took no pleasure in the operation; to him it was fratricidal and divisive though he accepted its necessity. All French Equatorial Africa was now behind de Gaulle, enormously strengthening his hand.

Chad, Libya and Tunisia

De Gaulle next sent Leclerc to Chad. From the end of the nineteenth century, French strategists had argued that this mountainous and impoverished area of Africa was nevertheless pivotal – from it moves into North, West, East or Central Southern Africa could all be made. In the improbable circumstances of 1940, they were to be proved right. In addition, Chad was the only territory of Free France touching on Axis territory, the Italian colony of Libya; Free France could resume the fight. De Gaulle in fact believed that the British would be chased out of Egypt and Chad would be a forward defence post for sub-Saharan Africa. Leclerc arrived in Chad on 2 December; he began talking of offensive operations against the Italians the next day, his objective the remote oasis of Kufra in south-east Libya.

His position was not easy. An aristocratic metropolitan cavalryman and the tough but less formally disciplined, often decidedly unconventional, colonial infantrymen needed time to learn to respect each other. Leclerc found it necessary to adopt a less abrasive style than he had used in Cameroun, but soon his energy, dedicated determination, modesty and clear thinking won the colonial officers over. The problems were daunting. Such vehicles and French equipment as existed were old and dilapidated. Kufra was over 1,000 miles from Fort Lamy, most of the distance being trackless. The oasis, its fort forming part of the Italian southern defensive system, was also an airfield for raids into the Sudan and links with Italian East Africa. It had a well-equipped Italian garrison which included aircraft, a motorised company, infantry and light artillery to a total of some 1,200.

CENTRAL NORTH AFRICA, CHAD & LIBYA

MEDITERRANEAN SEA

TUNISIA

■ TRIPOLI

● Mizda

● Benghazi

● Ghadamès

A L G E R I A

L I B Y A

Sebha ●

Murzuk ● ● Um en Araneb

F e z z a n

Kufra ●

E G Y P T

Tibesti
Mountains

N I G E R

C H A D

Lake Chad

S U D A N

N I G E R I A

● Fort Lamy

M Fugmann Nicklinson

0   100   200   300 Miles

CAMEROON

Map 2. Central North Africa, Chad and Libya

Action had to be immediate as Saharan conditions only permitted operations between December and March. Even in these months, conditions were bad enough, some mountainous terrain, then stone strewn or sandy plateaux and finally desert. Sandstorms could blow up quickly, the days were hot but nights could be cold. Water and fuel provision were major logistic difficulties. The British offered specialist desert warfare advice, but were not able to help much more than with limited air support. Overall, the British doubted the wisdom of the operation. Leclerc's assets were ninety-nine vehicles, many being requisitioned civilian ones, some 100 Europeans and 200 African soldiers, four mortars and two 75mm guns (in the event one only was taken, there being insufficient ammunition). But two misadventures occurred. First a patrol sent into north Chad to try to deceive the Italians was betrayed. And then a British Army Long Range Desert Group (LRDG) patrol arrived in Chad, tasked to attack Murzuh, in south-west Libya. This attack was a success but cost the life of one of Leclerc's best officers, Lieutenant-Colonel d'Ornano, who had accompanied the group.

Leclerc's column, formed into a small three company battalion, set out on 31 January 1941. The British LRDG patrol had offered to accompany it and was given a forward reconnaissance role. In this mission it was ambushed by the Italians, its commander being taken prisoner. Most of the remainder, judging that the element of surprise was lost, withdrew to Egypt. Leclerc was undismayed both by this setback and the difficulties of the journey – at its worst, the terrain permitted only a few miles advance per day – and, with an advance guard, he arrived at Kufra on the evening of 7 February. He at once shot up installations on the edge of the oasis and drew the conclusion that it was possible to infiltrate the area. The main body of Leclerc's column arrived on the 17th and 18th and fought some sharp encounters with the Italian motorised company supported by the Italian aircraft. Leclerc was in the thick of the fighting which resulted in the Italians being put to flight. Leclerc then began a siege of Kufra's fort, El Tag. The infantry garrison felt itself abandoned and its morale was further undermined by occasional mortar and field gun fire, Leclerc switching the firing positions to give an impression of greater numbers. On 1 March, the fort hoisted the white flag. Brusquely refusing any form of parley, Leclerc entered it, demanded and accepted a surrender. At a cost of four dead and twenty-one wounded, Free France had achieved its first land victory over the Axis. The symbolic significance was enormous. A large plain tricolour, and a smaller one with the Cross of Lorraine added flew over the fort. Leclerc addressed his column in a short but famous oration known as the *Serment de Koufra*, vowing with *passion* to fight on until the French flag again flew over Strasbourg cathedral.

For Leclerc personally the success was timely. The implications of the decisions that he had made for himself over the previous nine months had imposed a strain despite the outward calm; success confirmed that the decisions had been correct. He now had a victory, a charisma and self-confidence; he was more prepared to listen, discuss and explain. The continuing passionate intensity of conviction was however to be seen in his frugal life-style, eating little, sleeping only a few hours each night, no alcoholic drinking, and in occasional impatient outbursts. More serious signs of the stress of his lonely command, a stress exacerbated both by a Vichy court's sentence of death with confiscation of property passed upon him and anxiety over his family, and the legacy of his malaria, were occasional sharp and severe attacks of shaking. He concealed these with difficulty. One may surmise that moments of doubt were confided, and resolved, in prayer. He personally remained very modest with a simple and unaffected uniform. For a long time and until directly ordered, he even refused to wear the stars of a *général de brigade* to which rank he was promoted by de Gaulle in August 1941. He considered the promotion abnormal and in general suffered from a lack of personal communication with de Gaulle. But his leadership was never joyless, his headquarters were always lively and cheerful and a warm welcome awaited all Frenchmen who joined him.

A little after the taking of Kufra, an RAF aircraft dropped a copy of one of de Gaulle's publications which gave an account of the siege in the grounds of the Hauteclocque chateau in France.

Leclerc needed all his talents for de Gaulle's next design, the occupation of the Fezzan. The aim was that France renewed should occupy a province of enemy territory with French forces and, in military terms, also support a British entry into Tripolitania. The major physical problem was that of terrain. Chad's Tibesti range, passable only on camel paths which, on the Italian side, were fortified, stood in the way. But the psychological one, that of 'Forgotten army' *cafard*, was as difficult for him to surmount, necessitating frequent visits to remote outposts. On one of these, his aircraft ran out of fuel in the desert and only the miracle of petrol siphoned from a passing lorry saved him.

Rommel's repulse of Auchinleck's 1941 offensive set any Fezzan occupation back almost a year. The best Leclerc could achieve was a very successful fifteen day foray into the Fezzan in late February and early March 1942, again supported by the British LRDG; in the course of this, four Italian outposts were overrun by French columns, their stores either taken or destroyed and their garrisons taken prisoner. But Leclerc's subordinate commanders also gained terrain and combat experience – speed, radio silence, movement by night, concealment by day, desert craft. Just as important, they gained increased respect for their commander, who ate the same rations and slept sheepskin-covered under the cold starlight as they did.

After the Fezzan raid, Leclerc was appointed commander of all French forces in Equatorial Africa, de Gaulle flatly refusing to allow him to be placed under direct British command. Leclerc found this appointment irksome as it required desk work in Brazzaville and, as a consequence of de Gaulle's political activities in London, some friction with the British, a nation whose soldiers he liked but of whom as a whole he was jealous. He was also disturbed by the poor quality and controversial nature of Free French propaganda. Following a brief visit by de Gaulle, Leclerc found it necessary to issue to his officers a very clear and direct statement on de Gaulle's aims and his own total support for them. After the Allied landings in North Africa, for example, neither de Gaulle nor Leclerc had any respect for the temporising generals in Algiers or the scuttling of the French Navy at Toulon, subjects on which not all immediately shared de Gaulle's views.

The complex logistic preparations for the Fezzan operations continued throughout the summer, harassed occasionally by Italian air attacks or small forays from Vichy French Niger. Stores were acquired or purchased from the Belgian Congo and the Union of South Africa. The operation's timing was all important: too early could lead to destruction, too late would be purposeless. The British promised to give Leclerc eight days' notice to move; in the event, Leclerc was reprimanded by de Gaulle for this arrangement and it was de Gaulle who, on 28 October after Montgomery's Alamein victory, ordered him to move. Leclerc's force, 500 Europeans, 2,700 Africans (with another 1,400 in transport companies) and 350 vehicles supported by twelve aircraft, all formed into three columns, commenced its epic march across the Fezzan on 16 December. The force was almost immediately attacked from the air; this effective strafing and harassment continued until mid-January but failed to stop the French progress. Movement was mainly in the evening or by night, with frequent halts to dig out vehicles trapped in sand. In operations from 28 December to 4 January, the strong Italian post at Um en Araneb was taken by two columns arriving from opposite directions. Leclerc, although badly weakened by fever, personally directed the last phase. Sebha, the provincial capital, fell to the French on 12 January. Resupplied from the air, Leclerc's forces took Mizda on the 22nd and Ghadamès on the 26th. On the 13th, his advance guard first contacted the 8th Army; on the 26th as his columns entered the suburbs of Tripoli, Leclerc staked his claim to administer the Fezzan and to participate in the forthcoming Tunisian campaign. Montgomery, greatly impressed by Leclerc and his force, despite its grimy, sun-blacked and hirsute appearance in ill-assorted uniforms, gave Leclerc clothing, stores and weaponry. Leclerc himself accepted a British battledress but retained his battered makeshift *képi*, covered in a *tirailleur*'s desert scarf, and with two nickel stars, taken off the bushjacket of an Italian soldier, loosely pinned on.

Arrival on the frontiers of a French possession garrisoned by soldiers of very recent loyalty to Vichy was to present Leclerc with new dilemmas. For some time he and his force, now designated as 'L Force' by the British and strengthened by a company of Greek patriots, became a player in the power contest waged between the largely American supported Giraud and the best of the traditional *Armée d'Afrique* on the one hand and the largely British-supported de Gaulle, to whose movement Leclerc remained passionately loyal, on the other.

In the actual Tunisian fighting, L Force, after a period of rest and retraining, was deployed from 20 February 1943 on the left flank of the 8th Army. On 24 February, L Force took up positions under Stuka attack at Ksar Rhilane to cover Montgomery's assault on the Mareth Line. On 10 March, the force was subjected to a ferocious German armoured attack seeking to outflank the 8th Army. Leclerc, who had been warned by Montgomery in advance of the attack but had refused to withdraw, controlled a flexible defence from a small sandbagged command post concealed in dunes. To Montgomery's surprise and subsequent gratitude, the attack was repulsed with the help of the RAF, and L Force covered an advance to Gabès on 29 March. The force remained on the British left flank to occupy Mezzouna on 9 April. Thereafter, attached to the newly formed *1ere Division Française Libre*, L Force was deployed in the Djebel Garci area to form part of the western flank protection for the final operations against the Axis in Tunis, Bizerta and Cape Bon. Incidents in the campaign further illustrate Leclerc's character as a leader. He would exaggerate the number of men under his command so as to ensure they were given a key role. On one occasion, where overstretched French companies could barely man positions taken over from British battalions, Leclerc flew into a towering rage because one sub-unit commander had failed fully to reconnoitre his front. A little later he returned and with an embarrassed smile apologised; hands on the sub-unit commander's shoulders, he gave his usual explanation that he knew his temper was impossible but that he did daily try hard to curb it. He then added that he knew he planned and executed tasks that appeared out of scale, but this was reasonable as they succeeded. As before, Leclerc led from the very front, often under fire which he totally ignored, demonstrating his orders with battle maps drawn in the sand with his long walking stick. During and after the campaign some French citizens in Tunisia tried to lionise him, but he particularly disliked any form of popular personality cult and withdrew further into himself.

If the military mission was clear, the political role was the reverse. The French authorities decreed that for the Tunis Victory Parade, formations would be represented proportionate to their strength, a decision which would have meant a totally insignificant representation for L Force and which Leclerc refused to accept. The British instead showed their respect for Leclerc by including L Force vehicles at the head of the British contingent. The Force was reconstituted as the nucleus of a new *2e Division Française Libre*, together with its former parent, the *1ere Division*, it began to pull in both the young French *colons* and *evadés* from France and, applying for transfer, French soldiers from the *Armée d'Afrique*, drawn by its attractive mix of the glamour of success and British rates of pay. The *Armée d'Afrique* establishment became both jealous and apprehensive: two divisions loyal to de Gaulle in French North Africa were seen as politically dangerous. To Leclerc's chagrin, his former chief, Giraud, treated him very coldly, calling him 'Hauteclocque' and showing little admiration for his achievement. Other *Armée d'Afrique* officers were openly hostile, blaming Leclerc for the strife in Gabon. Leclerc was ordered to move his division back to Tripolitania, an order which, in a rage, he at first refused to obey.

For two months these French forces remained banished from French North Africa and direct contacts with other Frenchmen, Leclerc living in a small tent. But during that time the steady stream of Frenchmen wanting to join them increased in number and, above all, de Gaulle established his ascendancy in Algiers. The Allies were looking ahead to 1944 and the invasion of France. De Gaulle was secretly determined that a French *Division* should enter Paris with, at its head, units of a Free French tradition. A *Division* had to be prepared, that of Leclerc was the obvious choice both on account of Leclerc's record and the very large number of Frenchmen who had volunteered for it. Accordingly, in August 1943, Leclerc's Division was moved to Rabat in Morocco – with as few contacts as possible en route in Tunisia and Algeria. Leclerc was promoted to be a *général de division*, but he once again refused to put up the insignia. He was not told of de Gaulle's project, though he had some inkling of it, and he only allowed himself to put up his third star in Paris a year later. The *Division*, now bearing the title in which it achieved fame, the *2ᵉ Division Blindée*, was given the full weaponry and equipment of an American armoured division – Sherman and Honey tanks, armoured cars, self-propelled guns, other field artillery, anti-tank guns, small arms. Leclerc set in motion an arduous training programme.

The personnel of the *Division*, too, was changed. The Africans, to the disappointment of many, were returned to Black Africa as it was judged that European conditions would be too difficult for them. Initially, Leclerc would have preferred his regiments to be formed entirely from Free Frenchmen, but he soon saw that his division must bridge and not widen gaps. His views broadened to a recognition that there were good patriots other than those who had rallied to de Gaulle; moral cowardice lay only with their leaders who had deceived and betrayed. The *Division*'s composition therefore could reflect all interests. The original Chad *Tirailleurs Sénégalais* unit was given a proud new title, the *Régiment de Marche du Tchad (RMT)* and its ranks filled with *evadés* and some European and North African volunteers. The *RMT* and two of the *Division*'s tank regiments, the *501ᵉ Chars de Combat* and the *1ᵉʳ Régiment de Marche de Spahis Marocains*, all with soldiers from the same sources, represented the Free French element; the *Spahis Marocains* had undergone the same process of *blanchiment* as the *RMT*. A *Chasseurs d'Afrique* regiment and one of the artillery units came from the *Armée d'Afrique*. Another armoured regiment revived the traditions of the metropolitan French army as the *12ᵉ Cuirassiers*. Engineer and other support units were drawn from a variety of sources – sailors, marines, volunteers from Lebanon or Pondicherry. All the tanks and vehicles of the *Division* had painted upon them a map of France. The map on the vehicles of the Free French tradition regiments included a Cross of Lorraine, this later became the badge for the whole *Division* by general agreement and in Leclerc's own phrase 'enlarging the circle'.

Inevitably, even though all were volunteers, there were unpleasant incidents and sharp clashes, especially at first. On one occasion, Leclerc refused to punish severely two soldiers of the *501e CC* who had been caught by a captain singing a rude song about General Giraud. The affair created a great fuss. Leclerc addressed his staff and the local regional staff in bitter terms pointing out the soldiers concerned had spent three years fighting while most of those present had not. The address was badly received, old *Armée d'Afrique* hands once again attacking Leclerc and describing him as a condottieri. On another occasion, Leclerc told his Marines unit that they had done nothing in the war and would have to regain their honours and the nation's respect. But in Morocco and then, after an uncomfortable but safe sea journey, also in England, Leclerc stamped firmly on the bickering in time, and by his own personality welded together one of the finest fighting formations fielded by the French Army. The training, the conversion of bush and desert soldiers to modern armoured warfare with strange American equipment and doctrine, was no easy matter, but in itself it carried a unifying excitement and the realisation that the *Division* was to be an élite. The training ended with a great parade, presentation of colours to the regiments and the divisional badge to each soldier. Leclerc's model was the fusion of the best of the army of pre-1789 France with that of the post-Revolution volunteers.

Normandy, Paris and Germany

In the autumn of 1943, de Gaulle openly hinted to Leclerc that the Allies might accept his *Division* in the forthcoming plans for the Normandy landings. Leclerc immediately began lobbying for its transport to Britain. This brought a visit from and a furious row with de Lattre who, not unnaturally, wanted Leclerc's *Division* for his own 1st Army, which was to land in the South of France. But Leclerc continued his lobbying and, with the support of de Gaulle, secured the transport for the *Division* in April 1944. On arrival in Britain Leclerc was saddened to learn that his division was not going to fight alongside the British. But he was more than consoled when he was told of its inclusion in the US Army's Third Army which, under a fellow cavalryman, General Patton, was to have the break-out role after the Normandy landings.

Leclerc's style of command and choice of staff officers was distinctive. His subordinate combat team commanders were either officers, like Dio whom he had known from Chad days or Colonels whom he trusted implicitly, Langlade, Billotte, Guillebon and Remy. His staff officers were very largely reserve officers – for Leclerc pre-war regular French Army staff training was very suspect. They were given very precise instructions and Leclerc would then question to check the instructions were understood. He himself refused any particular comfort, living simply in a caravan, but he took great care to know well each of his staff officers and their major problems. When the *Division* was completing its training in Yorkshire, he allowed himself a very occasional relief. He would slip down to London for a concert of classical music of which he was very fond.

On 1 August, the *Division* disembarked at Utah Beach in Normandy, an emotional occasion. At this point, Patton's Army was preparing for its breakthrough and, after defeating a German attack, the Third Army's advance from Avranches rapidly gathered speed in the first week of August. Leclerc's *Division*, with three American divisions, formed the US Army's XV Corps, commanded by General W H Haislip, a French-speaking, attacking soldier with whom Leclerc immediately formed a close, mutually trusting, partnership. The French units contributed a special élan to the Corps, and Leclerc drew freely on his own local knowledge of the terrain and its personalities both for help and for suitable all-French celebrations to which he attached importance. As a good cavalryman, he also had the ability to find his opponent's weak spots and drive into them. For Leclerc the rapid advance was a fulfilment; he described it as akin to seeing 1940 in reverse. As before, he was always near the fighting and often under fire, directing his own artillery or tank movements. He had at first tried to command by means of a forward headquarters of some five or six key officers with support staff and a rear headquarters for the rest. He soon found the forward headquarters too unwieldy and it was reduced to just one or two vehicles. He kept his personal staff to the minimum so that he could move more freely about the battlefield. Very often, he commanded from his jeep alone; orders being sent by radio or by a liaison officer. These latter knew that they would later rejoin him on the main axis of advance. Tense with nervous energy before a battle, when in the thick of it, Leclerc was always perfectly calm and at peace with himself, an attribute much admired. The mood could however change later to a violent outburst of temper if subordinates had failed to meet expectations.

The first advance, over seventy miles in four days, was relatively easy going as far as Le Mans after which the 3rd Army turned north to cut off the Germans in the Falaise area. Almost encircled, two German armies fought desperately to keep open their eighteen mile wide escape route. Here Leclerc made one of his few errors, exceeding Haislip's instructions he let his armour continue to advance on a road near Argentan that Haislip had earmarked for petrol supplies. The traffic confusion delayed the American advance so enabling the Germans to prepare defences. From these and others concealed in the Ecouves forest the Germans fought tenaciously, the *Division* taking casualties and losing tanks, but establishing a bridgehead across the river Orne. The Americans then decided that Patton's 3rd Army should try and cut the Germans off further east. Leclerc's *Division* and one US division were to be detached to serve under the US Army's 1st Army in the V Corps commanded by Major-General L T Gerow, an officer very different from Haislip. These two divisions were tasked to cover the southern flank of the advance eastwards necessary for this. Leclerc ignored an order to withdraw south of the Orne and a little later the Americans and French resumed their pressure on the south side of the Falaise Gap. It was narrowed to six miles, and together with the Allied forces to the north and unceasing air attacks, French and American artillery shattered the retreating Germans.

Subsumed to the fortunes of the campaign, however, was also the internal French power struggle. De Gaulle, although at the head of the French provisional government, was still not yet fully accepted by the Americans; nor had he any mass following – even among the Resistance – in the France that was being liberated. As French *départements* were freed, de Gaulle had been putting in his own administrators, to the annoyance of the Americans who had had other plans. French Communists, strong and well organised, wanted to be the liberators of Paris in order to develop wider designs. The Allied Supreme Commander, General Eisenhower, had promised that Leclerc's *Division* should enter the city, all other factors so permitting. But at this stage of the fighting, both Eisenhower and Montgomery saw Paris as more likely to be a liability, absorbing military resources and food supplies; the city might best be by-passed. But for de Gaulle, an immediate French entry to Paris was even more vital than he had assessed earlier; not only would it play an important part in restoring French national self-respect, but it was the best, perhaps only, safeguard against a divisive repetition of the 1871 *Commune* uprising. Leclerc's view was not very different, he had developed an apprehension that revolution was in the air and was passionately concerned that Free French units that had fought since 1940 – and neither the Americans nor de Lattre's Army moving up from the south – should be the first into the city. He saw the Free French movement as a national regeneration and the sole hope against revolution. He even went so far as to refuse to carry out a local attack ordered by Gerow, which he thought in any case to be tactically unsound, in order to be prepared for a drive on Paris.

The hands of the Americans were forced to some extent by Hitler, who wanted von Choltitz, his garrison commander, to destroy the city, and very much more so by the Communists, who controlled a large proportion of the city's resistance movement and had initiated a limited-scale uprising on 19 August, despite de Gaulle's orders to wait. A precarious truce was negotiated between von Choltitz and the Communists the next day but this broke down on the 21st. It was nevertheless endorsed by de Gaulle's representative in the city on the day after, the 22nd. The situation had become very tense and very complex, different emissaries from both the Resistance and a mediating Swedish consul-general appearing at different American headquarters, while street fighting worsened in the city.

The situation was resolved firstly by Leclerc who, frustrated by American refusals to let him advance on Paris, had decided to act on his own. On the 21st he ordered a reconnaissance group to 'patrol' towards Paris, an order he was told to revoke by an angry Gerow but which he refused to do. De Gaulle then promptly endorsed Leclerc's action, having previously told Eisenhower that he personally might order the *Division* to Paris in any case even if the Americans objected. On 22 August, Eisenhower accordingly authorised a full scale march on Paris by the *2e Division Blindée*, which was further urged on by words of encouragement from de Gaulle at Rambouillet and the fear of an American division approaching from the east that had to be outraced. Eisenhower's authorisation was at least in part based on a fear of other armies going their own way, following a French example.

The *Division*, 12,000 men in some 3,000 vehicles, moved on Paris from the west in three columns commanded by Dio, Billotte and Langlade, the move beginning at 6.30 am on 23 August. Each column had a battalion of the *RMT* with a squadron of the *Spahis*, Dio's column included the *Cuirassiers*, Langlade the *Chasseurs d'Afrique* and Billotte the *Chars de Combat*. The main attack was to be from the south after a feint from the south-west. Some stiff resistance was met from several German positions on the axes of advance, the German

88 mm guns destroying a number of Leclerc's tanks. On the evening
of the 24th, it looked as if the American division might win. Leclerc
ordered a small team from the *RMT* and the *Chars de Combat* to
enter Paris somehow or another and hold on; this column found the
Port d'Italie unguarded and by 9.30 pm had crossed Paris to reach
the Hotel de Ville. Bells pealed far into the night and, early the
following morning, Leclerc's columns entered the city in force to a
rapturous welcome, Lieutenant-Colonel Massu, a Chad veteran,
being the first to salute the Unknown Warrior at the Arc de Triomphe. Choltitz formally surrendered to Leclerc, after some face-
saving skirmishing, in the afternoon. Leclerc, in accepting the
surrender, was of course again breaking Allied Command instructions that such surrenders should be to the Allied Command only.
Sniping continued in Paris until the evening and was not finally
ended until the next day. On that day, the 25th, with the shooting
still occasionally to be heard, de Gaulle walked from the Arc de
Triomphe to Notre-Dame Cathedral, Leclerc following a pace or
two behind and the route lined by the *Division*. But then, and in the
days that followed with all their adulation, Leclerc remained personally modest, often retiring, refusing to become involved with any
group or faction. For him the greatest satisfaction was a brief visit to
his family, his two elder sons instantly joining units of the *Division*,
the younger of the two falsifying his age.

But in this ceremonial lay the germ of trouble. De Gaulle wished
to keep the *Division* in Paris to contain any Communist take-over bid.
Gerow did not like Leclerc's division and was furious at the French
celebrating while his other formations were fighting. He had ordered
the *Division* out at once with a task to clear the Germans from the
northern suburbs. But de Gaulle insisted, and even succeeded in
securing Eisenhower's agreement, to the further fury of Gerow; only
part of the *Division* was briefly committed to the suburbs. Nearly two
weeks of revelry, however, began to have its effects on the *Division* and
Leclerc, increasingly anxious to return to the front, wrote an imploring letter to Haislip. De Gaulle wanted Leclerc's *Division* to join
de Lattre's *1re Armée* but was met by a flat refusal from Leclerc at his
most fiery. To Leclerc even de Lattre was a man who had served Vichy
but the refusal annoyed de Gaulle who from then on visited Leclerc
only very rarely. However a triumphant Leclerc took his *Division*,
strengthened by hurriedly trained or retrained recruits secured in
Paris to replace the six hundred killed in the liberation of the city,
back to the XV Corps which was moving towards Alsace. The *Division*

was tasked to take Colmar and Belfort, de Gaulle later persuading Eisenhower that Strasbourg be added.

The *Division*'s first battle since Paris showed the tactical skill of Leclerc at his best. The newest German tanks, Tigers and Panthers, were so well protected that the 76 mm gun of the American Sherman tank could not penetrate the front armour. Manoeuvre, in and out of cover, firing at the tracks from cover or from the flank, together with on call air-to-ground support, was the only solution. Leclerc applied this at Dompaire near Epinal between 12 and 14 September, so damaging a German armoured formation that it was unable to mount an attack that had been planned. There was also the satisfaction of a link-up with units of de Lattre's *1re Armée* moving up from the south. But thereafter operations slowed until November on account of heavy rain, mud, logistic difficulties and the German defences in the Vosges foothills which the *Division* encountered after crossing the Moselle and the Meurthe.

For Leclerc the aim remained that of the *Serment de Koufra*, Strasbourg. At American request, so as to enlarge their bridgehead across the Meurthe, he launched a very well-planned attack on 30 October. This not only gained the required ground but, to the admiration of the Americans, took the town of Baccarat before the Germans could blow its bridge across the Meurthe. Haislip next ordered him to clear forests to the east, an order Leclerc refused. For him Baccarat opened the route to Strasbourg and there followed what was to be Leclerc's most brilliant tactical battle, one to form a standard subject of postwar French Tactical Schools and Staff College studies.

The liberation of north Alsace, as planned by the American 7th Army's commander, Patch, envisaged a first or rupture phase from 13 to 18 November to be carried out by two American divisions, an exploitation phase across the north end of the Vosges to the Saverne passes by Leclerc's *Division*, and a rapid debouch on to Strasbourg itself. Although technically the city was not part of the Division's mission, which limited Leclerc to the passes, Haislip appreciated the symbolic significance for him and secured Patch's acquiescence to letting Leclerc have the first chance. The initial American two division attack was stopped by the Germans, the weather precluding air support; Haislip sought Leclerc's help. Leclerc had made a meticulously careful study of the ground and the German positions. Despite appalling weather conditions, he sent two powerful columns across the Vosges to take Saverne from the east. The columns, headlights switched on and vehicles bumper to bumper, used country roads and tracks, by-passing the German positions to the total surprise of the German commander. Then, despite the main road to Saverne still being blocked by the Germans and hence the necessity for all vehicles and supplies to use mountain roads, Leclerc ordered his *Division* to charge for Strasbourg and the Kehl bridge over the Rhine on five axes of advance. The order was only issued after his Intelligence officer had assured Leclerc that the Germans could not counter attack within two days; the dash began in rain and fog at 0715 on the 23rd. Brushing aside or circumventing the German defences, the columns succeeded in entering the city from the north a little after 10 in the morning, again to the surprise of the German command. By mid-afternoon the Tricolour flew from the cathedral, and a promise made at a remote oasis in Libya had been fulfilled. The whole attack was a classic bounce and bound armoured operation that split the German front in two, compressing one Army, the 19th, in an exposed salient. Flushing out small urban stayback parties of Germans and taking the forts surrounding the city, however, was to last several days. Some of these Germans, on occasions in plain clothes or disguised as policemen, or alternatively operating as snipers firing down from rooftops, killed several French soldiers. Leclerc had to threaten reprisals against captured German civilians, a threat that, in the event, was not carried out.

At this point, General Eisenhower made a questionable decision, yielding to pressure from Patton to thrust into the Saar rather than securing the Rhine line by eliminating the German salient. This decision was to prove costly later, and the Colmar pocket salient became a serious brake on operations. The salient was now only under attack from one flank, the south, by the French *1ere Armée* under de Lattre, an army in a serious state of exhaustion. Leclerc's *Division*, also now battle weary, together with an American division was ordered to link up with it; both were placed under de Lattre's command. Devers, the American Army Group Commander, seriously under-estimated the strength of the Germans in the salient and wanted Leclerc to make an attack southward to cut the Germans off. Leclerc refused to carry out such an attack, committing his division only to more limited fighting on the northern flank of the salient. He argued that the American plan, although essentially imaginative, required him to fight over terrain unsuitable for an armoured division and more infantry would be essential. But also present was his fear that the operation would lead to his permanent subordination to de Lattre. On the northern flank, the *Division* met well-defended German positions and, despite continuous attacks, could make little headway in what was essentially an infantry task.

The German Ardennes Offensive

With the opening of the German Ardennes offensive the *Division* was hurriedly moved to Lorraine to contain German attempts to break through into Alsace. There followed some sharp fighting in bitter cold. While so deployed Leclerc learnt that the Americans believed it might be necessary to withdraw temporarily from Alsace and Strasbourg, the overstretched Devers having advanced to the Saar in support of Patton and the Colmar pocket still containing a powerful German force. Predictably, he reacted strongly, sending an urgent plea to de Gaulle and warning his staff that, as a matter of honour, the *Division* might have to defend Strasbourg to the last themselves. The issue for the French was far wider than Strasbourg itself. The loss, even temporary, of Strasbourg would have called into question de Gaulle's credibility, with probable consequences for civil order in Paris. But, in circumstances examined later, the crisis was resolved.

These and other events in December 1944, however, had raised again the whole question of the employment of Leclerc's *Division*. De Gaulle still wanted it to join de Lattre's *1ere Armée*, so that all French units were serving in one powerful command. Once again, Leclerc objected. In a long plea to de Gaulle, Leclerc argued that the *Division*'s crusading zeal was special, that it contributed a French presence in a different sector, it was structured to work with the Americans, and that it was treated in all matters of rapid re-supply by the Americans as one of theirs. De Gaulle rather frostily commented that Leclerc's arguments were exaggerated and not based on reason; Leclerc in reply observed that virtually everything he had accomplished since 1940 could be seen as exaggerated and not based on reason. De Gaulle gave way, consenting to the *Division* rejoining Haislip's XV Corps in Lorraine. There, for the first two weeks of January, the *Division* fought on the southern front of the Allied counter-offensive. Leclerc was later to be criticised for his refusals, it being argued that had his armoured division joined de Lattre's Army as Devers wanted earlier, the German Colmar salient would have been destroyed sooner, so releasing more divisions for operations in Germany. The argument is unsound in view of Devers' serious underestimate of the German strength, together with the problems of supply, weariness and the winter difficulties precluding effective air support.

Behind Leclerc's arguments lay other factors. Leclerc's *Division* with its generous American re-supply not unnaturally aroused jealousy in de Lattre's Army. The *Division*'s often unorthodox methods, it would, for example, for preference not hand in a broken down vehicle in exchange for a new one but keep the new one and tow the old one along for spare parts – and its frequent rough and ready appearance also attracted criticism. In turn, Leclerc had a prejudiced perception of de Lattre's style, which he regarded as outmoded, with undue attention to elaborate routine and paper work handled by elegant staff and liaison officers. Leclerc feared that his *Division*, which he saw as the spirit of a new, reborn, France, would be tarnished by association with the old ways. He also, unfortunately, did not like de Lattre personally. This dislike was in part one of personality clash, the aristocrat in Leclerc, and his natural modesty, recoiling from the extrovert brilliance of de Lattre, and in part one of memories of 1940, Leclerc never really trusting any French general who had served Vichy. In addition, there had been a mishap on the ground. In December, de Lattre had lent Leclerc's *Division* two units for a particular small village clearing operation which had failed, at a considerable cost in lives – Leclerc was away at the time.

In January, however, after the end of the Ardennes offensive, the *Division* was taken from XV Corps again. With a promise that the move be temporary, it was placed under the command of de Lattre's II Corps commander, General de Monsabert, for the final operations to clear Alsace of the Germans. Leclerc protested to General Juin, then Chief of Defence Staff, in vain. Friction ensued. The *Division* lent an armoured group to support an attack on the small township of Grüssenheim planned by de Monsabert. Another incident followed. The group commander assessed that both de Monsabert's plans were unsound and his infantry too exhausted; after one abortive attack, he refused to continue unless the plans were recast. Leclerc supported him and stormy meetings with de Monsabert and then de Lattre ensued.

These months, January and February 1945, were months for infantry rather than armoured fighting, particularly in the hilly terrain of Alsace. But from 23 January to 9 February the *Division* continued loyally to support de Lattre's reduction of the stoutly defended Colmar pocket, its armour moving southward up the Rhine to link up with de Lattre's *1ere Division Blindée* in an outer pincer movement. A little later the *Division* was withdrawn, first to Lorraine and then to Chateauroux in Central France, for a period of much needed rest and regrouping. To Leclerc's annoyance, elements of the *Division* were used to help reduce Royan, one of the remaining Atlantic coastal areas still held by the Germans and one which commanded the approach to Bordeaux. But de Gaulle's use of the *Division* in France itself had a wider purpose, its moves across France and its use on the coast was meant to show more and more Frenchmen the part that their own army was playing in the Liberation, important in view of the indifference shown in some regions. De Gaulle had evidently intended that Leclerc should command a new III Corps, of which the *Division* was to be the nucleus. He was promoted and given a headquarters, but the project was overtaken by events. In April, Leclerc's *Division* was released to take part in the last act of the drama, the entry into Germany. Once more, and for the last time, the dash and style that had been the *Division's* hallmark took Leclerc and his men in nine columns through the Augsburg area of Germany, to the Bavarian mountain retreat of the former Führer, Berchtesgaden.

The *Division* lost 1,687 killed, of which 108 were officers, in its advance from Normandy to Bavaria. But both as a symbol and as a fighting force the *Division* and its commander had ensured a unique place for themselves in the history of France.

TUNISIA

MEDITERRANEAN SEA

Bizerta

TUNIS

Medjez el Bab

Pont du Fahs

Bône

Grande Dorsale Mountains

Mountains

Sousse

Thala Kairouan

Orientale Dorsale

Tebessa

Sfax

Mezzonna

ALGERIA

Gafsa

Gabès

MARETH LINE

Ksar Rhilane ● Médenine

Bir Djeneien

LIBYA

| 0 | 50 | 100 Miles |
| 0 | 50 | 100 | 150 Kilometers |

Ghadames

M Fugmann Nicklinson

Map 3. Tunisia

4

North Africa and Italy: General Juin

The administrative effort required to organise and transport large numbers of *Armée d'Afrique* regiments to France kept a frustrated Juin at Algiers until December 1939. In that month he gained his way and arrived in northern France to command the *15ᵉ Division d'Infanterie Motorisée* – a well-equipped formation of three infantry regiments with modern artillery and armoured reconnaissance units, but with only limited anti-tank sub-units and no tanks at all. Juin spent the early months of 1940 training his *Division*, borrowing tanks to simulate the lessons that he thought should be drawn from the Polish campaign.

May–June 1940; Prisoner of War

When the German blitzkrieg opened on 10 May, Juin's division, as part of General Blanchard's 1st Army, was ordered to move into Belgium and hold the line of the Dyle river near Gembloux, as part of the defence of Brussels. It was at this time still assessed that the main German attack would be through Flanders; the real German intention of a massive armoured thrust through the Ardennes was not foreseen. The 150 kilometer move to the Dyle was difficult, much movement had to be by night and upon one route already filling with refugees. At Gembloux two divisions of Blanchard's Army held up two of the best German tank divisions supported by air strikes throughout the 14th and 15th, but overall the pressure on Blanchard's Army forced a withdrawal. Juin's *Division*, still in good shape, was then ordered to retire towards Valenciennes as part of the proposed Escaut defensive line. Established by the 19th, the *Division* enjoyed four days of respite until the 24th when massive German attacks on this line began; worse still was the fact that the forces in

Belgium were now encircled by the German Ardennes break through and dash for the sea at Abbeville. A further withdrawal to the Lys, followed by yet one more to the suburbs of Lille, were ordered. These were carried out amid mounting chaos, the Germans having completed a virtual local encirclement of Lille. The six *Divisions*, some but remnants, others like Juin's still battleworthy, that were trapped in the area attempted a break out, but only one column – of units from Juin's *Division* – was successful. The remainder fought in the suburbs of Lille until ammunition ran out, Juin ordering his main body to cease fire in the late afternoon of the 29th, after the last artillery shells had been fired. The Germans granted full military honours to the defenders of Lille; Juin himself was taken to OFLAG VIB, the massive Königstein Castle in Saxony, a prisoner of war cage for senior French officers. Life was not uncomfortable but tedious: Juin took refuge in bridge, and mulling over the cause of the defeat. He saw these as complacency following a bad peace treaty, the complacency leading to a failure to modernise the army or to think in any terms of offensive action *'la sclérose doctrinale'*. It was not a place where questions of loyalty or the possibility of continuing the war from North Africa were immediate; as prisoners, these officers had no options. Juin's whole character and temperament however rested upon a concept of obedience and discipline; for him there was no doubt that Pétain's government was the lawful authority and was trying to manoeuvre in France's best interests. As part of this the Pétain government still controlled French North and West Africa and had installed Weygand as Delegate General and Commander-in-Chief. For those not entirely convinced by Pétain, Weygand provided an inspiration as an officer who was using North Africa to rebuild a French military capacity, either to hold North Africa against anyone, the Axis powers, Spain, Britain or de Gaulle – seen as an irresponsible adventurer – or to re-enter the war at the right moment.

Command in North Africa Under Vichy

The Germans – but not the Italians – were content with Vichy French control in North Africa. By their perception, Vichy secured the Maghreb against Britain at no cost to Berlin. Vichy was allowed to keep a sizeable army in the three North African territories and Weygand pressed Vichy to attempt to secure the release of Juin as a *'Spécialiste de l'Afrique'*. In June 1941, this was arranged, following a personal request by Pétain. Overtly, Juin's release was represented as part of a one for one exchange for the repatriation of thirty German sailors, survivors of a warship sunk in the Mediterranean who had been picked up by a French ship and taken to Tunisia. Initially the Germans objected, arguing that a general was worth more than a sailor; but impressed by the resistance to the British entry into Syria, they gave way; though it is said that Hitler later tried to have the deal revoked, wishing to keep Juin in captivity. On his release, he was immediately appointed to the command of all troops in Morocco, assuming the command, as a *général de division*, in September.

Almost immediately Juin was plunged into the crises that followed the death, in an air crash, of Vichy's Minister for War General Huntziger, and German demands for the replacement of Weygand by an officer more pro-Axis. Admiral Darlan, as Minister for Defence, wanted Juin to succeed Huntziger. Juin refused saying that he was only prepared to serve in an African command. Darlan, however, supported the Germans' demand for Weygand's removal, forcing Pétain's hand by threat of resignation, though not conceding to the German's preference, the bitterly anti-British General Dentz. Weygand was profoundly revered in North Africa. Vichy realised that his dismissal would be deeply resented and assessed that Juin was the only possible successor likely to command full obedience. Accordingly, in November 1941 Juin found himself promoted again, to be a *général de corps d'armée*, in command of all French land forces in North Africa, but not West. In addresses to officers he repeated with controlled *passion* the well-known words of Lyautey in August 1914, when Lyautey reaffirmed that despite the war, no ground in Morocco would be given up, '*Messieurs, la séance continue....*' His personal style was generally one of caution, prudence and loyalty to Pétain which did not endear him to watchers among the Allies and was later to carry penalties. But his loyalty to Pétain did not prevent his offering advice that he knew might be unpalatable, as when in March 1942 he advised Pétain against appointing General Bridoux, a collaborationist selected by Laval, as Minister for War.

The post in North Africa was, however, no quiet backwater. In December 1941, Juin found himself as acting head of a French mission, face to face with an angry Goering in Berlin. The German leader wanted to know what the French in Tunisia would do if the Afrika Korps was pushed westward out of Libya – Auchinleck's Crusader offensive was at the time at its most successful. Goering sought the use of Tunisian ports, roads and railways, and a free entry for the Afrika Korps. Juin's reply was that under international law the Germans should be disarmed, which heightened Goering's humour. Then, on the pretext of wishing to secure the Tunisia-Libya border, Juin asked for additional forces, with the political issues referred to Vichy. The meeting ended a little later, Goering saying that if the French would not co-operate in an Axis defence of Tunisia Hitler would turn to alternative solutions. The matter never reached a crisis as Rommel checked Auchinleck's advance, but Juin was furious when, on his return to North Africa, he found that Darlan had authorised the use of the Tunisian port of Gabès by Axis shipping. After the war, allegations were made that Juin was complicit to this deal, with rumours of documents hidden in German archives. But no such documents have ever been produced and the German General Warlimont's record of the meeting clearly notes Juin as saying that such decisions lay with Vichy and not with him. On his return to Algiers, he secretly set his staff about the preparation of four sets of plans for four contingencies – an Axis or Spanish attack on Morocco, an Anglo-American attack on Morocco, an 8th Army entry into Tunisia in pursuit of the Axis, and an Axis surprise occupation of Tunisia. One copy of the plans for this last contingency reached Darlan who ordered their immediate destruction. Vichy's action heightened Juin's suspicions that if Rommel was pushed back into Tunisia, Vichy would, in practice, not order the disarming of the Afrika Korps. This, in turn, would bring about a British pursuit entry into Tunisia, which, like Syria, might then become a battlefield.

More painful still was a sharp and increasingly open quarrel with de Lattre, who had been appointed, under Juin, commander of French forces in Tunisia, but whose removal was being requested by the distrustful Germans. Before his own arrival, Juin knew that de Lattre was to be removed, but de Lattre himself was not told. The two men almost immediately disagreed over the best strategy for the defence of Tunisia, Juin favouring defence in depth using the Tunisian hills, while de Lattre wanted to fight an offensive defence near the Libyan border. Juin argued that this was beyond combat and logistic capacities of the small French garrison, which would be destroyed.

Underlying the difference between these two outstanding officers were some of the basic fissions within French society and the Army. De Lattre was of course preoccupied with his own local command, Tunisia. But Juin, both as commander of all French forces in North Africa and himself a Constaninois *colon*, had a wider view – if the small French garrison in Tunisia were destroyed on the Libyan border, eastern Algeria would be wide open. De Lattre believed units from Algeria and Morocco should be sent to southern Tunisia, but this would have been a breach of the Armistice terms. Juin saw the main threat as Axis, the German and Italian forces retreating from Libya reinforced by the arrival of fresh Axis forces in Northern Tunisia; in these conditions, he saw Tunisia's garrison holding the hills, both as a foothold for France in Tunisia and as a screen for Algeria. De Lattre acknowledged that a threat existed to northern Tunisia but seemed unprepared to accept that it was not possible to reinforce the garrison. His planning was concentrated almost exclusively upon circumstances in which the remnants of Axis forces would be contained as virtual prisoners in Southern Tunisia, or were virtually destroyed by the British in Libya and arrived in flight. Behind de Lattre's planning was a contingency that Juin interestingly and probably wisely refused to face. De Lattre would have been prepared to use his forces to say 'no' to any demand by victorious British forces to enter the territory; the prevention of a German entry into Unoccupied France was no doubt uppermost in his mind. In a debate attended by both their staffs, Juin sharply imposed his views on de Lattre. But at the same time he used much of de Lattre's argument to seek men and material from Vichy.

In January 1942, at the very end of a visit to Tunisia, otherwise happy and socially successful, Juin abruptly told de Lattre that Vichy had decided that he was to go. De Lattre exploded with fury. Juin later reported that, friends though they were, they could not work together as a team. He nevertheless strongly recommended that de Lattre be promoted. But relations between the two were never quite the same again.

Throughout the first nine months of 1942, Juin came to believe the most likely threat to French North Africa to be either an Axis pincer assault, air landings in Morocco linked to an incursion from Tunisia, or an Italian coup to seize Tunis itself. He nevertheless used arguments about Allied attacks to try and persuade Vichy and the Germans to strengthen his forces. In the summer, he assessed an Allied commando raid of the Dieppe type followed by German occupation as a counter-measure to be a possibility but he did not envisage a permanent Allied landing. He remained excluded from the small groups of French soldiers and civilians to whom the Americans came to divulge their plans. The Americans appear to have excluded him as they were suspicious of the circumstances of Juin's release from Königstein, and also doubtful over whether Juin had not made secret concessions to Goering in December 1941. The Americans also held an unjustified suspicion of Weygand whom Juin was known to admire. But Juin did talk with the American consul-general, Murphy, about American reactions in the event of an Axis ultimatum or invasion. Murphy promised American assistance to Juin. Darlan, the Commander-in-Chief of all Vichy's forces, and Juin both doubted their capacity to help, although Juin did appoint staff officers for liaison work with Murphy. But elsewhere Murphy was pursuing parallel and more frank negotiations with those privy to the Allied landings plans. Despite the intelligence reports of the Allied troop convoys, Juin himself remained firmly convinced that the Allied plan was for a seaborne landing in western Libya.

Command in North Africa With the Allies

He was therefore caught by surprise when he was informed very early on the morning of 8 November that Murphy wished to see him. On his arrival, Murphy informed Juin that massive American and British landings were about to take place and implored Juin's co-operation. Juin, who disliked being woken at night, was in a bad temper; he protested that Murphy had not been frank earlier and that his orders were to resist any power whatever entering North Africa. He eventually agreed to contact Darlan, in Algiers at the time, who took the same stance. In Algiers, however, they were overtaken by events. The local French commander, General Mast, had been privy to the plans and had arranged for the arriving Americans to be unopposed and met by volunteers tasked to assist in occupying key terrain and installations. There were, in consequence, only a few incidents of shooting. Juin moved to his field headquarters and ordered the advancing Americans to be screened and watched but not engaged. At half past four in the afternoon, Darlan ordered all French units in the Algiers area to lay down their arms. It had been a most difficult sequence of events for Juin. His views on discipline and obedience pulled him in one direction; yet Algeria was his home, and he no more wanted the Americans in Algeria than he wanted the Germans in France. But of the two, his personal preferences remained for the Allied cause and the Americans; unfortunately, his own hopes, of a German aggression that could have led to an American arrival as a legitimate counter, had not happened. Above all he wanted to avoid fratricidal strife between Frenchmen.

Juin's authority was, however, confined to Algiers at this particular juncture as Darlan, fearing that Juin's freedom might be curtailed, had advised Vichy to delegate full powers to local commanders in Tunis and Morocco; these took different and less fortunate action resulting in some stiff fighting in Morocco and western Algeria and the unopposed arrival of Axis aircraft in Tunisia. Darlan refused to give a general cease-fire order, fearing that it would provoke a German entry into Unoccupied France. On this second day, the 9th, the situation was further complicated by the belated arrival in Algiers – after a dramatic escape from Königstein and submarine journey – of General Giraud, who was senior to Juin in rank, and the American General Clark. Juin initially declined to accept Giraud's authority. But in conditions of some drama – immediately following a noisy and destructive German air-raid and a *crise de nerfs* on the part of Madame Juin – Juin agreed at a late night meeting to accept Giraud's authority if so required. At a further meeting, on the morning of the 10th, Clark demanded that Darlan issue a general cease-fire. Juin asked the Americans to withdraw from the room. He then spoke very plainly to Darlan, warning him that if he refused to order a cease-fire, the Americans would attempt to disarm the French units near Algiers and destroy the units elsewhere. He added that if this decisive moment for France was not used, the Germans would arrive in strength in Tunisia and, further, that the morale of the *Armée d'Afrique's* indigenous soldiers would be damaged beyond repair. Darlan gave way and the order was issued, the copy to Tunisia including an additional instruction to deploy the garrison to shield Algeria. The order was received and obeyed in western Algeria, but did not apparently reach Morocco, where fighting continued. But later in the day, an order suspending Darlan was received from Pétain who claimed to assume all authority himself and ordered continuing resistance to the Americans and British. This order was followed by one on the next day, the 11th, giving full authority over all French forces in North Africa to General Noguès, the Resident-General in Morocco. Noguès had not been informed in advance of the American landings, though some of his subordinates had attempted to prevent resistance to the Americans. These latter Noguès had placed under arrest and wished to execute. In respect of Tunisia, Juin reiterated his orders that the small garrison of General Barré be re-deployed to the Dorsale mountain ranges to cover eastern Algeria where fresh American landings were taking place. But he did not feel he had the authority to order the garrison to engage the arriving Germans. The news of the entry of the Germany Army into Unoccupied France resolved this dilemma for Juin. No one could any longer affirm that Pétain was a free agent.

Many hitherto Pétain supporters felt that he should have left for North Africa in protest against the German incursion. After consultation with Darlan, who claimed that he had received a secret message from Vichy stating that Pétain still recognised him as commander of all forces, despite the previous disavowal, Juin ordered all forces to open hostilities against the Axis in co-operation with the Americans during the afternoon of the 11th.

The tangle of command and authority was however still not unravelled. Juin's immediate subordinate, the commander of the 19th Army Corps, and his air force commander, Generals Koeltz and Mendigal, both insisted that only Noguès had the legitimate authority from pre-Occupation Vichy to order their forces into action and that neither Darlan, Giraud nor Juin could do so. Their argument was not simply obstructionist, they held that only a legitimate authority could keep firm control of Morocco at a time of threats from the Americans, the Axis and Spain. Juin was obliged to prepare an order suspending his previous one, to the fury of Clark, while awaiting discussion with Noguès. Clark's fury was however needless, as Juin's chief signals officer had on his own initiative decided not to transmit the suspending order.

Although Noguès halted the fighting in Morocco on the 11th, his own preference, linked to his own ambitions, was for a period of neutrality benign towards the Allies before any participation in the war; he also objected to the presence of Giraud. With these views he flew to Algiers on the 12th to meet Juin and later Clark, Darlan and Murphy. Both meetings were stormy. Juin's difficulties were temporarily increased by a message from Barré to the effect that with his units on the move he was in too vulnerable a position to begin fighting; a little later a second signal arrived demanding precise instructions, as an encounter with the Germans was imminent. Juin despatched a reply in plain terms ordering the opening of fire. The following morning, at a meeting at the Hotel Saint Georges, Juin, by sheer force of personality (his voice harsh and his disabled arm twitching), overcame Noguès's hesitations, virtually forcing Noguès to shake hands with Giraud. The agreement of all, Giraud, Darlan and Noguès was now secured; all French Forces in North Africa were to be committed to the Allied cause and Juin immediately ordered the call-up of the 1934 to 1939 conscript classes. Darlan also came up with a further message which he claimed to have been sent personally by Pétain in the conditions of greatest secrecy restoring him to his former powers – and so restoring to him legitimacy at Algiers. But throughout all this confusion, Juin had played a deft hand and was now to reap well-deserved reward, important commands on fields of battle.

While his seniors jockeyed for prestige and power in Algiers, Juin, as Commander of the *Détachement d'Armée Française* (*DAF*), returned to the area of his studies in the early 1920s, the defence of Algeria against an attack mounted from Tunisia. The situation was unpromising. The Germans were arriving fast by sea and air with tanks and bombers. The Admiral at Bizerta with about a quarter of Tunisia's 13,000 military garrison in the area, remained loyal to Vichy and did nothing to hinder them; indeed young school leavers were recruited into a French force to fight on the Axis side. Barré, for reasons both military and political – under renewed pressure from Vichy and still uncertain whom to obey – was still avoiding battle. He took his small force, the equivalent of five battalions with fifteen old tanks and no aircraft, into the hills west of Tunis. Other French units moved into the Grande Dorsale. Elements of the British 1st Army, after landing in eastern Algeria, were moving into western Tunisia but they were not strong. By agreement with Anderson, the 1st Army's Commander, Juin's *DAF* was given the two Dorsale ranges as its area of responsibility – confirmation albeit in slightly different conditions, of Juin's position in his dispute with de Lattre and in conformity with his own earlier plans. The 30,000 strong *DAF* comprised Barré's weak division, a hurriedly assembled small division formed in the Constantine area, and a few Saharan units. Its task was to prevent a German penetration into the Tebessa area of Algeria through the mountains and cover the right flank of the British.

After the repulse by German aircraft and heavy tanks, of the British late November offensive, tasked to take Tunis, the British wished to withdraw to a line west of Medjez el Bab. Juin disagreed with this, as such a withdrawal would open the route to Constantine; he secured, via Giraud, Eisenhower's authority to hold Medjez el Bab. As his *DAF* became reinforced, further small divisions from the Algiers area and Morocco arriving in late November and December, Juin also moved to try to seize the key heights in the Dorsale Orientale and in the Pont du Fahs area. In the latter, the Moroccans were frustrated by German armour and aircraft.

In this period, despite cold and incessant rain, Juin, in a Basque beret and mud-covered cape, cigarette end in the corner of the mouth, personally conducted operations, often at the front and under fire. His troops, mostly North African *Tirailleurs* and *Spahis*, were equipped to 1939 standards and scales in terms of weaponry, generally without air or armour support; they were also poorly clad against the elements, and their logistic support depended upon mules. They nevertheless fought with traditional *Armée d'Afrique* spirit; the Americans and the British were impressed.

By January 1943 the *DAF* had been increased in strength to over 70,000 men, an increase that coincided with an Allied perception that the command structure needed reorganisation. The newly arrived II US Corps, which was under British 1st Army command, was deployed south of the *DAF*, which was not. Juin offered to place himself under Anderson, and for this was rebuked sharply by Giraud. Juin contested the issue in a letter to Giraud which showed both perception and tact. He noted his own good relations with the British at combat command level and added 'British senior officers are what they are. What we think in them is stupidity or obstruction is often only the result of a slowness in, or absence of, imagination... Remember Foch's dictum that he never gained anything from the British, even when he was Supreme Commander, except by persuasion in a carefully nurtured atmosphere of mutual trust. They could not be given orders'. Matters came to a head in late January, when the poorly equipped *DAF* after heavy losses had to call on British and American armour to check a German offensive between the two Dorsales. Further, both the retreating Afrika Korps and the advancing 8th Army had arrived in southern Tunisia, Juin's proposal that American forces attempt to prevent a linkage between Rommel in the south and von Arnim in the north having been turned down by the Americans. In the new command structure that was worked out, Juin participating, the *DAF*, now the *19ᵉ Corps d'Armée*, was placed under General Koeltz, all under the command of the British 1st Army. Juin was promoted *général d'armée* and withdrawn to prepare a future French Expeditionary Corps for operations in Europe, though left with a supervisory right to intervene in connection with French forces in Tunisia if he felt it necessary. He did this most notably during the crisis following the German successes in the Gafsa area in mid-February 1943. Juin first put together a hurriedly assembled screen of French units to cover the 1st Army's right flank, but the Germans moved the weight of their offensive further north to the Thala area. The American II Corps commander lost his nerve and envisaged withdrawal from Tebessa, which would have opened the way to Juin's home, Constantine, and all eastern Algeria, for German armour. Arriving dramatically at the II Corps Headquarters, Juin told the astounded Americans that if they would not hold Tebessa somehow or other the French, including himself and his staff, would do so. American resolve was stiffened by this display of *passion* and air attacks on the advancing Germans were mounted; a subsequent German change of plan, concentrating their forces to the south, fortunately defused the crisis.

The squabblings of the French in Algiers, American dislike of de Gaulle, Giraud's total lack of political perception, and the outdated equipment of the *DAF*, together with continual French demands on the Americans for modern equipment, had led the Allies to view the French disparagingly at the outset of the campaign. Juin's sound common sense and professional abilities eroded these attitudes and prejudices. Patton, Clark, Eisenhower and Alexander were all impressed by Juin and liked him as a man, a regard to prove very important over the next two years. Equally important were Juin's final instructions to the French general commanding in south-east Algeria, that the Free French Forces of Leclerc and de Larminat, arriving with the British 8th Army, were to be accepted on equal terms and fully regarded as fellow French soldiers. This order was unfortunately not always observed, prejudice remaining on both sides. Juin himself refused to be committed to any political camp, a refusal sometimes misunderstood, particularly by supporters of de Gaulle.

There was to be a sour post-script to Juin's activities in Tunisia. The French perceived the restoration of a firm French protectorate administration in Tunisia as an immediate priority the moment the campaign was over; the Vichy administration was discredited and they mistrusted American intentions. General Mast was selected by Giraud to be Resident-General but was almost immediately injured in an air accident. Giraud asked a reluctant Juin to act as Resident-General until Mast was recovered. The Bey of Tunis, Moncef, was a young man who had only acceded to the throne in 1942. He was known to have sympathies with nationalist groups but in the very difficult conditions of the Axis occupation he had only tried to steer a prudent course with the Axis commanders in the best interests of his people. The French authorities in Algiers, however, had decided on his removal, the Axis occupation period acting as a veneer over the real reasons for their decision – Moncef's sympathies with the nationalists and a wish for a showy French reassertion of authority. Juin was told to select a successor and then convey this decision formally to Moncef who had little idea of what was in store; he had in fact been retrieved by Juin personally following detention by British military personnel.

At a meeting, attended by Juin and staff in full uniform, together with the Bey and his advisers also in ceremonial robes, Juin first tried to induce the Bey to abdicate of his own free will. The Bey objected, declaring he had committed no fault. Juin, the weakness of his case adding to his exasperation, then gave an angry ultimatum and withdrew. The Bey accepted the inevitable a little later. Of the event, Juin wrote later that it was '*un acte impolitique*' imposed upon him by the 'pseudo government' in Algiers and that the Bey had always been loyal with no serious faults for which he could be blamed. But Juin had no subsequent qualms about his other major political act as Resident-General, his refusal (despite American pressure) to receive the militant nationalist leader, Bourguiba, a refusal that led Bourguiba to depart to Cairo for safety.

A little later, while still in Tunis, Juin received a letter from de Gaulle written in Olympian but friendly style, congratulating him on his contribution to the Tunisian campaign and requesting that Juin come to see him. De Gaulle, by this time and despite American opposition, had acquired much of the real power in Algiers, Darlan having been murdered and Noguès, and others who had prevaricated in November, having been discredited. De Gaulle respected the competence of his former *promotion* contemporary of Saint Cyr; in turn Juin realised and accepted that de Gaulle was the new legitimate political authority of a united *France Combattante*.

But difficulties and the wide differences of approach between the Free French of 1940 and the *Armée d'Afrique* of North Africa in November 1942 remained. Leclerc, as already noted, had paraded with the British and not the *Armée d'Afrique* units in the Allied victory parade in Tunis, viewing the *Armée d'Afrique* as former collaborators. Giraud was still seen, despite his political naivety, as the legitimate successor to Darlan by the *Armée d'Afrique*, and de Gaulle had not yet fully succeeded in shunting him away from political power. He remained with de Gaulle as joint head of the governing Committee for National Liberation. Chairmanship was rotated and each appointed his followers as members – a recipe for friction and one described by Juin as *pagaille* [shambles]. Disharmony and tensions were perpetuated by acrimonious rivalry in recruiting the *evadés* who were arriving from France, rivalry in securing British and American equipment or more basically rations and welfare packs and uncertainty among the Free French forces of their careers, their honours, their higher level of British Army pay, even their pension prospects, in an Army in which they were but a minority. It was rumoured that only Free French units would join the Allied entry into Europe, the *Armée d'Afrique* remaining in North Africa for garrison duty. As a concession to the interests of two different groupings, and in the hope of bringing them together, two different Chiefs of Army Staff were appointed, Juin for the units of North and West Africa and de Gaulle's general, de Larminat, for the Free French forces. Juin accepted this arrangement with reservations, and after two weeks resigned. He argued that the rivalries served only to confuse and discourage Frenchmen who simply wanted to fight the common enemy. After a further row between de Gaulle and Giraud, a unified military staff was established at the end of July, Juin being enabled to return to his work of preparing the expeditionary Corps. He had first however to face thinly veiled accusations from de Larminat. These, directed at *'spécialement les officiers généraux'*, alleged that in the previous November resistance to the Allies had continued despite Darlan's orders for a cease-fire and that the efforts of Frenchmen anxious to help the Allies had been obstructed. De Larminat sought their retirement and appearance before any enquiry. Juin only learnt of this attack upon him on the day it was to be discussed by the important Permanent Military Committee established and chaired by de Gaulle. Juin, who was a member of the Committee, refused to attend, de Gaulle struck the subject from the agenda and de Larminat was kept without employment for a while. At Vichy, an order signed by Pétain dismissed Juin and stripped him both of his Legion of Honour and French nationality. Juin, on hearing of this burst into laughter and added 'Kind of them not to sentence me to death'.

Command in Italy

Juin's work in preparing the *CEF*, French Expeditionary Corps, in the period June–September 1943 took place at a time of two great debates among the Allies that vitally affected his work, but in which he personally had no say. The first was one in which no Frenchman at all had any voice, the purely Anglo-American strategic decision making – what should be the next Allied moves. In the second, Giraud represented, very effectively, French interests in the negotiations to secure equipment, and shipping space priority for that equipment, for the French forces. Important though the French contributions to the Italian, and later North-West Europe campaigns were to be, these summer 1943 debates foreshadowed the conditions under which French forces had to fight throughout the years 1943–45 – in accordance with an overall strategy in which they had no voice and dependent on Allied, in practice largely American, goodwill. These were constraints and frustrations that contributed significantly to post-1945 French military and political thinking.

The *CEF* was initially planned to be a formation of one armoured division, the *1ere Division Blindée*, (*DB*), of General du Vigier, and two infantry divisions, the *2e Division d'Infanterie Marocaine*, (*DIM*), of General Dody, and the *3e Division d'Infanterie Algérienne*, *DIA*, of General de Monsabert, all composed almost entirely from the *Armée d'Afrique*. It was also planned to include in the Corps a *Groupe* of *tabors*, small battalion size units of the Moroccan irregular *goums*. Juin removed all the units selected from the Algiers area into Western Algeria, and in sweltering heat set about training and exercising with the new American equipment as it was delivered, the deliveries greatly raising morale.

After making some preliminary studies on the possible use of the *CEF* in a campaign in Corsica and Sardinia, Juin was given a firm directive in early September. The *CEF* was to participate in the Italian campaign, initially two divisions to arrive in the winter, with further divisions to follow when logistics so permitted. Juin himself accepted an invitation from General Clark, now the American 5th Army commander, to visit the Italian battlefield where he was struck by the severe limitations imposed on the British and American armoured and motorised forces by the terrain. He quickly appreciated the special contribution the *Armée' d'Afrique* infantry divisions, with their experience of hill and mountain warfare in North Africa, would be able to make. The *2e DIM* and *3e DIA* were accordingly ordered to prepare to move, the first elements were to arrive in Italy in late November. In August and September, Juin was heavily involved in the planning, and post-Italian surrender hurried re-planning, of an all-French invasion of Corsica. The force was, however, not to be commanded by him. In October, Juin found himself involved in a delightful interlude. At the request of Eisenhower, he and Patton, now commanding the US 7th Army, were sent to Corsica for a few days as part of a deception plan. It was hoped that the Germans would believe an Allied landing in the Gulf of Genoa was being prepared, a landing to involve Patton's Army and Juin's *CEF*. The two generals carried maps and false plans and engaged in rather conspicuous 'reconnaissance'. For Juin it was also an occasion to visit Ucciani, his mother's home village, where he was given an emotional and effusive welcome – all watched by an astonished Patton. But on 25 November 1943 the interlude over, Juin arrived at Naples to begin a nine month command which would earn him a place of honour for ever in the history of his country.

Juin's situation was not promising and the absence of any American staff representation or official welcome on his arrival underlined it. The re-equipment programme for his divisions had met the needs of regiments in very varying measure. Some were well re-equipped with weaponry but short of the personal equipment needed for soldiers to survive in an Italian mountain winter, others had not yet received some, or in the case of most of the *goums* even any, of the weaponry. Although Clark personally had a high opinion of Juin, many Americans distrusted all French generals and their attitude towards the *CEF* was one of doubts over its fighting value outside Africa. Juin himself was a *général d'armée* but had decided to revert to a grade of *général de corps d'armée* for his *CEF* role, assessing correctly that an officer styling himself French Army Commander would not be accepted. Juin correctly saw that the major command functions required of him were the establishment of credibility – that French forces would fight and fight well – and assertion, and that that point having been made, French generals would play a greater role in future Allied decision making. This assertion might, and in the event did, entail heavy casualties. His eventual aim, a full French Army in Italy with its own logistical arrangements and an equal voice at Allied conference tables, was one that required time and proven battlefield success. But it was to be his fate that the whole Italian campaign was viewed as secondary to, even as a foil to, the Normandy landings project, Operation *Overlord*.

Juin's national-political role had to be discharged along with the two other normal facets of generalship, sound and successful tactical handling of troops and a personal style of leadership that inspired all ranks to give of their best. Here Juin held assets in his hand. The mountain areas of southern Italy were not dissimilar to Morocco in the context of tactics – mobility on foot, infiltration and junior leader initiative.

From his experience in the Rif and 1930s' campaigns in Morocco, Juin also knew a great deal about mountain artillery and mountain logistical supply, in particular the value of mules. Furthermore, he was commanding divisions composed largely, at ordinary soldier level, of North Africans whom he knew and who knew him, and who at this stage had not yet suffered in Tunisia a casualty or other attrition rate serious enough to affect morale. The French officer and NCO cadres were the pick of the *Armée d'Afrique*. Frenchmen and North

Africans alike – Juin's special Orders of the Day were issued in French, Berber and Arabic and aroused the same enthusiasm – saw the fighting to come as the first step to liberating *La Patrie*.

Juin's role in the campaign is best examined under the separate headings of tactics and personal leadership. In the former, as only a Corps commander, he was never his own master. Only when his expertise was recognised could he play a full role; in the latter, he rates as a very great leader of men.

At the outset, the Americans envisaged using the French forces simply as unit reinforcements. Juin firmly controlled his strong sense of resentment and of having been deceived. Recognising that the American perception of the French was one of excitability and that with only two divisions in Italy his position was weak, he pursued a careful discreet policy; in this he was soon helped by Clark's chief of staff, General Gruenther. Clark's Army was held in check by the German 'Winter Line' of the Garigliano and Upper Volturno rivers. An American attack on a key escarpment, the Pantano, on 1 December had suffered a bloody reverse in which a division was largely destroyed. Juin proposed that the *2ᵉ DIM* replace the American division. Clark agreed and in seventeen days, but at considerable cost and despite snow storms, the *2ᵉ DIM* supported by *goums* and *Armée d'Afrique* mountain artillery took the Pantano and the range beyond as well. Their reward was a sector of the line on the right of the 5th Army's front for the *CEF*, Juin in command, from 3 January 1944.

Clark's operations in December had run into severe difficulties. He had hoped initially to crack the German 'Winter Line' in order to reach the Rapido river, and then crack the much stronger 'Gustav Line' in order to reach terrain from which his armour could dash for Rome from the Liri valley. Juin felt the plan over-ambitious but was overruled. His *CEF* was given the secondary role of advancing to the Rapido, covering the American right flank. The weather conditions were appalling, many of the poorly equipped *Tirailleurs* suffering from frostbite in the freezing rain. Despite very tough resistance from Austrian mountain troops, Juin's two *Divisions* reached their objectives five days ahead of time, receiving warm congratulations from Clark whose other formations were held by the Germans and had suffered heavy losses.

Cassino blocked the Americans' way to the Liri valley. Juin, always an advocate of manoeuvre, wished to advance further to Atina and then turn west to strike at the German communications behind

Cassino, but he was not given the additional troops necessary for such a move and was forced to halt. Further, the Anzio landings, designed to draw German units away from the Gustav line, were in trouble and there was an urgent need to prevent any reinforcement of German troops opposing the landings. An American frontal assault on Cassino, supported by a *CEF* assault on another massive dominant mountain feature in the north, the Belvedere, was therefore mounted. The Belvedere was daunting, steeply sloped in itself with bare summits, protected by two rivers and encircled by other heights, it formed a key and heavily protected feature of the Gustav line. De Monsabert declared its seizure impossible, but Juin felt the whole question of French honour and credibility was at issue and that the attack must take place. The attack, led by the *4e Régiment de Tirailleurs Tunisiens* lasted eight days. Particular features were taken, lost and retaken in violent fighting, the whole forming an epic in French military history.

The American attack was less successful, at one point Juin having to request Clark to press on further as otherwise he would be too dangerously exposed to remain on the Belvedere. Clark next replaced the American units in front of Cassino by Indian Army and New Zealand formations, but their valiant frontal assaults and later those of the Polish Corps attained only limited success. This came as no surprise to Juin who consistently but vainly put forward his preferred turning solution. He also lobbied Algiers for reinforcements, his requests arriving at a time when formations were already being earmarked for the forthcoming Normandy (*Overlord*) and South France (*Anvil*) operations and so meeting opposition from, among others, de Lattre. Juin countered this argument by observing that an advance further up the Italian peninsula was essential to secure a southern France landing. Juin initially received an Italian formation – which in the event fought well – and the first *tabors* of General Guillaume's *goum* irregulars, men born and bred in the Atlas mountains. Then, in February, arrived General Sevez's *4e Division Marocaine de Montagne (DMM)* and after a personal visit from de Gaulle, a fourth *Division*, not of *Armée d'Afrique* but of Gaullist origin, General Brosset's *1ere Division de Marche d'Infanterie*, which persisted in using its former Gaullist title, *1ere Division Français Libre*. With certain Corps and specialist units, Juin was now commanding a force of some 120,000 men.

The mud of late winter and early spring reduced the scale of activities on the Italian front. During this interlude the Allied forces were re-deployed, the *CEF* being moved westwards to a sector

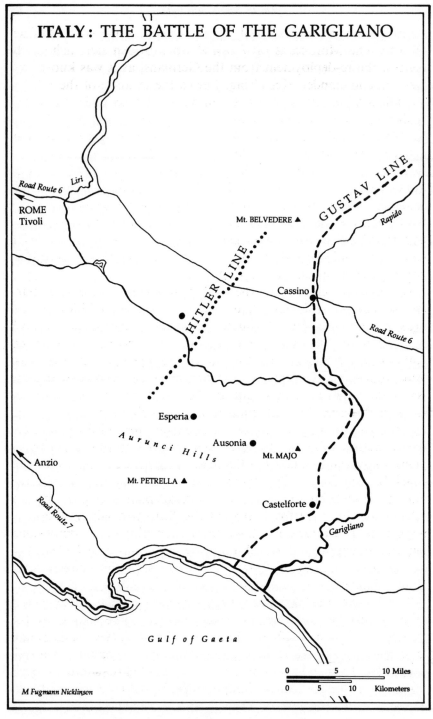

ITALY: THE BATTLE OF THE GARIGLIANO

Road Route 6
Liri
ROME
Tivoli

Mt. BELVEDERE ▲

GUSTAV LINE

Rapido

HITLER LINE

Cassino

Road Route 6

Esperia ●

Aurunci Hills

Ausonia ●

Mt. MAJO ▲

Anzio

Road Route 7

Mt. PETRELLA ▲

Castelforte ●

Garigliano

Gulf of Gaeta

0   5   10 Miles
0   5   10   Kilometers

M Fugmann Nicklinson

Map 4. Italy: The Battle of the Garigliano

running from the confluence of the Liri and Garigliano rivers to Castelforte. The Moroccans of *4ᵉ DMM* wore British steel helmets to conceal the re-deployment from the Germans, as it was known the German commander, Kesselring, viewed the location of the *CEF* as an indication of attack. Before the move, the British had won a small bridgehead across the Garigliano, the bridgehead lying at the foot of Mt Majo behind which lay the Aurunci mountain range. The German defences were formed by two lines of minefields, fortifications, flame throwers and supporting artillery, the Gustav Line, which followed the Garigliano but looping back to Mt Majo, and the Hitler Line, some ten miles further back and covering the entry to the Liri valley but leaving the Aurunci. These mountains they assessed as impassable and so left unfortified. Nevertheless, they were a range from which Germans could sweep down on the right flank of the Americans, so holding the American II Corps in check.

No commander in Italy knew more about mountains and manoeuvre than Juin. He immediately seized on the possibilities of turning the German position through – and over – the Aurunci, so both opening up the Liri valley from the south-west and covering the right flank of the Americans operating on the easier ground near the coast. Juin and his staff laboured to produce an operational plan. The British favoured a major assault further north with a *CEF* attack as support. The Allied commanders were also at first sceptical as to the feasibility of Juin's plan. Other arguments in the Allied debate were less attractive – who might be the first to enter Rome (no part of Juin's plan), or to whom might fall the heaviest casualties. Gruenther and Clark backed Juin while Alexander remained sceptical but allowed Juin to launch his offensive in an overall plan that provided for attacks all along the front, that of the British remaining the most important. This arrangement, which was something of a compromise left Juin unhappy; and to add to his worries at this time, he learnt of de Gaulle's exclusion of Giraud, who had supported him so well, from office and power in Algiers.

The Battle of the Garigliano, as Juin's offensive is known in French military history, was the first large setpiece battle fought by the French Army since 1940. The four *CEF Divisions*, the *goums* irregulars, and the all-important eight mule supply companies were all committed; food and ammunition for five days fighting were pre-positioned by night. The attack plan provided for a three *Division* attack, *4ᵉ DMM* and the *goums* on the left for the Aurunci, *2ᵉ DIM* in the centre, *1ᵉʳᵉ DMI* on the right. The *3ᵉ DIA* was placed initially in reserve on the left but was tasked to cross the lines of communication of *4ᵉ DMM* and act as a second echelon for *2ᵉ DIM* in the centre. The Germans were aware an attack was being prepared, but were deceived successfully in respect of the date and the scale.

The initial attacks began at 11 pm on the night of 11 May with no preliminary artillery bombardment, in order not to compromise the British plans. This was to prove a mistake. One attack was to be by the *1ᵉʳᵉ DMI* on the right tasked to break through the German lines and cut off the retreat of the Germans pushed back by the second, a major assault on Mt Majo by three regiments of *Tirailleurs Marocains* of the *2ᵉ DIM*. These advanced into battle singing the '*Marseillaise*' and the old *Armée d'Afrique* '*C'est nous les Africains*', the Moroccan soldiers chanting '*La Allah ihl Allah*'. However the attack suffered very heavy casualties. By dawn, it had been stopped. In the morning, Juin made his way to the front through parties of returning wounded, dead mules and in full danger of German counter attacks, to see for himself. He took almost the whole day to assess the situation before he made his most critical battlefield decision. At stake were not only men's lives but, in the event of a fruitless attack crippling the *CEF* with heavy casualties, the whole credibility of French military renaissance. The factor that decided him was intelligence reports indicating that the Germans had no reserves, while he himself had. He directed that during the coming night the entire Corps artillery would first fire in support of *2ᵉ DIM* and then in support of the further *4ᵉ DMM* attacks. Moonlight enabled the artillery to fire just ahead of the attacking troops. Success followed and was matched by success also on the *1ᵉʳᵉ DMI* front as well. By 1 pm on the 13th, the Germans were in general retreat from the Gustav to the Hitler Lines, many trapped by the French pincer becoming prisoners or abandoning their guns and equipment.

On the 14th, it was possible to begin the second phase of Juin's plan, the sweep into the Aurunci, initially the Petrella feature, by *4ᵉ DMM* and the *goums*, and, Mt Majo being taken, the launching of the second echelon *3ᵉ DIA* towards Ausonia and Esperia to cut off the retreat of the Germans. The *3ᵉ DIA* was supported on its right flank by the advance of *1ᵉʳᵉ DMI*, the first, and supremely rewarding for Juin, example of close co-operation between an *Armée d'Afrique* and a Free French formation. The operation was made exceedingly difficult by ferocious German resistance, the mountainous terrain and the destruction of the few roads. The logistics were daunting and the rather slower rate of advance by the British on the *CEF*'s right also added to

Juin's worries. But by 21 May, the Germans were in full retreat from the Hitler Line. Two days later, the advancing Americans linked up with the Anzio bridgehead forces.

The Aurunci having been cleared by the *CEF*, the final advance on Rome could begin amid some jostling between the Americans and the British for the prestige of entry into the city. Despite the enormous contribution made by the *CEF* to these operations, Juin played a modest hand. He proposed that the *CEF* should advance towards the Tivoli mountain area to the east of Rome, a proposal that included Route 6. This met with British opposition as they wanted the road as their main axis of advance on Rome, an advance in which the French Corps would play only a subordinate role. Matters were however decided by the slow rate of the British advance. Juin simply pushed the *3ᵉDIA* and *2ᵉDIM* through the Lepini mountains, after which *3ᵉDIA* crossed Route 6 and linked up with the *1ʳᵉDMI* near Tivoli. Their right flank again covered, the American 5th Army could enter Rome. Clark decided on a formal entry in which he would include his Corps commanders in his own vehicle; Juin was given the seat of honour next to Clark. Celebrations followed, including an audience with the Pope, a reception at the re-opened French Embassy, a parade by the *2ᵉDIM* and a congratulatory telegram from de Gaulle, amid many others.

But for Juin the success suddenly rang hollow. British caution and the American's obsession with being the first to enter Rome greatly hindered effective follow-up of the defeat of the Germans. Worse, he himself was informed that the *CEF* was to be withdrawn from Italy to prepare for the South of France landings (Operation *Dragoon*). Juin's arguments, supported by the British commanders, that the Italian triumph should be exploited and the overall Allied strategy be one of a giant pincer to meet in Central Europe, were set aside. For Juin, the Southern France project was a characteristically French error 'more imaginative than objective'. But among those sharply critical of Juin, on national as well as strategic grounds, was de Lattre. He even observed, with asperity and rankling memory of his replacement by Juin in Tunisia, that some senior French officers of the Vichy era only began to think about helping the Allied cause after 1942 and were now risking the capability of the French Army to participate in the liberation of France by committing it in Italy. Whether this Italy-to-Vienna strategy could have succeeded remains debatable. Although the Germans had been badly mauled, it is by no means certain that the Allies could have mustered sufficient shipping to reinforce their forces in Italy to a measure capable of defeating the Germans on a very narrow front. In the case of the French troops, de Gaulle assessed that liberation of the *métropole* must take priority; the Americans were not able to provide equipment sufficient for both a *CEF* in Italy and a French force for the South of France.

For Juin these decisions were bitter. He lost his *CEF*, which he had formed, trained and commanded, and his devoted staff. Giraud, when joint chairman of the Algiers committee, had promised de Lattre an Army, de Gaulle had later agreed – some have claimed de Gaulle preferred the prospect of two successful commanders to one very successful one. There was not to be another field command for the *CEF*'s *Patron*, as Juin was called. After an initial grumbling outburst, Juin accepted the situation with great dignity and loyalty.

There remained but four weeks of command for him. In that period, the *CEF* was given a sector of the front directed towards Siena, which Juin was anxious to capture as little damaged as possible – one of his divisional commanders issued an artillery order 'No firing beyond the 18th Century'. He entered the city, undamaged, on 4 July and after a splendid Bastille Day celebration, the withdrawal of the *CEF* divisions began. Visitors to Juin's headquarters included de Gaulle and a somewhat embarrassed de Lattre; after a brief pilgrimage to Assisi, a short respite in Rome, and numerous cordial farewells Juin departed for Algiers.

The warmth of the many farewells highlighted how Juin, as a leader of men, had inspired a remarkable devotion from soldiers of many different lands and cultures. His leadership – unlike that of de Lattre – contained no ingredient of fear and was essentially modest. With the brief exception of the first phase of the Garigliano battle, when he used a castle for convenience, Juin commanded from tented headquarters. Wisely eschewing *la vie du chateau*, he limited his own personal comfort to a box body vehicle. Despite the miserable conditions of rain, snow, sharp winds, freezing cold and mud, Juin's headquarters was a happy place for the men – and women – who worked there. Staff were ordered to look clean and smart and no complaining was allowed. The lessons of each engagement were carefully analysed, learnt and passed downwards to units, contributing to the tactical skills increasingly displayed. Frequently '*Le Patron*', and his chief of staff, Carpentier, would be invited to the *popote*, communal camp fire, of one section of the staff or another, and the old *Armée d'Afrique* songs would fill the

Italian sky. After dinner, Juin would relax by playing bridge, and his staff were told firmly only to awaken him at night in an emergency.

Almost every day, Juin would visit a part of the front. On many occasions he was in the firing line, on one he was nearly captured by the Germans and on another he was obliged to abandon his jeep under heavy machine-gun fire. He would also send out liaison officers from his headquarters to front line units to observe and report on particular needs. His own visits were always characterised by his good humour, plain soldierly speech – and jokes – concern for his soldiers and, wherever possible, prompt follow-up action to meet requests. He was also very firm in bringing the wild *goums* of Moroccan irregulars back under discipline and control after several excesses of mass rapine and pillage. Of this period of command, personal stories abound. Two or three may be told. A pharmacist officer was driving a vehicle carrying blood plasma bottles along a narrow mountain road ravaged by shell holes and winter weather. The officer found himself followed by a battered jeep, horn sounding intermittently. He refused to accelerate, fearing for his cargo, and stopped to make a well known gesture of irritation at his follower. Eventually the road widened, the jeep overtook the vehicle. From the back of the jeep Juin with a laugh and cheery wave threw over a package of *bastos* – Algerian cigarettes. At the height of the Garigliano battle, when under quite heavy artillery and small arms fire, an over-excited medical officer very peremptorily ordered Juin, who was on a visit, to withdraw saying the front was no place for a General. Juin was amused and with a smile mildly replied 'Shut up doctor, I'll obey you when I am wounded'. Still laughing over the incident, he later remarked to his staff that he had not had such a reprimand for a long time. Also during the Garigliano battle, Juin's jeep advanced too far forward and came under German anti-tank and machine-gun fire at close range. Juin was quite unperturbed, merely remarking 'My word, we seem to have arrived among the Germans' adding advice to his anxious driver, to reverse carefully as if he was going to be killed, he would prefer a bullet to a motor accident. On his return to the French forward *Tirailleurs* positions, he distributed cigarettes, laughed the event off and joked over the Germans' poor aim. 'They couldn't hit a cow in a corridor, I was the cow'. Whatever his feelings as he flew out from Italy, he had proved himself the best of the Allied generals in the theatre, he had written a spectacular page in French military history and he had convinced doubting allies that France was firmly back in the war.

Chief of Defence Staff

His achievement was fully recognised by de Gaulle, who appointed him Chief of Defence Staff (*Chef d'État Major de la Défense Nationale*) after a brief leave period. Juin, in accepting the appointment, made it clear that he expected de Gaulle to support him and, in the event, de Gaulle found himself increasingly dependent on Juin's advice and ability to smooth feathers that he, de Gaulle, had ruffled. Juin had to assume his responsibilities in the exciting but confused conditions of the liberation of Paris, and it was some time before he could establish himself in Paris and move the Army's logistics and other staffs from Algiers. In this interim period, Juin was almost incessantly on the move. He was first directed by de Gaulle to assist in persuading the Americans to release Leclerc's Division for entry into Paris. He went to the headquarters of Patton's 7th Army, only to be told that Leclerc's Division had been transferred to Hodge's 1st Army. But while at Patton's headquarters, he met a strange deputation of two leading Paris financiers, the brother of the Swedish Consul-General in Paris and the ADC of the German commander in the city. These all urged an immediate entry to the city to avoid the threatened Communist-led uprising and German reprisals. Juin sent them on to Eisenhower with his full support; the outcome has already been noted. On 25 August, he himself entered Paris in the same vehicle as de Gaulle, the latter standing arms stretched out in a V sign while Juin remained seated with a pistol in his hand, as the city was far from being cleared. The next day saw civic welcomes and a service in Notre Dame – both still accompanied by sporadic firing and explosions.

Paris liberated, two delicate missions awaited Juin. The first was the placating of Gerow, US Army Vth Corps commander, angered by Leclerc's division remaining in Paris at de Gaulle's insistence. The second was Juin's meeting with an emissary despatched from Vichy by Pétain with a document which, in the event of his detention by the Germans, was meant to transmit legitimate authority. Juin took the document to de Gaulle who gave it no recognition.

A Provisional Government of France having been installed in Paris from early September, Juin set about the task of the virtual re-creation of the French Armed Forces. This was a task of immense difficulty in view of different political backgrounds – a new third factor being that of the Resistance 'French Forces of the Interior'. The FFI was superimposed upon the breach still not finally bridged between the Free French and the *Armée d'Afrique*. The material problems were as daunting as those of personnel, many areas of France devastated, fighting continuing in the north east, and desperate shortages of funds and equipment. Once again, Juin's work also carried a 'national-political' dimension, the need for credible French forces to balance against the Anglo-American hegemony. This need occasioned Juin to accompany de Gaulle on a visit to Moscow, a visit simply to make a point.

The two main day-to-day problems of the autumn were the related ones of maintaining and supplying de Lattre's Army, equipment for further French forces, and the FFI. Using all his tact, Juin regained the confidence of de Lattre by supporting him to the maximum. Many Americans still felt that French units would be best kept in logistic or lines of communication roles, there being sufficient armoured and mechanised units, or at least as many as the shipping situation could support. They were not receptive to French wishes to unite their different groupings into modern forces well equipped for battle against the Germans or for imperial security, and they further distrusted the origins of many of the FFI. This, in fact, was but an umbrella organisation that loosely co-ordinated some 400,000 men from a variety of political backgrounds, varying from Communist to former Vichy Army or Navy personnel. Not all of them wanted to continue fighting the national enemy. Some were keen to fight political enemies at home, others wanted no further fighting after the liberation of their home area. The most difficult were in the south-west of France where revolutionary communes were dispensing a totally arbitrary justice; On Juin's orders, *Spahis* cavalry regiments were brought from North Africa to suppress them. De Gaulle and Juin wanted more than the eight divisions approved in 1943 in order to absorb the best of the FFI personnel. Juin prepared a careful plan and submitted it to the Supreme Allied Headquarters, with success. This plan amounted to the provision of equipment for forces, mostly FFI, totalling in effect a further four divisions, these to be committed to sealing off the German garrisons cut off on the Atlantic coast or in the Alps. In terms of actual personnel, Juin ensured that members of the Army's own resistance organisation, officers, NCOs and cadres of the French Army, either 1939 or Vichy personnel who joined after November 1942, received preference in the amalgamations of FFI contingents with the Army.

By the end of the year, Juin had also re-established the traditional military region headquarters throughout liberated France; these furthered the task of the integration of the FFI, together with new conscripts, into restored military units and combat formations. In addition, foundations for a restored Air Force were laid and the process of re-integration within the Navy continued.

Despite a fatiguing programme of tours and visits to supervise his work, Juin also found time to look ahead to the future. For him the Rhineland crisis of 1936 had highlighted a weakness noted by Foch as early as 1925. The lesson was that the restored French Armed Forces must have an immediate intervention capacity as well as units for imperial garrison duties and a conscript metropolitan army. The 1936 situation, in which any effective action would have required a general mobilisation, must not be repeated.

The turn of the year 1944-45 saw Juin faced with the implications for France of the Germans Ardennes offensive. The details of the tactical problems are set out in the next chapter as they primarily affected de Lattre; all that needs to be noted here is that at Eisenhower's Supreme Allied Headquarters it was felt that a temporary evacuation of Strasbourg, and much of Alsace only recently liberated, was inescapable. Pressure was brought at all levels, de Gaulle telegraphed Roosevelt and Churchill and ordered de Lattre to detach forces to occupy Strasbourg if the Americans withdrew, and order already anticipated by de Lattre. On 2 January Juin was sent to Supreme Headquarters to inform Eisenhower of this French decision. Eisenhower, however, was away and Juin's representations had to be made to his Chief of Staff, General Bedell Smith. Juin initially pointed out the consequences for the people of Alsace, in particular the vengeance of a returned Gestapo and the propaganda scoop that the Nazis would make; these arguments cut no ice. Juin then announced that the French Army would hold the city. Bedell Smith, angry, replied that in the event of such disobedience the French Army would be denied ammunition and petrol, to which Juin riposted that in such circumstances de Gaulle would forbid American usage of French railways and signals facilities. The following day Churchill visited Supreme Headquarters and strongly supported the French arguments. Eisenhower gave way and the orders for withdrawal were changed; although the German offensive was slowing down, cover by the US VI Corps of the French left flank was essential. The event did, however, occasion another of the minor brushes between Juin and de Lattre, the latter arguing that Juin's intervention at Supreme Headquarters and his conflicting loyalties had jeopardised his relationship with his superior, the American 6 Army Group Commander.

Juin's representations, if anything, appeared to have strengthened the respect in which he was held at Supreme Headquarters. When, in January 1945, he protested against a heavy air attack on Royan, one of the remaining German held Atlantic coast pockets, an enquiry was ordered. He was consulted by Eisenhower on the plans for the Rhine crossing and suggested certain changes, in the event accepted. He successfully defused, among others, particularly sharp disagreements between Supreme Headquarters, who wanted to use certain French security and pioneer units in occupied German territory as part of an overall plan, and de Gaulle, who insisted that these should remain under French control for use in an eventual French Occupied Zone and also upon the principle of and size of a French zone, a principle which had at that time not been fully conceded. Juin was, however, pushed by de Gaulle personally into accepting operations, purely for the sake of national pride, against the German Atlantic coast pockets in April 1945. These operations cost lives and were not necessary on military grounds, the pockets being largely neutralised and the end of the war being near.

The German surrender found Juin in the United States, as part of the French delegation attending the conference inaugurating the United Nations Charter. His advance was required on the section of the Charter relating to United Nations Forces, their composition, logistics and rights of passage. He was not greatly interested. The United Nations was already a forum for ill-informed attacks on the colonial powers. Juin was experiencing a foretaste of a post-war world, very different from the world of his first fifty-six years of life.

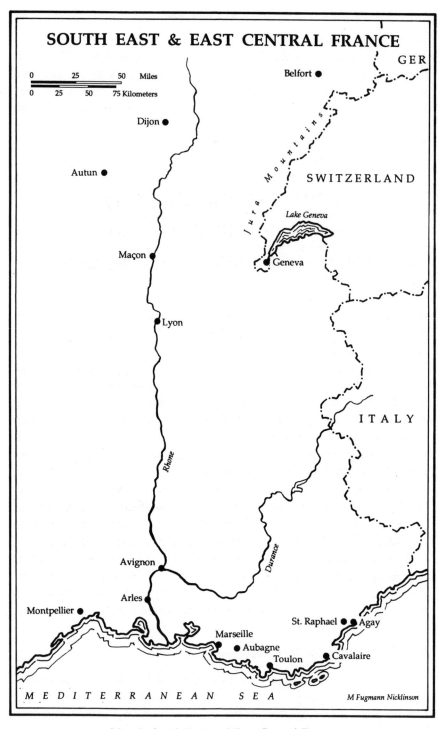

SOUTH EAST & EAST CENTRAL FRANCE

GER

Belfort ●

0   25   50 Miles
0   25   50   75 Kilometers

Dijon ●

Autun ●

Jura Mountains

SWITZERLAND

Lake Geneva

Maçon ●

● Geneva

Lyon ●

ITALY

Rhone

Durance

Avignon ●

Arles ●

Montpellier ●

St. Raphael ● ● Agay

Marseille
● Aubagne
Toulon ● Cavalaire

MEDITERRANEAN   SEA

M Fugmann Nicklinson

Map 5. South East and East Central France

5

The First French Army,
The Riviera to the Danube:
General de Lattre de Tassigny

After an autumn and early winter's work of staff planning for the 5th
Army headquarters, General de Lattre was appointed to command
the *14ᵉ Division d'Infanterie* in January 1940. This *Division* had been an
'active' rather than a reserve formation and was supposedly one of the
best in the French Army; it comprised two regiments of infantry, a
two-battalion *demi-brigade* of *Chasseurs*, a reconnaissance group and
divisional artillery. The soldiers of the *Division* were mostly recruited
in Alsace.

Until April the *14ᵉ Division* was holding a sector of the French line
opposite the Saar. Despite its reputation, de Lattre found the *Division*
infected with the general malaise of the French Army at this time,
apathy, inadequate provision of essential welfare services, such as
canteens and showers, and worst of all, accepting German
ascendancy in patrolling. He threw himself into organising facilities,
replacing poor quality officers, improving training, and directing
patrolling and counter-bombardment. To set an example, he
accompanied one patrol to take Mass in a deserted church in
no-man's-land. In April the division was sent to rest.

May–June 1940; the Armistice Army

The opening of the German offensive on 10 May led to hurried
recalls from leave and then to a period of the utmost confusion. The
French command came slowly to realise the threat presented to them
by the German onslaught on the Meuse and on the 13th de Lattre's

Division was ordered to move, part by road and part by rail, to Rheims; on their arrival, the forward units were then immediately ordered to reinforce the Sedan area. There directions became more specific in an order made a little later; de Lattre's *Division* was to be included in an ad hoc grouping of one other division plus the remnants of the French 9th Army, all under General Touchon. This force was tasked to plug the gap opened by the Germans between the French 9th and 2nd Armies, through which the tanks of General Guderian were pouring. But this clear mission was obscured by the fog of war, units arriving a company or so at a time, others periodically out of contact, and groups of soldiers from other divisions retreating south in disorder. De Lattre had also the increasing physical harassment, for everyone including himself and his staff, of German dive-bomber attacks and developing German panzer encirclement movements. Signal communications broke down and orders to regiments had to be conveyed by liaison officers.

De Lattre displayed all the qualities of a great commander. He remained undismayed, obtaining the best results he could from each of his subordinates, one being urged, another quietly ordered, a third commanded in plain terms. He wished to remain north of the Aisne near Rethel to impede what he correctly assessed as the main German drive, to the east. Touchon reluctantly allowed him to retain a small detachment at Rethel but, by the 17th, the bulk of the *14ᵉ Division*, strengthened by one or two other units cut off from their parent formations, was holding a thirteen mile sector on the south banks of the Aisne and the Aisne Canal. The *Division* fought notably well, containing the German attacks which attempted to dislodge them over a four day period. In his headquarters at Rethel, de Lattre himself devised new tactics to meet those of the German armour. These abandoned the unrealistic linear doctrine in favour of an all-round concept based on mutually supporting defended zones, usually villages, and a mobile reserve.

The Germans, concentrating on their victorious dash for the sea and cutting off of the British and French forces in Belgium, did not mount a major assault on the Aisne until 9 June. On that day, the German 12th Army attacked. De Lattre's *Division* held firm for two days, repelling three German divisions and counter-attacking with vigour. However, other divisions on the flanks of the *14ᵉ Division* gave way, to the fury of de Lattre who was obliged to withdraw in conditions of great difficulty to the Marne. He conducted the withdrawal in a box formation to avoid the *Division* being split. Even so, Guderian managed to cut off a small part north of Chalons.

But the line of the Marne could not be held in face of the German onslaught, nor in succession could lines on the Aube or the Loire. The *14ᵉ Division*, now reduced to only some 1,500 men, had to retreat steadily southward amid all the difficulties of refugee-congested roads, burning towns and villages and constant air attack, this often destroying bridges that were needed. The *Division* not being motorised, de Lattre had, too, continual dangers on his flanks. But amid all the general disintegration and demoralisation of the French Army, de Lattre continued to insist on discipline and smartness in the *Division*. The Armistice found him at Clermont-Ferrand, inspanning into the *Division* any organised bodies of men willing to continue fighting, and still desperately trying to improvise defences.

Although de Lattre had been taught by de Gaulle's father at school and had served with de Gaulle at Saint Cyr, in Paris and in the 5th Army, de Lattre did not follow him, though evidence exists that he frequently considered doing so. His wife admired de Gaulle's stand. But de Lattre had also a strong loyalty to Weygand. He had no doubt that Germany remained the enemy but at a deeper level de Lattre decided that regeneration must spring from within France itself. In particular he believed that an appeal must be made to the nation's youth, a concept not natural to Frenchmen of the period. But, as a disciple of Lyautey, he saw a mission for himself in this social role.

The Armistice provisions permitted the Vichy régime to maintain a metropolitan Army of 100,000 men in Unoccupied France; this was seen as a bulwark against any Communist uprising. The metropolitan Army was forbidden from possessing armour and heavy artillery and severe limits were placed on training, not much more than small arms, minor tactics and signalling being allowed. De Lattre was one of a fortunate minority of French generals not taken prisoner. His record in the May-June campaign had earned him the award of Grand Officer of the Legion of Honour, conferred upon him personally by Weygand, and promotion to *général de division*. He was appointed to command the *13ᵉ Division Militaire*, the Puy de Dôme Military District in the Massif Central.

Here de Lattre was able to put into practice his theories on basic training, theories which he believed were strengthened by the May-June catastrophe. He saw the Armistice Army as one of teams and followers, to be a nucleus but specifically not an élite for a future expansion. The physical and spiritual training of these teams was to be of especial concern and overriding priority, even if military skills could not be developed. For this purpose he took over a castle and land at Opme, on the Gergovie plateau near Clermont-Ferrand. The choice was symbolic as well as practical, for near Opme the Gauls had defeated the legions of invading Rome. He had to overcome arguments that there existed already two junior leader units and that the Vichy government was launching its own national youth movement, the *Chantiers de Jeunesse*. De Lattre insisted that Opme was to be special, and with his usual disregard for such minor matters as budgetary provision, set out to build his training centre, complete with new spacious barrack blocks, swimming pool and sports stadium. On his first cadre course, young conscripts of the especially disillusioned 1940 group and a few released prisoners, provided willing labour. They were drawn, after careful selection, from different regions of France and different socio-economic groups. Later courses included the cadres of the units of his District.

Opme's course was aimed to produce men with a restored pride in France and its Army, despite the recent humiliation. These men were to act as a leaven in an Army of the future; de Lattre, with remarkable prescience, forecast 1944 as the year of fulfilment. The setting was both theatrical and grand with much of the training in good open countryside. Both these conditions were very different from the usual dreary high-walled urban barracks that crushed the pre-war conscript. Emphasis was placed on a peak of physical fitness, on past French military glory and on discipline, initiative, comradeship and team work, the latter either on training or in community singing of patriotic songs – even *Vous n'aurez pas l'Alsace et la Lorraine* – in the evenings. On de Lattre's 'campus' were also students of Strasbourg University, transferred to Clermont Ferrand; these and distinguished visiting speakers, all gave Opme its remarkable vitality. Success in the training developed self-confidence and a small start in rebuilding confidence in the Army's commanders. De Lattre saw his methods as superior to those in formal education which relied on memorising academic facts. For him historical facts, or more correctly his own selection of them, were to be translated into an ethos of optimism, enterprise, patriotism and action.

De Lattre, his family installed in the castle, inspired the training with his customary vigour, at the same time taking care that Opme did not attract the attention of the German Armistice Commission. Opme took most of his time, but within his region he organised several small mobile infantry sub-units of the Armistice Army. He also maintained very discreet contact with General Cochet whom he knew to be planning a resistance movement.

In July 1941, Weygand requested that de Lattre should be appointed to command the French forces in Tunisia, and in September, de Lattre, much invigorated by his work at Opme, arrived. The somnolent, easy-going colonial life-style of the units that formed the French garrison was abruptly and brutally shattered. All units were inspected, inefficient officers ruthlessly posted away and within the limits of funds, equipment and the eyes of the Italo-German Armistice Commission, a vigorous training programme begun.

A version of Opme for cadres was opened at Salammbô on the shore of Lake Carthage. Salammbô's courses – for a variety of officers and NCO cadres – were more military than those of Opme. But, as at Opme, de Lattre prescribed both 'direct' instruction, physical, tactical, communal work and discussions, and 'indirect' which he saw achieved by the historic site, dress and discipline, and in the communal life, all ranks messing and living together equally and engaging equally in communal manual labour. To reassert French prestige, de Lattre's car was generally escorted by a troop of *Spahis* in ceremonial scarlet, the troop being commanded by the great nephew of Abd al Kadir, the great opponent of the French in the 1840s. De Lattre also developed the policy of Weygand, and then Juin, of hiding away weapons and equipment from the Germans and secretly training units and commanders.

Juin's appointment as Commander-in-Chief of all French troops in North Africa did however lead to the sharp differences of opinion, already examined, between himself and de Lattre. The latter was possibly already a little jealous of Juin's superior rank, particularly as he himself had hoped to become Vichy's Army Commander following the death of General Huntziger in November 1941. The defence of Tunisia quarrel and Juin's somewhat tactless handling of Vichy's decision to bow to German pressure and recall de Lattre (see Chapter 4 pages 68–9) worsened the strained relationship.

Although promoted to a *général de corps d'armée* de Lattre's posting in France was a 'holding' one below the level of his rank – command of the *16ᵉ Division Militaire*, the Montpellier Military District. He took this posting, apparently to a backwater, in a mood of dejection realising he was under suspicion and being closely watched. But it was to prove the most dramatic period of de Lattre's life. Predictably, his first move was to open another Opme style training centre at Larzac, his views on the moral state of France and the social role of the Army strengthened by the worsening general metropolitan atmosphere of defeat and apathy. The life of the units in his command centred around what military training was possible, particularly night exercises; food growing which was combined with physical exercise; initiative training in many forms, and ceremonies, local and national. In these his smart units showed up others of the Armistice Army which were more apathetic. But all this, together with his inaction following Vichy instructions to prepare coastal defences (against a supposed Allied landing) and his selection of officers of known anti-German views for his staff, brought him under increasing surveillance. The local Vichy régime security officer recommended that de Lattre be 'neutralised'.

De Lattre's position in this highly charged political situation was very difficult. Although some Vichy officers watched him critically, he maintained contacts with other senior officers and other personalities within the Vichy system who thought as he did and, in one way or another, sought secretly to help the Allies. One of the touchstones for action for these officers was any German invasion of Unoccupied France which they saw as ending any claim Pétain and Vichy could have as a legitimate government. De Lattre was, in fact, given a secret directive by Admiral Darlan, Commander-in-Chief of all Vichy's forces, appointing him Army commander for the whole of the Mediterranean coast area should the Germans invade. Darlan's motives here and at other times are obscure. This author would simply speculate that Darlan, as a sailor, would have appreciated the grand strategic significance of two decisive battles in 1942, the US Navy's victory at Midway and the Royal Navy's Malta Relief Convoy victory of August 1942, and that he was preparing to change sides. Other evidence tends to support this. In accordance with this directive, de Lattre and his staff prepared a plan and made certain provisions to hold a bridgehead of resistance on a line Alps-Cevennes-Pyrenees facing north. The project seems to have been more one of national honour than military sense, the Allies were not in a position to offer effective help. De Lattre saw it entirely as a matter of honour.

The arrival of the Allied invasion fleets at Gibraltar and the landings in French North Africa that followed brought the tension to crisis. Darlan, who had given de Lattre his secret directive, was in Algiers and in no position to support, and Vichy's early reactions to the Allied moves, drafted by a combat-minded general, were warnings to military district commanders to be prepared to move out with weapons ready to fight. De Lattre also contacted those concerned within his role under Darlan's secret plan, securing promises of support from some commanders and officers but suspicion from others.

Resistance, Arrest and Escape

When the Germans crossed the demarcation line on 11 November 1942 de Lattre issued orders for action in accordance with the plan. But as he himself was about to move, the Vichy War Minister, Bridoux, telephoned him ordering that no troops should move out of barracks. De Lattre ignored this order and tore up a written version of it from his immediate superior at Avignon, General Langlois, that arrived a little later. All his *passion* was now unleashed. He went to Confession, said farewell to his loyal wife and son and set out with his headquarters staff, two platoons of infantry, and two guns to a pre-arranged troop concentration area in the eastern foothills of the Pyrenees. But, unknown to him, several of his subordinates had informed Langlois that de Lattre was proposing to disobey the 'no movement' order; these and Langlois himself went on to issue local counter-orders cancelling those of de Lattre. Bridoux ordered de Lattre's arrest. In the field it was very soon clear that no troops were arriving and that gendarmes were out searching for de Lattre. In a typical gesture of loyalty to those who had supported him, de Lattre discarded the option of an escape to Spain and reported to a gendarmerie post. There, after refusing a dubious telephone offer of a return to his command, he was arrested.

After a comfortable spell in prison at Toulouse, he was moved to one less comfortable near Lyons in preparation for his trial. On 9 January 1943 and before a special State Tribunal rather than a Court-Martial – such Tribunals were a Vichy procedure usually accorded to political offenders – de Lattre was charged with 'treason and abandoning his post'. The latter charge could not be escalated to 'in face of the enemy' because Vichy could not allow the Germans to be an enemy. He was allowed limited legal assistance but he also defended himself with all his customary communication skill. Among much general oratory on the role of the Army, de Lattre pointed out in particular that, by confining the troops to barracks, the government had thrown away one of the few cards in its hand. In the end, the treason charge was dropped and de Lattre was sentenced to ten years imprisonment for abandoning his post. He was however not demoted as the prosecution had sought and Madame de Lattre had earlier obtained a personal promise from Laval that he would not fall into German hands. De Lattre viewed the Tribunal with contempt, in particular two of its members, an admiral and his superior in May 1940, General Touchon.

In prison, de Lattre was very heavily guarded and at the outset treated harshly. His wife and others used their contacts at Vichy to secure an improvement and from February, when he was moved to Riom, he lived in reasonably comfortable cells, though remaining in solitary confinement.

He was visited, not always under particularly close supervision, by his wife and Bernard. He overtly spent his time gardening in a little courtyard, in reading generally, and, in particular, in reflecting over certain Catholic texts written for young men. He also conducted a form of distance learning instructional correspondence with Bernard, now aged fifteen and being privately tutored. Covertly, de Lattre was planning escape. His first attempt in May 1943 failed. Undaunted, de Lattre and Bernard devised a new plan for which Bernard smuggled in vital tools and some rope concealed in books, washing or flowers.

Escape was no mean achievement for a man aged fifty-four. Movements of sentries had to be studied. One inside guard corporal who had served under de Lattre in 1940 was prepared to help, as was an outer wall gendarme. The escape itself, on the night of 2–3 September, involved, as preliminaries, weakening the window frame high up on the cell wall and, using a towel horse, practising squeezing through a narrow space. Standing on piled furniture, de Lattre removed the window frame on the night of the escape and hacked through the bottom part of the iron bar that lay beyond it. He then squeezed through the narrow space and slid down the rope to a narrow courtyard lying between the inner and outer walls. Warned in advance by the guard corporal, Bernard arrived with a rope ladder for the outer prison wall; the prison wall's sentry was distracted by the outer wall gendarme noisily feigning drunkenness. Accompanying Bernard to greet de Lattre on the freedom side of the prison wall was de Lattre's driver from the *14ᵉ Division*, with two cars and with false papers for the general in the name of Dequenne, de Lattre's former divisional clerk killed in 1940. They had somehow earlier satisfied patrolling gendarmes.

So, disguised as Dequenne, a private tutor, with Bernard as his pupil, de Lattre hid for a while on a Puy de Dôme farm where he grew a beard. But local arrests indicated that the farm was becoming unsafe. After a few days travelling by train and making contact with the Lyons underground resistance, he and Bernard were taken to a field near Mâcon on the evening of 17 October. There, with the field guarded by armed Maquis members, he and others were picked up by a British aircraft and flown to Britain, a move that had been planned by the British Special Operations Executive for some time. Bernard, on whom the strain of events had been severe, had unfortunately to be left behind for the moment. As Robert Laurent, and with the help of friends, he moved to Paris where he was able to contact his mother who, as Mademoiselle Suzanne Lalande, had also arrived in the capital and was to hide in a convent. Pretending to be his aunt and claiming that 'Robert Laurent' was the son of French settlers in Tunisia, she arranged for the boy to enter a Jesuit school in Rheims, the school's Father Superior delighted to help and keep the secret.

In Britain, de Lattre faced several unexpected and confusing problems. First was his relationship with de Gaulle, with whom even pre-1940 he had not always seen eye to eye. To the credit of both, they both put their pride in their pocket. Second was the most suitable employment for him. Some move – from where came the initiative is unclear – appears to have existed to task him with co-ordination of the resistance movements. While he was prepared to brief London on the resistance, such a role was not to de Lattre's taste, and he spent his first weeks of freedom energetically lobbying British, American and Free French personalities for the creation of a powerful French Army in North Africa. He himself would not be content with anything other than a field command. The third problem was his damaged lung, for which a brief spell in the Middlesex Hospital proved necessary.

Command of the 1ᵉʳᵉ Armée Française; Operation *Dragoon*

On his recovery, de Lattre flew to Algiers where he both cemented his rapprochement with de Gaulle and renewed his friendship with Giraud. The latter was now fast losing political influence but retained much local military power; this he used to secure de Lattre's promotion to *général d'armée* and appointment to the command of what at that time was referred to as the *2ᵉ Armée*, all the French forces in North Africa. It was not until April 1944, however, that de Lattre was officially told that this force, under the title of Army B, would be landing with the Americans in the South of France (Operation *Dragoon*). But even before being given this role, de Lattre, immediately and with all his customary energy, explosions of fury and at times ruthless exercise of authority when he required particular individuals or equipments, threw himself into the task of fashioning the Army. Here de Lattre, like Juin and Leclerc, had to face all the problems of forging Gaullistes, former Vichy personnel, escapees and others into one unified purposeful organisation; de Lattre however had the added difficulty that many of the best units and cadres were either with Juin in Italy or earmarked for Leclerc's *2ᵉ Division Blindée*. This difficulty perhaps underlay his cavalier manner, the sobriquet '*Le Roi Jean*' first came into use at this time. His own style seemed to be one of a daily drama òr quarrel, entertainment of visiting important personalities in the grand manner, and then an all night work-in. Another training centre for officers and NCOs, reflecting de Lattre's highly personal style, was opened at Douera. Inefficient commanders were replaced and below-standard units received punishing training programmes.

The preparation of Army B faced several interrelated problems, men and equipment, and the commitment in Italy of Juin's four divisions. De Lattre wanted weapons and equipment not only for divisions to be used in the landings and others immediately to follow, but also for what he hoped he would find on arrival in France, thousands of young Frenchmen anxious to re-enter the war. He was also prepared to dispense with some of the service and support units that the US Army included in all its divisions. But the Americans had their own logistic and other problems, and many in Algiers were still not fully convinced of the value of French troops or of any popular enthusiasm following liberation. De Lattre was, unjustly, blamed for overstating his case. Eventually, the Americans agreed to equip and supply a force of five infantry and three armoured divisions; these totals however included Juin's *Divisions* and that of Leclerc, destined for Normandy. For some time, the Americans and British contested the concept of a wholly French Army, which the French countered by formally confirming de Lattre's appointment as an Army Commander. But neither the overall American control nor the French almost total dependence on American supply were conditions to de Lattre's liking. He felt with *passion* that the Americans had little understanding of the fact that he was commanding a French Army setting out to liberate its homeland; friction was inevitable.

To de Lattre it was also essential and obvious that Juin's Corps of four battle experienced *Divisions* and numerous *goums* should be brought back from Italy and placed under his command. As already noted, Juin objected and de Lattre replied in some irritation. But if Juin had been correct in the dispute over the defence of Tunisia, in this argument he was overruled, with justification, by both de Gaulle and the Allied command. Juin's divisions joined de Lattre in July giving him the *1ᵉʳᵉ Division Blindée* under General du Vigier, the *5ᵉ Division Blindée* under General de Vernejoul and the *9ᵉ Division d'Infanterie*

Coloniale (DIC) under General Magnay in addition to the four returned from Italy, Brosset's *1ere DFL*, Dody's *2e DIM*, de Monsabert's *3e DIA* and Sevez's *4e DMM*.

In this period of preparation, however, two events occurred that enormously cheered de Lattre. The first, in May, was the escape from France of his wife and son. Bernard had not settled well at Rheims and was showing symptoms of disturbance; he was also approaching the age when he might be drafted for forced labour in Germany. Their journey, which was requested by London and organised by the Resistance, involved numerous new aliases, police and Gestapo checks and, for security reasons, separate crossings of the Pyrenees, still under deep snow. Both eventually arrived in Algiers, Bernard immediately joining the training centre at Douera.

The second was a subsidiary military operation decided upon by the Allied Command – that French troops should take the island of Elba. The operation was originally to have been commanded by the French Army Corps Commander in Corsica, Martin, acting under the Allied Commander-in-Chief, General Sir Henry Maitland Wilson. De Gaulle intervened, and demanded a French Army Commander as a move in the dispute still on-going at the time as to whether there should be an Army-level French formation. De Lattre was appointed, and in the light of recent reports of German strengthening of the garrison, immediately requested a postponement of the assault for four weeks. This was conceded but his second demand, for the one French parachute unit, was turned down despite his threat to abandon the whole operation. Both issues occasioned friction, but de Lattre was determined that there should be no risk of failure and that he should have the maximum force available.

In the event the attack proved well planned. It was launched on 17 June, with the full co-operation of the Royal Navy whose admiral, Troubridge, de Lattre liked. It was a complete and quick success. De Lattre's force included the *9e DIC* of mainly Black African troops, some 2,000 Moroccan *goumiers*, and a *Bataillon de Choc*, a commando-style unit of picked men together with a few additional commandos. The *Bataillon de Choc* and the commandos, landing in small parties quietly and in darkness, destroyed almost all the dangerous coast heavy artillery defences. The main landings met with heavy and damaging opposition on the beaches from 88 mm guns; this had however been foreseen by de Lattre's staff and an alternative landing place was then used, the main body landing safely. Within forty-eight hours the stiff German resistance had been overcome.

In the planning for the August Riviera coast landings (Operation *Dragoon*) de Lattre had to fight his corner on a number of issues. On three he lost. His preference would have been for landings on either side of Toulon in order to take it more quickly than the planned twenty-four days. This was ruled out as too hazardous and a stretch of coast between Cavalaire and Agay, not covered by the most powerful of the German coast defence batteries, was selected. He also wanted French troops to be the first ashore, but they were assessed as un-trained for an assault from the sea and de Gaulle personally forbade the use of the French parachute unit. On other issues, he won his points – that despite heavy German coast defence batteries, naval gunfire must support the landings for some time and that in the event of strong German resistance in coastal pockets, the French forma-tions would not be broken down to contain them. In the first of a series of disputes with his deputy, de Larminat, de Lattre refused to concede tactical command of the forward units. In a firm but tactful corre-spondence with de Gaulle he insisted that the Moroccan *goumiers*, with their unique mountain warfare abilities and mule-based logis-tics, must be used in the campaign despite their record of rapine in Italy. The story of the *goumiers* was typical of de Lattre; he remarked to his staff 'When we speak of 1,000 *goumiers* we think of 2,000 and we embark 6,000'. There was also a sharp dispute with General Patch, the US 7th Army Commander, about the break out phase. De Lattre wanted a wheeling movement by French forces to cut off the Ger-mans, but Patch seemed to believe that this project was to spare them the tough nuts of Toulon and Marseille. A final peculiarly French and delicate problem for de Lattre was to rally behind him the four divisions in Italy who were devoted to Juin. This he achieved by retaining Juin's chief of staff, Carpentier, and all his divisional com-manders. Further, de Lattre tried to impress on all cadres his admir-ation both for the French successes in Italy and for Juin personally; not all Juin's staff were receptive.

The plans for the landings provided for preliminary French and American and some British Special Force and Airborne landings to neutralise coastal batteries and carry out demolitions. This was to be followed by a US Army three division landing with, accompanying them, the lst Combat Command of du Vigiers $1^{ere}DB$, all fully sup-ported by ships and aircraft and timed for each morning on 15 April. A first French echelon of the $1^{ere}DFL$ and $3^{e}DIA$ with certain other units was to land twenty-four hours after the American assault. This was to be followed four to eight days later by the $9^{e}DIC$, several hundred *goumiers* and certain other units. The Americans were to thrust inland towards the Durance and Rhône Valleys, the French were to take Toulon and Marseille. Both cities were well fortified and the capture dates were assessed as about 4 September and 25 September respectively.

The initial landings went largely according to plan, only one beach not being secured. Amid great emotion, de Lattre, accompanied by his staff and by Bernard, landed on French soil on the evening of the 16th. The immediate local German resistance proved less strong than had been expected and de Lattre was faced with his first major decision as a large formation commander – whether with his first echelon to risk a dash for Toulon, with its circle of fortifications set in the steep hills and a garrison of some 25,000, or wait as both prudence and the overall Allied plan counselled, until the second echelon had arrived – but in so doing lose the element of surprise. As with the decisions Juin had had to make in Italy, the issues were not purely military: prestige of success or the political consequences of a reverse were also at stake. A speedy capture of Toulon and Marseille would enable him to keep up with the Americans. Characteristically, de Lattre opted for an immediate attack, de Monsabert's *3ᵉ DIA* was to traverse the inland heights and encircle Toulon while the *1ᵉʳᵉ DFL* was to attack the heavily fortified coast approach. An unexpected asset was the arrival, earlier than originally planned, of elements of the *9ᵉ DIC*; these were placed in the middle, along the St Raphael-Toulon road. Not without difficulty, de Lattre persuaded Patch to approve his plan. There followed very stiff fighting, but by the 21st, Toulon had been encircled by de Monsabert and by the 26th the city and dockyard had been cleared of Germans by the *9ᵉ DIC*.

Exciting though all this was, de Lattre, from the start, kept in sight the further objectives, Marseille, as strongly held and fortified as Toulon, and the Rhône valley. Again taking a risk, on 20 August de Lattre ordered the 1st Combat Command, which had been returned to him, to move on to Aubagne, just east of Marseille; the Moroccan *goums*, newly arrived, began to infiltrate and clear the mountainside gun positions and pill boxes. Clear thinking remained necessary, however: the Toulon fighting was at its height, the Americans were in need of help in the Aix area and du Vigier's *1ᵉʳᵉ DB*, the remainder now ashore, was required for the Rhône. De Lattre ordered de Monsabert and the *goums* to clear the Marseille suburbs only, but events then gathered their own momentum. The Marseille Resistance in the city centre rose in revolt, the 1st Combat Command penetrated towards the Old Port, de Monsabert moved *3ᵉ DIA* units in to support them, and the fall of Toulon on the 26th released further French forces. On the 28th, after a final assault on the Notre Dame de la Garde feature by Algerian *Tirailleurs* of de Monsabert's *3ᵉ DIA*, supported by heavy artillery fire, the Germans surrendered. The rapid capture of the two major French ports had been a brilliantly skilful feat of arms. The German lost several thousand dead and 37,000 men taken prisoner. French casualties killed or wounded totalled 4,000. A remark of de Lattre's highlights his own personal role 'To go to Monsabert's post was a dangerous sport which frequently forced one to crawl on one's belly'. The *Armée* itself gained a great sense of elan. Almost immediately the *1ᵉʳᵉ DB* whose leading units were already in Arles and Avignon was regrouped together for advance further up the Rhône; more of France was to be freed.

The next stage of operations, following hard on the heels of the retreating Germans, was, in purely military terms, not too difficult until the foothills of the Vosges were reached. Four hundred miles were covered in three weeks, despite some tenacious German delaying actions, particularly in the Autun and Dijon areas. Emerging, however, were a number of exceptionally difficult part-military, part-political and part-personal problems with which de Lattre had to cope as the fighting in the Vosges became severe.

The first of these related to the command structure. With all his divisions on shore, De Lattre could now assert an independence from Patch as an Army Commander in his own right. Within his Army now proudly styled the *1ᵉʳᵉ Armée Française* he could compose two army corps, the I Corps on the right, given to General Béthouart and the II Corps on the left, given to de Monsabert. De Lattre found it impossible to work with his deputy, de Larminat, and had him removed – a subsequent enquiry fully supported his action. But de Lattre's *1ᵉʳᵉ Armée* remained part of the US Army's 6 Army Group under General Devers, with whom de Lattre was to have many a theatrical altercation. Later in September, Devers's Army Group, in turn, came under the command of Eisenhower at SHAEF, the Mediterranean-link being logistic only.

An early issue between de Lattre and the Anglo-American command was the role and axis of advance of the *1ᵉʳᵉ Armée*. The Americans, with no consultation, wanted de Lattre to move westwards into Languedoc. De Lattre believed in the light of his victory in Provence that a rapid concerted movement by his *Armée* northward up the Rhone with the American VI Corps on the right of his main body and his *Armée's 3ᵉ DIA* to the right of the VI Corps on the Alps foothills, might cut off the retreating Germans. He was above all keen not to be hemmed in by the Americans but to keep level with their advance. The Americans doubted their logistic capability for de Lattre's plan but did give the *1ᵉʳᵉ DFL* pride of place in entry into Lyons, France's third largest city, on 3 September. The city's liberation was also marked by a fine sweep by the *1ᵉʳᵉ DB* round the west to the north, capturing over 2,000 Germans. De Lattre sent a small detachment temporarily into Languedoc, he himself gaining immense personal satisfaction from a visit to Montpellier.

A severe constraint, to worsen as winter approached, was de Lattre's virtually total logistic and fuel dependence on the Americans. Dependence was compounded by weather, shipping delays and port congestions, in de Lattre's own words '... the Germans most effective ally: the empty fuel tank'. De Lattre had, for example, frequently to take lorries from one formation to move or supply another, and field and electrical engineering equipment was also scarce; he never had the almost instant resupply enjoyed by Leclerc. As the campaign extended, so worsened also the replacement problems of worn-out and damaged equipment. Much of de Lattre's time during the campaign had to be spent in fighting the French corner, with attrition on nervous energy and temper.

De Lattre also found himself faced at Army command level with the same problems created by the FFI that Juin was facing at national level. The capture of Toulon and Marseille had highlighted the role that FFI Resistance units, at their best, could play; the advance northwards up the Rhone was also greatly helped by FFI groups. But the 'vibrant and tumultuous', to use de Lattre's own words, mentality of Resistance, even if shorn of political ideology, was very different to that of professional soldiers, a difference most evident in discipline, informality and variety of groups and a heterogeneity of cadres, but extending also to day to day problems of uniforms, pay, medals and equipment. In addition to those groups of marked political or regional allegiance, others were overtly anti-Army, seeing themselves as a new French revolutionary army. Others were simply jealous or resentful. The French army's regulars, veterans of Tunisia and Italy, often viewed the self-promoted Maquis leaders and their scruffy ill-disciplined guerillas with disdain, particularly if, untrained as they were, they were not steady under fire.

Further, as time passed and the weather grew colder, both early and suddenly, it became evident that some of the *Coloniale* and *Armée d'Afrique* units, particularly those including personnel who had fought throughout the 1943–44 winter in Italy and almost continuously ever since, were becoming exhausted. Many still had only summer uniforms. More dangerous still was a growing atmosphere among the north African soldiers, particularly those from Algeria, that they were being exploited by the French who were themselves not making a fair contribution, a *'sentiment terriblement dangereux'* in de Lattre's words.

This sentiment was compounded by the apparent apathy which de Lattre's troops frequently encountered as they moved further into France. By the end of the year, the morale of the *1ere Armée* had fallen very low. De Lattre wrote a letter of alarm to Diethelm, the Minister for War on 9 November. In it he noted first the fatigue of many of the regiments, the inadequacy of uniforms and food in the cold weather and complaints over pay. But he added that the underlying and more grave causes were the general feeling that the nation was not interested in its army, and that those who had not joined the FFI groups being incorporated in the army were living a life of comfort and ease. De Lattre repeated these warnings in a letter to de Gaulle on 18 December, also emphasising the view of the North African troops that they were doing all the fighting.

To de Lattre these issues were interrelated; the best of the FFI must be brought into the fold of a rejuvenated French Army, for preference his *1ere Armée*, in accord with the ethos of Douera. The African soldiers had to be relieved by Frenchmen, who must then be seen to be liberating their own country. He accordingly set up special supply depots and training centres for the thousands of young FFI members who joined the *1ere Armée*, mostly voluntarily but a few as a result of a conscription decree. Some 75,000 had joined by the end of November 1944, a further 62,000 joined by May 1945. The original re-equipment agreements with the Americans had not provided for this. The Americans were persuaded to provide a modest scale of light weapons and equipment for 52,000. But this provision, together with improvisations, use of old French or captured German weapons and in respect shortfalls of clothing American generosity at regimental levels, failed by some way to meet all the needs. All, too, had to be done in the midst of heavy fighting.

In unit terms, FFI groups initially restructured into approximately battalion size, were first drafted on to the *1ere Armée's* regiments; success varied, affiliations with armoured formations being generally happy but incorporation in infantry regiments creating friction. De

Lattre next began a process of *blanchiment* that extended into February 1945 whereby first the Black African, Caribbean and Pacific units and sub-units of the *9ᵉ DIC* were replaced by FFI units en bloc, and then later some of the more exhausted of the North African *Tirailleurs* regiments also. The North African divisions became mixed, with two indigenous regiments and one metropolitan. Parades were held at which rifles and equipment were formally handed over. At first the FFI units retained the African names of their predecessors, but they were soon re-designated with numbers and names of traditional metropolitan regiments. To his great pleasure, de Lattre was able to form a whole division of FFI units early in 1945. It was given the number 14 – that of de Lattre's 1940 division. The process was not always smooth. Some African units resented their withdrawal as victory approached; some FFI units in the event proved unreliable, on occasions having to be encircled and disarmed. De Lattre himself was criticised for the tolerance he showed to the FFI. But overall de Lattre could justifiably claim it as a great moral victory '...of synthesis and French brotherhood'. Other emotive frictions also surfaced occasionally. In January 1945 the Gaullist *1ᵉʳᵉ DMI* made exaggerated claims in the press on its role in the Alsace fighting. A furious de Lattre caused a number of heads to roll.

Finally de Lattre had a personal worry. Bernard, although still under seventeen, was serving with a cavalry regiment; in fighting around Dijon, he was wounded, fortunately not severely.

Winter Fighting in Alsace

The link-up between Devers' Army Group and Eisenhower's main force was made simultaneously by several units, but among those linking were advance detachments of Leclerc's *Division* and de Monsabert's Corps. At this time, the deployment of the different 6 Army Group armies on the ground could be reshaped to its final form. Amid some difficulty, as all concerned were in contact with the enemy, the American VI Corps was taken out from the middle of the *1ᵉʳᵉ Armée*. The *1ᵉʳᵉ Armée* was given as its role the extreme right flank of the Allied advance, tasked for Alsace. In this role the *1ᵉʳᵉ Armée*'s rapid advance was checked in late September by the German defence of the Belfort Gap, the pass between the Jura and the Vosges which, if lost, exposed both Strasbourg and all Wurtemberg.

The Americans envisaged de Lattre's Army, whose logistic and attrition difficulties were evident, limiting itself to being a cover on

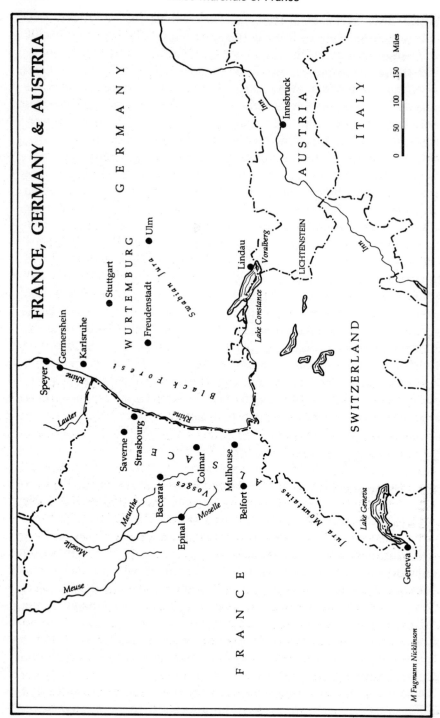

Map 6. France, Germany and Austria

1. General Leclerc and General Montgomery, near Tripoli, January 1943 (*Courtesy Imperial War Museum*)

2. Generals de Gaulle, de Monsabert, Juin and de Lattre de Tassigny, Italy, July 1944 (*Courtesy ECPA*)

3. General Juin, Italy, 1944 (*Courtesy Imperial War Museum*)

4. Generals Alexander, Clark and Juin, Siena, July 1944 (*Courtesy ECPA*)

5. General Leclerc, Paris, August 1944 (*Courtesy Imperial War Museum*)

6. General Leclerc, Normandy, August 1944 (*Courtesy Imperial War Museum*)

7. General de Lattre de Tassigny and his son Bernard, South of France, August 1944 (*Courtesy ECPA*)

8. General Leclerc de Hauteclocque, Ho Chi Minh and Jean Sainteny, Hanoi, March 1946 (*Courtesy ECPA*)

9. General Juin arriving as Resident-General, Morocco, May 1947 (*Courtesy ECPA*)

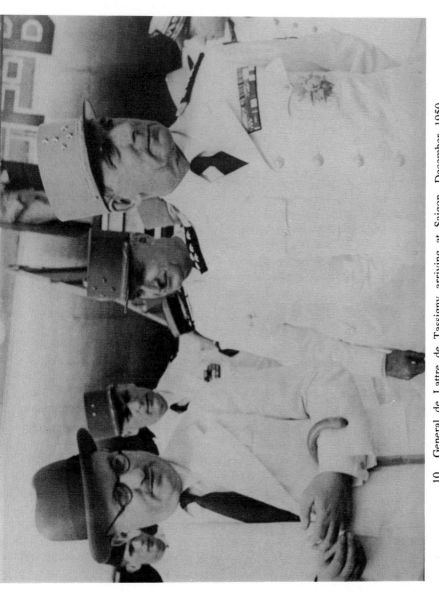

10. General de Lattre de Tassigny arriving at Saigon, December 1950
(*Courtesy Fondation Maréchal de Lattre de Tassigny*)

11. General de Lattre de Tassigny with General Salan and Colonel Beaufre planning the defence of Tonkin, December 1950 (*Courtesy Fondation Maréchal de Lattre de Tassigny*)

12. General de Lattre de Tassigny with Colonel Edon inspecting a recently recaptured Tonkin village, April 1951 (*Courtesy Fondation Maréchal de Lattre de Tassigny*)

the right flank of the Allied Armies, this flank itself not the main concern of Supreme Headquarters. Such a role did not suit de Lattre, especially in view of his personal fondness for Alsace. He planned to by-pass Belfort, the bulk of II Corps going north, with only a small detachment in contact with the fort, and with I Corps for the south. The latter received additional artillery to batter German defences on the Doubs river. De Monsabert received a fresh Moroccan division and other units, but found himself continuously pulled northward to cover the right flank of the Americans whose main interest was in Lorraine. De Lattre's view was that this 'warping' was a major factor enabling the Germans to built up strong defences in Alsace. And, indeed, although attacks were pressed throughout late September and an unusually wet and miserable October, the German defence proved too strong. An attempt to switch the main weight of attack from the left to the right flank also failed, and the advance came to a halt.

After further strong representations to Devers, de Lattre was permitted to try again in November, though just before his attack an enraged de Lattre had vehemently to resist a Supreme Headquarters project that two of his divisions, the 1ere *DB* and the 1ere *DFL*, be detached to take Bordeaux. He secured postponements, and in the event the 1ere *DB* never left him. The new attack plan provided for a reinforced I Corps main armoured attack, mostly to the south of Belfort, in order to try to enter the Rhine Valley, while II Corps initially was to mount an elaborate deception plan, together with small scale infantry attacks in the Vosges. Belfort was to be invested for later reduction. All the preparations had to be made in great secrecy, and in appalling weather conditions.

In thick snow, the attacks were launched on 14 November taking the Germans by surprise. Two weeks of stiff fighting, in which eight French divisions and additional Army and specialist troops and *goums* were involved, followed. The 1ere *Armée*, continuously urged on by de Lattre, achieved success, but not the total success for which de Lattre had hoped. I Corps units reached the Rhine in five days, Belfort finally fell on 25 November and an attempt by the Germans to mount a counter attack, splitting the two Corps, was repulsed, but the breakthrough into the Rhine valley was not achieved. The two French Corps linked up between Belfort and Mulhouse, but this encirclement was small scale. De Lattre's hope, that the Americans would be sufficiently strong to exploit Leclerc's capture of Strasbourg and sweep south for a far bigger encirclement could not be fulfilled, and nine divisions, together with the latest and most powerful German armour, remained in the Colmar pocket.

As noted earlier, the force assembled to attack the Colmar pocket from the north, Leclerc's Division and the US Army's 36th Infantry Division, was inadequate. On the southern and western sides, de Lattre had finally to accept the departure of the *1ere DFL*, with the *1ere DB* still under threat to follow. De Lattre's *Armée* also faced an acute artillery ammunition shortage. The German defence was aggressive and de Lattre's three week long assault, beginning on 6 December, could only make very limited gains. Morale fell to its lowest. De Lattre's request to Devers for two more divisions met an irritated refusal. The situation was then already being overtaken by the opening of the German Ardennes offensive and the need for the redeployment of Devers' two divisions to support Patton's counter attacks. De Lattre was warned that his *Armée* might have to withdraw to the Vosges, though he was given the *1ere DFL* back.

De Lattre was as violently opposed to any withdrawal from liberated Alsace as Juin and Leclerc. To counter any 'psychosis of retreat' he issued orders that reaffirmed the holding of the Belfort gap and Strasbourg, which city in a letter to Devers he described as symbolic of the resistance and rebirth of France. He sent a copy of this letter as a balm to de Monsabert with a very firm injunction to do as he was told and stop protesting about the redeployment of his units. From a purely military point of view, however, not only was Strasbourg difficult to defend but any attempt to do so could lead to the cutting off of French and American forces in north Alsace. It was in this context that on 2 January Eisenhower ordered the thinning out of troops preparatory to a withdrawal, an order that met with a furious '*Ca non!*' from de Lattre. Despite the weariness of his *Armée* and his own suffering from a feverish chill, he promptly set about military preparations to defend Strasbourg. He also added his personal pressure to that of Juin and de Gaulle at Supreme Headquarters. Both these two immediately confirmed his action in planning the defence of the city. De Gaulle's tone was unnecessarily sharp as, through a breakdown in communication, he at the time believed de Lattre would follow the Supreme Headquarters' orders. The sharpness only added to de Lattre's worries.

Firmly but courteously setting aside the protests and grumblings from its commander, General Guillaume – a trusted old friend from Moroccan days of the early 1920s – de Lattre ordered the exhausted *3e DIA* to Strasbourg. This indomitable division had been due for a rest, some units had been in action continuously since August. De Lattre, although still unwell, tirelessly directed the city authorities and the local FFI to prepare for a last-ditch defence; he also, not without altercation, pushed Devers into covering his left flank. The German assault on the city – a southward thrust by the main Germany Army and a northward thrust from the Colmar pocket – opened on 7 January. Fighting raged for two weeks, both sides suffering severely, before the German offensive ran out of steam. It was eventually stopped by the *1ere DFL* in the south, the US VI Corps in the north, American air to ground support – and the resolution of de Lattre in command.

There remained the Colmar pocket with its eight divisions and other troops, the final lap in the *1ere Armée's* Liberation campaign. De Lattre's plan, which he saw as the best counter to the German threat to Strasbourg, was for a massive pincer movement. II Corps of three French divisions and the US XXI Corps of two American Divisions were to move in from the north west and north, while I Corps of three French divisions would attack from the south-west and south. He was given back Leclerc's division, together with a tired American division from the Ardennes, to join II Corps. He himself had a newly arrived French division for I Corps. I Corps was to start operations early on 20 January, partly to draw off German troops from the II Corps front, where the attack was to begin on 23 January. De Lattre wanted an earlier date, partly to ease the pressure on Strasbourg but more particularly to avoid being left behind containing the pocket while the Americans entered Germany. As before, the Germans were confused by a careful deception plan. The conditions were exceedingly difficult in respect of the terrain, bitter blizzards, three feet of snow, frozen oilpipe lines, damaged roads and railways and broken bridges. The Corps headquarters, too, were over a hundred miles apart compelling de Lattre to establish a forward headquarters for himself. The whole operation was a command and logistics nightmare.

Heavy German resistance checked the French and by the 24th even the usually optimistic Béthouart was counselling a halt. The divisions had taken severe casualties, air support was limited, men were exhausted and frost-bitten. De Lattre's answer was to request the help of an American Army Corps, the XXI, that he knew was not committed. The request was supported strongly by Juin in representations to Supreme Headquarters. Devers generously backed de Lattre, despite the misgivings of other American commanders. With XXI Corps entering the battle between the two French Corps, a slow

advance was resumed with the Germans continuing to resist
fanatically; Colmar was liberated by French and American forces
jointly on 2 February. The 'inner-pincer' of the US XXI Corps and the
French I Corps closed at Rouffach on the 5th and an 'outer-pincer' of
Leclerc's Division moving south with II Corps and the *1ere DB* moving
north linked up on the west bank of the Rhine on 8 February. By the
evening of the next day the only Germans across the Rhine in Alsace
were prisoners. The cost to the French forces had been 2,137 dead with
over 11,000 wounded, a considerable but not excessive price for this
final battle to clear France of its invader.

Entry into Germany

A much needed respite followed in which de Lattre himself returned briefly to Mouilleron to see his father. The *1ere Armée* was
reorganised and restructured with further *blanchiment* and the incorporation of the *14e Division*. A new cadre training centre, to which de
Lattre devoted much time and attention, was opened at Rouffach.
Rouffach combined military training with the further binding together of the FFI personnel and the regular soldiers. As always with
de Lattre, drill and ceremonial was given an important place in the
programme.

Once again, however, the future role of the *1ere Armée* was in doubt.
The main Allied military effort was to be a broad front advance
towards the Ruhr area; the upper Rhine was not seen as important.
The American 7th Army was to form the right flank of the broad front,
the French *1ere Armée*, it was thought, should extend its sector north of
Strasbourg and then follow the 7th Army into Germany. This was a
role, predictably, that de Lattre would never accept. Nor, for rather
different reasons, was it acceptable to de Gaulle, who wanted the
French Army to occupy a substantial area of Catholic south Germany, at least as a prestige zone of occupation and perhaps as an area
to be detached later as some form of French client state. But the
French *Armée* was not well equipped enough to cross the Upper
Rhine on its own, in face of strong German defences and difficult
terrain.

De Lattre embarked on a wily mix of political and military manoeuvre. Advancing northwards with the 7th Army, he quietly
extended his left flank by using his *goums* to clear a large forest. This
forest was technically in the 7th Army's area, but it enabled de Lattre
to occupy a sector on the south bank of the river Lauter, part of the

Franco-German border, abreast of the Americans rather than behind them. From this sector, on 19 March, de Monsabert was able to task two divisions to cross the Lauter into Germany and attack a section of the Siegfried Line. After six days of hard fighting, the two divisions broke through and reached the left bank of the Rhine. Devers, impressed, allowed de Lattre to participate in the crossing.

The Rhine, 300 yards across in this area, was a formidable obstacle to an army ill-provided with heavy engineering equipment. As early as the previous September, de Lattre had ordered his chief engineer to prepare for a Rhine crossing; with great difficulty he had assembled material that formed one bridge, but only one. De Lattre's assault plan provided for twoassaults on the night of 31 March near Speyer in the north of his sector, and near Germersheim further south. The Germersheim assault, by the *2ᵉ Division d'Infanterie Marocaine (DIM)* came under heavy fire while still in boats. At first it could only establish a toe-hold across the river though by the end of the day three battalions were across. The Speyer assault by the *3ᵉ DIA* was more successful; construction of the bridge, originally earmarked for Germersheim, was begun. Two days later the *9ᵉ DIC* achieved a third crossing still further south. By the evening of 4 April, de Lattre had four divisions of de Monsabert's II Corps across the Rhine and had taken Karlsruhe, but his I Corps further south still remained on the west bank facing Siegfried Line defences with the Black Forest behind.

Accordingly, de Lattre next directed II Corps to move southwards to clear the east bank of the Rhine, so finally securing Strasbourg and enabling the I Corps to cross the river. This accomplished, the Corps then began to move northwards as part of the concept of being the right flank of the Allied Armies. However, in pursuit of his own and his country's wider ambitions, de Lattre made a dramatic recasting of his plans, a move involving a total change of direction for I Corps. As a matter of urgency and ignoring any considerations of fatigue, he ordered both Corps to converge on the town of Freudenstadt, to the east of the Black Forest, by 18 April. From Freudenstadt II Corps was tasked to take Stuttgart and then move on to encircle the Swabian Jura, where German forces were assembling for a last stand, from the north. I Corps was given two tasks. The first was to complete clearing the southern Black Forest, a stiff task in itself as some 30,000 Germans still remained there. At the same time the Corps was also ordered again to change direction and move east, encircle the Swabian Jura from the south and take Ulm.

With brilliance and dash, I Corps crossed the Danube on 21 April 1945 even though operations in the Black Forest were still dragging on. Also on the 21st, de Monsabert's II Corps occupied Stuttgart and in the next five days completed the encirclement of the Jura, where the Germans surrendered. On the 24th, French and American troops jointly entered Ulm. Relieved of the Black Forest commitment by some help from II Corps, Béthouart was able to despatch two columns, one from the Black Forest area to the shores of Lake Constance and the Voralberg Pass, and one, also reinforced by II Corps, into Austria's Western Tyrol via the Inn Valley. At the time of the final German surrender, therefore, nine divisions of French troops were in occupation of a very large area of German territory and de Gaulle was well placed in negotiations over the size of the French Zone of Occupation.

For the reasons of wider French designs, this occupation had been achieved by a measure of poaching in areas earmarked by the Americans. Patch's 7th Army had earlier conceded Stuttgart to the French operationally but an irritated Devers demanded that the French withdraw immediately. Allied press reports deliberately minimised the French achievement. De Lattre refused to withdraw and was supported by de Gaulle, who further rebutted American proposals to relieve French units in the Palatinate. The French participation in the occupation of Ulm made the usually placid Devers exceedingly angry, and no amount of pleading by de Lattre of special Napoleonic historic associations served to calm him. Acrimonious signals and letters flew. It was not until 13 May, in reconciliation and amid other tributes that he paid to de Lattre, that Devers remarked: 'For many months we have fought together – often on the same side'.

French long-term designs for southern Germany could also be seen in the strict control of the behaviour of the French and Maghreb soldiers. With the exception of the occupation of Stuttgart, where there were some excesses by Algerian *Tirailleurs*, the conduct of troops was notably good. Where there were cases of looting of property or rape they were dealt with very firmly; in at least one case a Moroccan soldier was actually shot for rape. The German population was impressed – particularly when comparisons were made with the behaviour of other occupying armies.

The *Armée's* achievement had been considerable – tangibly, the liberation of nearly a third of France and successful battle against two German armies resulting in the capture of 250,000 prisoners. Less tangibly but as important, the *Armée* had made a huge contribution to the restoration of confidence in the fighting capabilities of Frenchmen, both within France and amongst her allies.

De Lattre, of course, had commanded a force over twice the size of that of Juin; Leclerc, to this point, had commanded only a division. De Lattre had had first to train himself to lead his *Armée* in a fast moving, modern, armoured warfare campaign, very different from the almost First World War fighting in Italy. His style reflects the size and complexity of his command as well as his own temperament; several features of this style merit further study.

Juin's headquarters had been that of the highly capable professional commanding in ordered, traditional style. The larger-than-life de Lattre commanded differently. For him command was matter of orginality and imagination, breadth of vision, grandeur and perhaps above all of drama. His headquarters were charged with tension, *passion*, but were also run with style. His chiefs of staff had to be aware of his fast changing moods and plans. He would by day physically control operations like the conductor of an orchestra, either on the ground by radio or by telephone, directing each player when his moment arrived and in the process displaying flexibility, daring and speed. He always used his forces economically, deploying them where they would be most effective. He would refuse to be drawn early on the detail of future projects and then would bounce a decision on staffs at very short notice. Daily operations orders would be redrafted some three or four times by his staff during the night, each draft inspiring de Lattre to think of some new move. He would dine between ten and midnight, work until five and eventually sign his orders in bed at six in the morning. He also believed in demanding of his men more than their apparent capabilities which, with his imagination in command, produced his successes despite the logistic shoestring. One of his biographers, Simiot, records that between 1 and 15 September, the period of pursuit up the Rhône Valley, de Lattre issued no less than fifty-seven operation orders. He gave the greatest attention to detail – his orders for the landings in the South of France, for example, were re-drafted seventeen times, emerging as a model, detailed, precise and clear. His following of the teachings of Foch was clear in his belief that Strasbourg would be best defended by an attack on the Colmar pocket.

As earlier, he thrived on debate, exchange of ideas. For the South of France landings he established a cabinet 'think tank' of five officers to study the major problems in detail and would spend long periods of time talking these problems through. He continued with a 'think tank' of civilians, some commissioned as reserve officers, in France; with these he discussed wider civil-military matters. His principal staff officers and commanders were likely to be summoned at any hour of day or night or they might find de Lattre arriving in their office, sometimes cajoling, sometimes in a *colère*. They were driven, at least in part deliberately, to a point of exhaustion; two generals were removed from their commands by de Lattre during the winter fighting.

Style in command was extended to soldiers. At Christmas 1944 de Lattre ensured each soldier at the front received a parcel of Christmas food and comforts, and he himself made a radio appeal to the French nation as a whole to think of their soldiers. His addition of the proud *Rhin et Danube*, with its Napoleonic associations, to the title of *1ere Armée Francaise* was meant to give each soldier a sense of having made an historic contribution to his country; a special shoulder badge was hurriedly mass-produced.

De Lattre's headquarters, at Besançon, Montbéliard and Guebwiler were the domain of a grand seigneur. Political or diplomatic guests were invited; on occasions quite senior officers with important business would have to wait while de Lattre talked to his guests. One of his staff officers commented that visitors were so many that they sat in droves on the stairs to his office, sometimes for several days. The food was good (though De Lattre himself ate little), the junior staff officers elegant, the female clerical support pretty, the vehicles well polished. The 'think tank' members looked after guests when de Lattre was otherwise engaged. He also arranged for a special press staff officer to give full briefings to the press every day, but for reasons on which one may speculate, the French press and special exhibitions gave more publicity to the Allies and to Leclerc than to the *1ere Armée*. Madame de Lattre, herself heavily involved in medical and welfare work for the Army, was particularly distressed by this.

Well might one French general, de Chambrun, say that Juin commanded with ability and intelligence by day while de Lattre commanded with genius at night. One of his chiefs of staff remarked also that he had never served anyone so difficult as de Lattre, but he would not want to serve anyone else.

The Armistice found de Lattre at Lindau on Lake Constance with Bernard, not far away, serving as a tank gunner. While de Lattre was celebrating the end of the fighting with his commanders and staff, there arrived a number of French political and military figures who had been deported by the Germans; among them was General Weygand. But at the same time a signal from Paris was received ordering the arrest of any who had served under Vichy, a further signal specifically named Weygand whom, it was clear, de Gaulle would never forgive. De Lattre was embarrassed and angry. He received Weygand joyfully as an old friend and chief, and only later told him of his orders. For their execution, he arranged for Weygand to return to Paris, but in dignity, accompanied by an aide de camp and after a ceremonial parade in his honour.

At the same time, de Lattre himself received express personal instructions from de Gaulle to proceed to Berlin where the formal military surrender of the German armed forces was to be made to senior American, British and Soviet commanders. These were General Spaatz, Air Chief Marshal Sir Arthur Tedder and Marshal Zhukov; for the Germans, Keitel was to sign. It was not intended that a French commander should be a signatory, to the fury of de Gaulle. The journey itself was uncomfortable and hazardous, de Lattre arrived very tired to find the room – in an east Berlin technical school – where the surrender was to be signed contained only three places, surmounted by national flags for the Allied commanders and one place for Keitel. De Lattre erupted into one of his most violent, almost uncontrollable, *colères*, with the result that a fourth place and a Tricolour hurriedly improvised from a Nazi flag, a sheet and a boiler suit were added.

De Lattre's claim to be a signatory was championed by Tedder, who was later supported by the Soviets. In the end, Tedder (as Eisenhower's Deputy) and Zhukov signed as contractors, with Spaatz and de Lattre as witnesses. The exact order was varied on different copies to please all. But at the ceremonial banquet that followed, de Lattre had again to make his point. At the outset, Zhukov toasted Stalin, Roosevelt and Churchill, a glowering de Lattre refused to eat or drink. An embarrassed Zhukov then made a second speech extolling France, after which a band played the *Marseillaise* and all was well.

On his return to Lindau, de Lattre reorganised his headquarters into a full vice-regal style, reminiscent of Lyautey's Residency in Morocco. A chateau was requisitioned, refurnished elegantly and its gardens magnificently laid out. A stream of important visitors, including the Sultan of Morocco, the Bey of Tunis, political leaders, academics and men of letters as well as his subordinate commanders were all invited to stay as guests.

De Lattre himself travelled around in a large car with motor-cycle escort, or, if on the lake, in an immaculate white yacht for which a special quay was built. Parades and ceremonies followed one another in all the towns and cities garrisoned by the *1ᵉʳᵉ Armée*. Military governors of towns or unit commanders who failed to provide an elaborate ceremonial and civic welcome for de Lattre on a visit received the full force of a *colère*, as did any unit whose men or vehicles were not immaculate. Devers was honoured with a twelve-hour long pageant concluding with an evening walk through a parade of 2,000 torchbearing *goumiers*. All de Lattre's love of theatre was now given its opportunity with lake and mountain scenery as a backcloth. French actors and corps de ballet were bidden to perform before military audiences.

There was, however, serious purpose behind this display. De Lattre wanted to bond his soldiers into a comradeship for the future, based on pride in their achievements. He also believed firstly that the Germans had to be shown that the French Army was a national force, not the handful of Gaullist fanatics commanding colonial mercenaries portrayed in former Nazi propaganda. Also, as with other Frenchmen of the time, the whole war experience had awakened in him a sentiment perhaps best described as 'proto-European', a still largely subconscious feeling of a need to reforge mainland European cultural links, especially among youth. For de Lattre, one of the roles of his *Armée* was to 'throw a bridgehead across towards German youth', a youth he saw as confused and needing moral guidance.

The early weeks of the occupation saw sporadic guerilla attacks and sabotage attempts on the French forces. These necessitated intelligence gathering, certain movement controls and a few cordon and search operations. Other lesser roles of de Lattre's *Armée* also merit mention. One was the care and humane treatment of the thousands of deported persons, including many Frenchmen who, for one reason or another, found themselves in southern Germany at this time. Many were very ill, the camps were infected with typhus and dysentry. Another was the return to France of an infinite variety of goods looted by the Germans. De Lattre's military administrators also embarked on the process of denazification of local authorities, police and schools.

On 24 July it was announced on the radio in abrupt terms that the *1ʳᵉ Armée Française Rhin et Danube* was to be dissolved and General Koenig, a *Gaulliste de la première heure*, appointed Commander-in-Chief of the French Army of Occupation. Although a restructuring of command had been forewarned earlier in July, the treatment of de Lattre appeared shabby with the post he was to be offered inferior to that of Juin. It must be admitted also that '*Le Roi Jean*'s glittering style at Lindau had attracted sharp criticism in Paris. De Lattre himself irritated de Gaulle. De Gaulle had nominated a General Staff general to be present at the Rheims surrender of the German Army. At this ceremony the other Allies had also nominated staff generals rather than commanders but the decision riled de Lattre who had earlier been promised the privilege. De Gaulle had, further, snubbed de Lattre at a Paris ceremony in June to commemorate his own 1940 broadcast. But one may perhaps speculate that de Gaulle's motives were not simply personal. France still seemed on the verge of a Communist revolution and de Gaulle no doubt still saw himself as uniquely placed to prevent it. In these perspectives, a charismatic rival with a military-political power base might be divisive and a hard decision might be necessary. De Lattre felt his own preference to remain in Germany to reorganise the civil administration, on which he had made specific recommendations, had been brushed aside. In strongly worded representations to de Gaulle, he specifically argued that the reputation of France in Germany and the morale of his *1ere Armée* suffered from the absence of major policy direction and rumours of his forthcoming removal circulating in Paris, the snub to him of 18th June, and the frustrations he was experiencing in securing honours and awards for his units and men.

De Lattre concluded his command on 4 August 1945 with a final pageant. Colour Parties from all the *1ere Armée's* regiments were drawn up on the banks of the Rhine at Kehl for a last salute from their Commander. Few present could have imagined that de Lattre would ever conduct a second equally remarkable campaign.

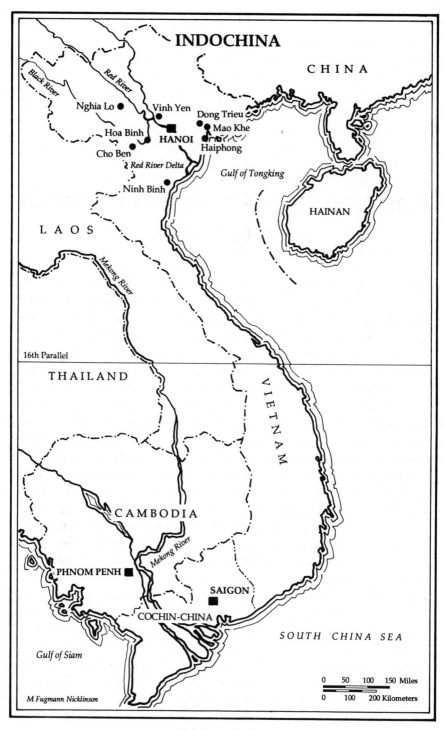

Map 7. Indochina

6

Indochina 1945–47: General Leclerc de Hauteclocque

General Leclerc de Hauteclocque, (Leclerc was added formally to his family's name in November 1945), was only forty-three when the war ended in Europe. In the relatively quiet period of October 1944 he had given much though to the post-war future of France, the nation's army and his own role. The war experience had left him with a new regard for the working man, many of whom had sacrificed much for France. He even arranged a strange dialogue between a worker priest and a trade union leader, both of whom had served in the Resistance. He was hoping to try and highlight some essential unity based on a moral regeneration, the Christian family and patriotism that would link the spiritual with the material needs of men. In this he was even prepared to admit that a few of the concepts of Vichy France, especially in the emphasis on family, might carry worth, though a proper legitimate authority for them was necessary. But he was seeking in vain, the war had sharpened class divisions that already existed and added new ones of Gaullist, Pétainist and resister. Leclerc's final contribution to his country was to be entirely different, a brilliant mix of political and military action to restore, as far as it was possible, France's position in Indochina. To his actions he added advice, perceptive and far-seeing but ignored, that, thereafter, French military force was only a card to play; the French Army could never secure a total victory. This acute perception was all the more remarkable coming as it did from an officer whose road to generalship had not been accompanied by the usual higher command staff courses of many years of experience. It came as a surprise to many who had been deluded by Leclerc's war years' prejudice against discussing wider national issues, apparently concentrating his mind only on his *Division*. De Valence, Leclerc's

aide-de-camp in Indochina, attributed his understanding and acceptance of the emerging Asian and, later, North African nationalism to a
genuine humanism that was the product of his religious beliefs; this
would certainly be in character.

To Recover and Re-establish French Sovereignty in Indochina

After Berchtesgaden, Leclerc led his *Division* as the vanguard of a
Paris victory parade on 18 June, the fifth anniversary of de Gaulle's
London appeal, and in an emotional ceremony handed it over to the
faithful Dio on the 22nd. It was not in his temperament to be a
spectator of events and he asked de Gaulle that he should be sent to
Morocco. De Gaulle replied that he was sending him to Indochina
because it was the most difficult of tasks. The headquarters of the
proposed III Corps became instead the headquarters for an expeditionary force to be formed from the *3ᵉ* and *9ᵉ Divisions d'Infanterie
Coloniale*. Unusually for a French *Coloniale* infantry division, there
were to be no *Tirailleurs Sénégalais* units. Leclerc forbade these,
aware of likely reactions in Asia. Leclerc was to be Commander-in-
Chief responsible to an overall High Commissioner. For this latter
appointment Admiral Thierry d'Argenlieu was selected in August.
Leclerc's mission was to recover and re-establish French sovereignty
in Indochina, but at the political level the only concession Paris was
prepared to make was a limited measure of internal autonomy to each
of the component states of Indochina within a French Union that
controlled all foreign affairs and defence matters as well as much
internal politics.

French Indochina was in fact a union of three quite distinct Asian
territories. Much the largest of these is Vietnam, a kidney shaped
territory of which the north was at the time called Tonkin, the centre
Annam and the south Cochin China. Vietnam's people are of a generally uniform Chinese appearance. The country's pre-colonial history had seen frequent conflict between north and south. Cambodia's
Khmer people are brown-skinned and of quite different religious and
cultural origins. Equally distinct are the mountain peoples of Laos.
The pre-war French power structure provided for an Emperor of
Annam – whose territory included some of Tonkin – and kings in
Cambodia and Laos all within a heavily French controlled Union
which included as components Annam, Tonkin, Cochin China, Cambodia and Laos.

In return for certain garrison and airfield rights, the Japanese had tolerated a Vichy French administration until March 1945. Then, following the collapse of Vichy and its replacement by a hostile de Gaulle, they seized full power in a brutal and bloody operation. With Japanese encouragement, the Emperor of Annam, Bao Dai, proclaimed the independence of Vietnam, in Cambodia Prince Sihanouk followed suit and there was a similar proclamation in Laos. Bao Dai's empire, however, faced a challenge from the Thai Nguyen area north of Hanoi, where a Communist-controlled 'League for the Independence of Vietnam', or Viet-minh, had created a 'liberated area'. Ho Chi Minh, the Viet-minh leader, also had a substantial following in central and southern Vietnam. Further, the Viet-minh was generally acting as a catalyst for the politicisation of the Vietnam peasant masses by means of violent social revolution at village and commune level, killing off and destroying the old traditional authorities who had worked willingly or unwillingly with the French. The situation was anarchic, the Viet-minh leaders were not speaking with one voice and some were prepared to do a deal with the French. Ho Chi Minh, although firmly Communist, appeared as one of the more moderate influences, restraining those more militant, such as Vo Nguyen Giap (soon to be known throughout the world as 'General Giap' and seen as a leading exponent in the art of guerilla warfare). The French all found the situation – sometimes threatening, sometimes conciliatory – difficult to assess; nor did they fully grasp the damage done to their prestige by the events of the war years. The Viet-minh had fought perfunctorily as guerillas against the Japanese but had gained some real credit from United States well-wishing opponents of colonialism by intelligence gathering.

By August 1945, the time of the Japanese collapse, the survivors of the Vichy French garrison had struggled through to Yunnan in south China where the Chinese, to suit their own purposes, did little for them. Under an agreement reached at the Potsdam Conference, at which France was not represented, Indochina north of the 16th Parallel was to be occupied by China, and south of this line by the British. The snub to France did not pass unnoticed in Indochina. The agreement reflected American anti-colonial prejudices and was an important contributing factor to the decades of misfortune that followed; the Japanese, however, were more minded to hand over their authority to Ho Chi Minh and they freely handed weapons over to the Viet-minh. In face of this and also in the absence of any French willingness to deal with him, Bao Dai abdicated. A large Chinese army arrived, pillaging ruthlessly on its way. It was formed of contingents whose loyalty was suspect and the Chinese government was glad to have abroad. On its arrival, it expropriated French property and humiliated the French in every possible way.

In late August, the French made an unsuccessful effort to reassert sovereignty by parachuting two small teams led by colonels, designated to be administrators for the north and south, into Indochina. In the south, Colonel Cédile was pushed aside by the local Viet-minh but left at liberty; in the north, Colonel Messmer was arrested by the Viet-minh, escaping to China only with great difficulty. Ho Chi Minh then moved into Hanoi, preparing for his September 22nd proclamation of Vietnam's independence, by which he hoped to pre-empt the Chinese rather more than the French. He was unable, however, to prevent the arrival in the north of the Chinese Army, which continued to behave like a victorious conqueror planning a long stay. The Chinese commander maintained the Chinese refusal to release the French escapees, and forbade all French shipping in waters north of the 16th Parallel. Ho Chi Minh's reaction was to accept the presence of another French administrator, Sainteny, and to try to broaden his political base by dissolving the Communist party (though retaining its cadres) and effecting a reconciliation with Bao Dai, now styled 'Principal Counsellor'. Opinions are divided on how genuine this move was. In the south, a British force arrived at Saigon on 12 September. The force was composed, however, of Indian Army as well as British units and its mission had at the outset to be limited to the control of the large Japanese garrison. Additional complicating factors were a French resident population and French servicemen released from Japanese camps, both in vengeful mood. These had openly insulted Viet-minh followers who, in turn, had perpetrated a horrific night of burnings and killings of some 150 French civilians. Leclerc, on his way to Saigon, immediately visited Mountbatten – the Supreme Allied Commander, South East Asia – in Ceylon and with *passion* sought authority for General Gracey to impose martial law. On 23 September Gracey went further, acquiescing in a take-over of government by Cédile. This latter event led to further fighting but the British and Indian units secured control, and a truce was negotiated. Meanwhile, Mountbatten strongly urged Cédile to negotiate with the Viet-minh.

In this unpromising situation, not clearly understood in Paris, Leclerc arrived at Saigon on 7 October. He had made a great effort to study the Indochina situation, consulting academics, soldiers and administrators of experience. He had also spent much time in India and Malaya in arranging British logistic support for his force on its way to Indochina; France was in no state to provide the necessary ships, vehicles, aircraft, fuel, stores, medical supplies or tropical warfare equipment. In Ceylon, he had been strongly advised by Mountbatten that post-war Asia was very different to the pre-war colonial scene, to which there could be no return; to this advice he had replied significantly 'What you say makes sense but is not French policy'. This contradiction was to dog him in the coming months. He had also had the satisfaction of representing France at the formal surrender of the Japanese on board an American battleship in Tokyo Bay, and then again at the surrender of the Japanese in Singapore. In Japan, General MacArthur had warned him that he could expect no direct American military help. Even less helpful was his first encounter with his superior, d'Argenlieu, who refused to discuss overall political strategy, insisting that Leclerc's task was simply that of military control.

Leclerc brought with him some of his most trusted officers from the *Division*, including notably Colonel Repiton-Préneuf, his intelligence adviser. But he had to wait until late October and November before the arrival of any troops, other than the one infantry regiment formed from released prisoners of war, to back him up. What follows is a remarkable series of minor operations carried out with diplomatic skill, limited forces, and little or no support from his superiors of the local French provincial administration, which wanted a much more emphatic reassertion. Leclerc's remark 'One does not kill ideas with bullets' shows not only his perception that any generalised conflict had to be avoided but also how far intellectually the able if narrowly professional, cavalry captain of 1940 had progressed. He came very quickly to appreciate that any military reconquest was out of the question, but that French troops could be used for a limited period to hold cities and the main lines of communication, thus reasserting a sovereignty which must then be used for political negotiation.

First, fearful that the truce might not hold out, he made an impassioned appeal to the French population in the south for order, emphasising that they must not look on the Indochinese peoples as enemies; this appeal was generally received poorly but nevertheless obeyed. Then, with the help of Gracey's troops and his one regiment, Leclerc began to reassert control over the Saigon area, the reassertion including the disarming and repatriation of the former Japanese garrison. He next tackled a crisis in Cambodia in very characteristic style. The king had had a Prime Minister, Son Ngoe Thanh, imposed upon him by the Japanese. Thanh had first broken all links with France and then begun plotting against the king himself. The king and his entourage wished to retain the French link and were also apprehensive that in any local political dissension Communist allies of the Viet-minh would seize power. Leclerc, on hearing of this situation from a relative of the king and the head of the French mission, flew to Phnom Penh, accompanied only by two aides. He instructed Thanh to present himself at the office of the British military representative. On Thanh's arrival Leclerc ordered him into a car, and without telling him where he was going bundled him into an aircraft and on to French detention.

Next, leaving British units to secure Saigon and using units of the expeditionary force as they arrived, Leclerc began the reassertion of French control over Cochin China. First the belt of Viet-minh insurgent groups that surrounded Saigon was broken, after which French columns fanned out very rapidly over the region. The rebel groups were not well trained and were equipped only with small arms and grenades; furthermore, they were divided amongst themselves. But they were already practising the style of the Indochina war, paddy-field peasant by day, guerilla by night. They could not stop the French penetration, but they were able to harass, often very effectively, either by ambushes and snipers or by destruction of roads and bridges. Leclerc's method was to push motorised or waterborne detachments forward quickly, sometimes at night, to take towns and villages by surprise, and then consolidate with infantry sweeps around the occupied areas later. The more powerful rebel groups were only disposed of with the help of artillery and aircraft. All members of the expeditionary force were given explicit instructions not to treat the local inhabitants as an enemy people but to make friends; all forms of looting or brutality were expressly forbidden on pain of severe punishment. By the end of November, most of Cochin China had been re-occupied and a network of defended areas established; in addition, units were entering both southern Laos and Cambodia. Northern Laos remained confused following the arrival of Chinese troops. The French presence was limited to a small contingent of troops operating almost as guerillas. In January, disembarking from the sea, French forces entered south Annam. The restoration of economic life could begin and, in respect of the three regions south of the 16th Parallel, was complete by the end of February 1946. It has to be said, however, that the Viet-minh were only pushed underground. They continued to organise, prepare and intimidate and occasionally massacre in the absence of any political solution. The total cost paid by the 50,000 men committed by Leclerc amounted to 630 killed and 1,000 wounded.

French military historians see Leclerc's re-occupation of Cochin China as an operation in the classic French colonial 'pacification' tradition, the *tache d'huile* method of Lyautey, rapid occupation followed by consolidation spread over a widening area, the restoration of economic life and the beginning of new economic development. But students of British military history will be also struck by the similarity of Leclerc's personal style in Indochina with that, a few years later, of General Sir Gerald Templer in Malaya, a rare British Army example of *passion*. That style's hallmarks were a lively high morale, dynamic energy with frequent sharp explosions of temper, charisma, awards of praise or blame in very plain terms, personal visits and a refusal to be deskbound, disregard of any personal danger, attention to and maintenance of standards of fighting, efficient intelligence gathering, communication of a sense of being part of a team, economic recovery when the fighting was over, and overall the realisation that operations were as much political, to recover confidence in France and French intentions, as purely military. French operations were presented with much justification as a liberation from the Japanese and from Viet-minh terrorism. Leclerc's style, as earlier, won him wide devotion, but it failed to convert his superior, d'Argenlieu, who had arrived in November 1945. It seems possible that, at this stage, Leclerc had not fully appreciated the growing strength of the Viet-minh underground.

Tonkin and Hanoi

The north, Tonkin and North Annam, remained as the major problem, requiring even more diplomatic skill and preparation. Leclerc believed his policy must aim at the speedy withdrawal of the 150,000 Chinese troops, together with the opening of negotiations with the Viet-minh, the departure of the Chinese, whose presence remained oppressive and extortionate, providing a common interest. Leclerc planned a three point strategy, diplomatic pressure by Paris upon the Chiang Kai Shek government and by his own officers on the Chinese command in Hanoi, to secure withdrawal, the building up of French military strength to a level that would be effective for the negotiating table and open negotiations with Ho Chi Minh. He appreciated that time might not be on his side as the longer the Chinese remained in the north, the more they were able to build up, or plain buy, a political following. He realised also that the position of the 30,000 members of the French community resident in the north was one of acute personal danger. In addition, tidal conditions at Haiphong limited the choice of days for any joint military-naval operation.

Military plans and preparations were made over the period November 1945 to February 1946, the total number of French troops rising to 65,000. Leclerc sent his own emissaries to Chunking and others to Paris to press for Chinese withdrawal at the international level. He was helped here by the changed needs of the Nationalist government for troops to fight the Communists and France's willingness to offer up for the sake of Chinese prestige the old pre-1939 trading concessions in Chinese ports; these factors led Chunking to promise withdrawal. Leclerc was, however, free of illusions. He knew that the Chinese would not go until April 1946 at the earliest and his own limited purpose was to create a climate in which the arrival of French troops in March would not spark off incidents. For his part, Ho Chi Minh, whatever his ultimate aims at that time might have been, (and his statements and actions suggest that they were much less extreme than they later became), was prepared to negotiate. He was, in fact, seriously alarmed by Chinese support of opposition to him and was now willing to recognise Sainteny. His terms for negotiation were a French recognition of independence and a promise that the presence of French troops would be temporary.

Leclerc's position, however, was complicated by the absence of clear support from Paris after the resignation of de Gaulle in January 1946 and, more serious, the hardline views and uncommunicative, withdrawn personality of his superior, d'Argenlieu. The High Commission, influenced by the numerous traditionally minded French colonial administrators and residents, still believed a strong military assertion would bring a complete military and political victory and restoration of a formal protectorate. Leclerc had no illusions about Ho Chi Minh and the Viet-minh. He realised that they were totally opposed to any long-term form of French control. But he believed that the needs of both countries could forge a new relationship, profitable for both and in keeping with the realities of post-war Asia which he had understood and accepted. The French contribution would include a *rayonnement* of French culture and ideas of social progress, but in a relationship between partners rather than one of protectorate tutelage. However, this clear realisation that an overall military victory was out of the question, though an effective military presence would influence the political settlement even if that was one of independence, was seen as defeatist by a growing number of critics.

The last weeks of 1945 and the first of 1946 saw, then, much overt and covert negotiating in which Leclerc was not always personally involved. D'Argenlieu sought a meeting with Ho Chi Minh, but the latter refused. On 6 March, Ho Chi Minh did, however, sign an agreement with Sainteny accepting the French arrival; by this agreement, Vietnam was recognised as a free state within the French Union and France undertook to withdraw progressively except for a few bases and depots, all troops within five years. A referendum on unity in one Vietnam was to be held in Tonkin, Annam and Cochin China. Negotiations on future status and on overseas diplomatic representation were to open with France. The Chinese in Chunking agreed to the progressive relief of their forces by French units in March. In Hanoi, General Salan and Sainteny negotiated with the local Chinese commander, of known independence of view, to accept this arrangement. These negotiations proved difficult. Not until the day of the landings, could Leclerc be sure to what extent the Chinese might oppose the French and perhaps seek to involve the Annamese as well in that opposition. Leclerc's views, however, are clearly to be seen in a telegram which he sent to Paris on 14 February, strongly advising that the French Government should promise, and use the word, independence. He stated that, after the landings, France would have recovered sovereignty throughout almost all of Indochina and would be able to fashion an agreement with the nationalists that would give them the independence they sought within a French Union. He believed such a promise would be welcomed internationally and please the Indochinese at the critical moment of the French arrival; he warned the alternative might be a protracted guerilla resistance campaign. Although he had some slight reservations about the terms that Sainteny had negotiated, he nevertheless thought that they were a *tour de force* in the circumstances. D'Argenlieu, fortunately in Paris and in no position to interfere, remained cryptic and the French government non-commital.

On the evening of 5 March, the French landing force entered the Haiphong River. They were met by fire from the Chinese, one landing ship being set on fire and others hit. Very reluctantly, Leclerc ordered fire to be returned, the exchange lasting just over thirty minutes. A Chinese negotiator then arrived, offering a cease-fire if the French squadron moved downstream. Leclerc refused and eventually, after a face saving delay of twenty-four hours, the Chinese accepted the disembarkation of an initial 5,000. The rest followed later, with no difficulty, though negotiations with the Chinese were to last another week before Chiang Kai Shek ordered his local commander to co-ordinate his withdrawal with the French. This withdrawal, even when agreed, proved dilatory. But the Tricolour was flying again in conditions acceptable to the Viet-minh but restoring effective French sovereignty over Tonkin, at a cost of only 37 dead. Each French Army vehicle carried both the Tricolour and the colours of Vietnam. When Leclerc moved ashore, he insisted that his guard be both French and Vietnamese. The day after the landing, Giap, Ho Chi Minh's principal lieutenant, met Leclerc aboard a destroyer. Giap expressed his admiration for the French resistance and the liberation of Paris; the two soldiers spoke frankly, with mutual respect. A little later, Leclerc met Ho Chi Minh who was greatly impressed by Leclerc's straightforward and honest approach. Of Leclerc, Ho later remarked that there was a Frenchman he could fully trust. Ho sought a mixed Franco-Vietnam commission to supervise the ceasefire and administration in both South Annam and Cochin China, but Leclerc refused in respect of Cochin China. He did however agree to scale down French operations and to try to contact the remaining rebels to arrange a ceasefire. He also fully supported Ho Chi Minh's request for early negotiations in Paris. In every way he could, Leclerc tried to limit French involvement in purely internal Vietnam affairs to what he thought was the essential minimum, and to try to build a new spirit of co-operation. He had, however, been disappointed when, upon his entry into Hanoi on 18 March, only French people greeted him. Elsewhere the speeches of Giap (who compared the Viet-minh consent to the return of the French with Lenin's surrender of territory to the Germans at Brest-Litovsk in 1917) and Ho Chi Minh made it clear that they saw their acceptance of the French return as bowing to a temporary necessity only; in some areas of Tonkin the arrival of the French met Viet-minh resistance. In others, however, Leclerc and General Salan were able to create a friendly partnership with the Viet-minh, Ho even visiting French units and being cheered by them.

Policy Differences and Departure; North Africa; Death

More serious still was Leclerc's growing rift with his High Commissioner. Although d'Argenlieu had been a Free French officer, his views on Indochina, widely shared in Paris and in the local French community, represented all that Leclerc distrusted. D'Argenlieu began to speak scathingly and without guard about Leclerc, on one occasion even suggesting that his meetings with Giap and Ho Chi Minh represented an Asian Munich. He sought the recall of Leclerc and Salan. Leclerc in turn was later to remark that those who had understood nothing in 1940 understood nothing of what was happening in Vietnam. Sainteny had promised Ho Chi Minh that the negotiations would open in Paris. Leclerc thought this essential, but d'Argenlieu stalled, and ensured that Paris stalled also. Leclerc, in strongly-worded telegrams to Juin, held this to be a breach of faith and likely to lead to an extremist challenge both to Ho Chi Minh and the French community. At a time when early negotiations in Paris were becoming a touchstone of French good faith for Ho Chi Minh, d'Argenlieu was instead trying to create a separate Cochin China state divorced from Hanoi. There were certain cultural and historical differences between Cochin China and the rest of Vietnam, but the magnification of these in favour of local non-Marxist moderate political figures began to push Ho Chi Minh, reluctantly it would seem, into the militant extremist wing of his movement. Leclerc considered this proposal for Cochin China to be a 'divide and rule' ploy and commented that it was both dangerous and farcical, but he did also rebut Ho Chi Minh's claims to include the territory, pointing out that the 6 March agreement had provided for a plebiscite. Overall, he felt that the status of that territory was an issue that could have been resolved by time and tactful negotiation.

In late March, d'Argenlieu returned to Indochina after a visit to France, his hand much strengthened by growing Paris support for a hard line; he began issuing orders to military units, by-passing Leclerc. Leclerc, in an important report dated 27 March, summarised what had been achieved with limited forces and reiterated emphatically that a military reconquest of Tonkin was impossible. He argued that any open breach with Ho Chi Minh would lead to overtly militant Chinese support for the Viet-minh, and that Ho was not far from breaking off the agreement and resuming a guerilla war. In fact, this was already the case in Cochin China, where the Viet-minh, goaded by d'Argenlieu's project, opened a very bloody guerilla campaign which the scattered French forces were too weak to contain.

The differences of opinion surfaced for all to see. At the end of March d'Argenlieu met Ho Chi Minh but all he would offer was local negotiations, not in Paris, but at a hill station in Annam. At these talks, Giap took a hard militant line, demanding nothing short of full independence including Cochin China. However, agreement was finally reached on a conference to be held in France. This was unfortunately delayed due to the instability of French domestic politics. The conference eventually took place in July and August in an atmosphere still soured by d'Argenlieu's creation of a government for a Republic of Cochin China, which Leclerc viewed with scepticism. With great difficulty, a *modus vivendi* agreement was signed in September in which Ho Chi Minh was forced into a number of economic and cultural concessions to France. These rankled among his hardline followers, Giap preparing for and initiating fighting, both against the French and with especial ferocity against the more moderate nationalists. Widespread terrorism broke out again, and was met by heavy repression by French forces, poorly trained and led. Ho Chi Minh's final attempts to stop the slide to disaster were delayed or ignored, almost certainly deliberately, by d'Argenlieu. After a street battle and naval bombardment at Haiphong in November, full open conflict erupted on 19 December. France had begun to tread the road to Dien Bien Phu in a war in which one of Leclerc's sons was to be killed – though after Leclerc's own death.

Leclerc had left Indochina in July. He believed that the mission with which he had been tasked was complete and that under d'Argenlieu he had no further role to play. He welcomed an official recall which he also had been seeking, but with great dignity he expressed no open criticism of or hostility towards d'Argenlieu. Some commentators have speculated on the reasons for his silence. These appear to have been his own modest recognition of his relative youth and rapid advancement, a tradition of loyalty, a measure of prudence and his lack of, or even interest in, political contacts.

During the Fontainebleau conference, Ho Chi Minh called without warning on Leclerc in Paris. Leclerc listened to all that Ho Chi Minh had to say, but was not willing to intervene. Almost certainly, he assessed that any intervention by him, already under a cloud for his liberalism, would do more harm than good. Ho Chi Minh also wrote Leclerc a letter of sympathy when his eldest son was wounded in Tonkin. Leclerc was however not deluded by the 'Unclo Ho' image that Ho Chi Minh could present to disguise his own authoritarianism, and earlier in June he had warned Robert Schuman, the president of the MRP political party, to watch out for duplicity.

After the 19–20 December outbreak of war, Blum, the newly installed Socialist Prime Minister, summoned Leclerc. The two men despite their very different backgrounds, spoke frankly, simply and honestly, understanding each other immediately. Despite objections from d'Argenlieu, Blum asked Leclerc if he would go to Indochina as his personal representative. Against advice from de Gaulle that the mission would be politically loaded, Leclerc departed for Indochina – after his first family Christmas for nine years. On his arrival, he made it clear that he had come only to advise, not to criticise and he refused to see Ho Chi Minh; in this his hands were tied, as the French Minister for the Colonies was also in Indochina. Ho Chi Minh nevertheless broadcast an emotive appeal to Leclerc, deploring the conflict and promising that an independent Vietnam would fully co-operate with France within a French Union. After visiting both the north and Saigon, Leclerc began to prepare his report. Firstly and immediately, he recommended that more Army units should be sent to Indochina. His wider recommendations followed his earlier analysis. Drawing on French history, he saw facing France an emerging revolutionary challenge as strong as Napoleon I had faced in Spain and Napoleon III had faced in Mexico; a political settlement, negotiated from a position of strength, was the only alternative.

On his return to Paris, Blum offered him the appointment of military commander in Indochina, hinting that at some unspecified later time Leclerc might succeed d'Argenlieu. On advice from both Juin and de Gaulle, Leclerc declined saying that he could not work with d'Argenlieu at all; de Gaulle also felt that any recall of d'Argenlieu would entail loss of prestige. It was also clear to all that the Blum government would not last and for internal French reasons it soon fell. Blum's successor, Ramadier, offered Leclerc the High Commissioner's post as a successor to d'Argenlieu. Leclerc was much tempted by this offer and set out conditions under which he might be willing to accept. These included first and foremost a clear statement of French government policy with, for him, full powers to implement that policy. He saw the options as either a military reconquest, for which an army of at least 350,000 would be necessary and so one he considered totally unrealistic, or negotiation based upon a limited strengthening of France's military position to a total of 115,000. Wherever possible, local decisions were to be left to the people of Annam and Tonkin, with an ending of French direct provincial administration and the opening of negotiations with the Viet-minh. In these, France should concede independence within a French Union, but retain certain key bases and ensure that minority communities were protected.

The bargain was never struck. Ramadier said, that, while he was sympathetic, he could not pledge a Parliament and Leclerc's various conditions would need detailed study. More significantly, Leclerc again sought the advice of de Gaulle whose knowledge of Indochina was based on briefing from d'Argenlieu. De Gaulle, in a stormy interview, strongly advised a complete refusal of Ramadier's offer, saying that to replace d'Argenlieu would be an *indélicatesse* between Free Frenchmen and even more important that he thought Leclerc would simply be used, to be saddled with the blame for any loss of Indochina. Leclerc then declined; to his close friends and associates he gave as his reasons de Gaulle's advice and his certainty that he would not be able to rely on continuous support from Paris. To the civilian appointed two months later, Leclerc urged '*Traitez, traitez à tout prix*'. In private conversation with Maurice Schumann, Leclerc went further, remarking 'Colonial empires all have their period of greatness but are destined to disappear sooner or later. Let us hope that ours will disappear in good circumstances'.

In reviewing events in Indochina later, Leclerc commented that d'Argenlieu's actions in 1946 had put light to the barrel of powder. Certainly he and Sainteny had been the only two leading French figures respected by Ho Chi Minh. Had Leclerc's advice been heeded and the 6 March agreement fully honoured, the disasters of the next seven years, perhaps of the next twenty-five, could have been averted. For the second time in his life, Leclerc de Hauteclocque had seen more clearly than almost all around him when a war should be fought and when it should not.

In 1946, Juin, then Chief of the Defence Staff, had sounded out Leclerc on a Maghreb appointment, Inspector of Land Forces in North Africa, hitherto not particularly prestigious. This proposal was now revived and Leclerc assumed the post in February 1947. To critics of Leclerc, it seemed demotion and a convenient exile, but this was not the case. Juin, with his Algerian background, was aware of the rising nationalism in North Africa; a vicious uprising in the Sétif area of Algeria in May 1945 had highlighted it. Juin wanted a secure and well-defended French North Africa for the defence both of France and the West generally. Leclerc was to be the man to re-activate the appointment which, at his request was soon logically extended to cover naval and air forces. Leclerc gladly accepted the challenge. In so doing, he was also aware that his rapid wartime promotion had both advanced him far ahead of his age, so arousing jealousy, and had imposed a strain on his health. Some pause in his career was clearly necessary to take stock and to prepare for wider national responsibilities. There was also another and much less obvious reason for his appointment, for which he was given an office in Paris. At this time, the Communist Party was exceedingly strong in France, particularly in the capital and other major cities. A Communist coup attempt was feared, and Leclerc, as the liberator of Paris, was seen as the most likely person to be able to contain and suppress it. Leclerc had little taste for this role and made it clear he would only consider it as a last resort, in the light of conditions at the time.

In the spring of 1947 he visited Morocco, Tunis and Algeria. There several officers and administrators warned him of the mounting political unrest. On his return to Paris, Leclerc expressed his anxieties to the Minister for the Interior, whose responsibilities included Algeria, making certain comparisons with Indochina. On one occasion, visiting a *colon* village in Algeria, he turned to a gathering of settlers and said 'And now show me what you are doing for your indigenous workers'. In the summer, he divided his time between his home, including family, hunting and music, work in Paris, learning about the background and changing situations in each territory, and ceremonial occasions. At these latter, his open modesty and natural simplicity of character remained uncorrupted by fame; one of his main concerns was arrangements for former members of his wartime *Division*.

In the autumn, he began again his inspections and visits to units in North Africa. It was a time of great difficulty for the French Army – pay was poor, funds and equipment were short, wartime divisions still festered and morale was low. The message brought by Leclerc in his own simple direct style was a call for imaginative, innovative leadership, the overcoming of problems and difficulties, and of 'having a go'. He liked exercises where the unexpected required junior – and sometimes senior – leaders to adapt and improvise. The juniors generally welcomed such challenges, the seniors preferred exercises well prepared and rehearsed in advance. Leclerc's visits were often controversial.

On 28 November, Leclerc was attending exercises in the western Oran area of Algeria. His aircraft, carrying himself and his staff took off from Oran for Colomb-Béchar. The weather was bad with wind and sandstorms, and the aircraft evidently lost its way in poor light when coming in to land; there was no prior message suggesting any problem. It flew into a rock, Leclerc and all its passengers and crew being killed. Rumours abounded that Leclerc had overruled a warning from the pilot, or that the Communists had sabotaged the aircraft.

They can be discounted, Leclerc never overruled his airmen, but his whole temperament was one in which risks were daily routine. His pilot may simply have decided that he would prefer the risk rather than offer a warning.

Leclerc's body was brought back to France. For the National Funeral it was taken to Paris along the route of the leading *2ᵉ Division Blindée* column of August 1944. After a service at Notre Dame, the final ceremony took place at the Invalides. General Leclerc de Hauteclocque's greatness and very special place in French history, as will have been seen, lay in the paradox of his personality, well summarised in de Lattre's tribute *'un imprudent magnifique'*. In him were, at times burnt, tensions; there were fires of patriotism that, in the Second World War, amounted to a fanatical crusading zeal; there were the post-malarial explosions of temper that he could not always control but always regretted and there was inexhaustible restless driving energy. But in moments of crisis, whether minor on a small scale battlefield or major at moments of great national decision, Leclerc was calm, concentrating, clear in thought and analysis, simple and lucid in expression. All those who knew and served with him comment on the strength of his faith and his total, unassuming and modest, selflessness. Of him, in a letter to his widow, de Gaulle wrote that Leclerc had not only been his companion in difficult and in good times, but had been a friend of whom he could say that no thought, no act, no gesture or single word had ever been marked, even with a shadow, by mediocrity.

7

Training, the Cold War, and Indochina 1950–51: General de Lattre de Tassigny

In July 1945, General de Lattre de Tassigny was offered the appointment of Inspector-General of the Army, an appointment that he at first regarded as honorific, below that of Juin and below the status he himself had earned as commander of the *Iere Armée*. He initially refused and asked to be retired. But he finally accepted the appointment when de Gaulle changed his mind and linked it with that of Chief of the General Staff, which he had previously refused to allow. Nevertheless, the change from a vice-regal life style and a large staff to, initially, a Paris flat, a meagre ration of petrol, three months of unemployment, and a personal staff much reduced, was a difficult one for him. He filled it in with the help of his wife by founding a veterans *Association Rhin et Danube* to care for the welfare of former members of his *Armée* and also to publicise its achievements, which he still felt to have been poorly recognised. In the years that followed, even returning from Indochina mortally ill, de Lattre would attend any *Rhin et Danube* association reunion that he could.

On one occasion in this period he accompanied de Gaulle on a visit to Germany. He returned alarmed at what were still de Gaulle's hopes – that it would be possible very quickly to create a French client state out of the Rhenish areas of Germany, and that France and this client state would together form the nucleus of a European state to check the advance of Communism. De Lattre believed that this project would annoy both the Western Allies and the Soviet Union, leaving France isolated.

Chief of the General Staff; Training

As Inspector General, he drew up a one hundred page document on the future of the French Army. This document was written with a sharp eye on the internal political situation at the time in which the Communists were very strong. De Lattre had been greatly impressed by the Red Army and by some of the Communist FFI. While he himself had no brief for Communism, he was half drawn and half frightened by it. He had also the memories of his own experience at the hands of extreme conservative officers in 1934 and 1942. The new French Army, he believed, must take from Communism what was good in order to resist what was bad; it must be fully democratic and national, therefore obviously a conscript rather than a professional force. National service was to be a period of schooling in citizenship for the youth of the nation. The pick of the conscripts were to be offered full military careers whatever their social origins.

On becoming Chief of the General Staff in the same year, de Lattre accordingly devoted his main efforts to his old love, training. This, as he saw it, would combine his long term design with the immediate need of fusing the different components of and wartime legacies within the Army and re-establishing bonds of confidence between nation and Army. He saw the problem as clearly as Juin, but his solution, different and characteristic, was one of training, which he put before re-equipment, for which he argued that France was not yet ready.

The system of the wartime camps, from Opme to Rouffach, was to be the basis, now to be extended throughout the Army. De Lattre threw himself into the opening of his new 'Light Camps' as they were to be called, with all his customary volcanic energy. His target was to have as many open as possible, in the event some twelve, in time for the May 1946 conscripts. His task was complicated by reductions in the size of the Army ordered by the government, which he contested with some measure of success, and the growing calls of demobilisation, of Indochina, and of elsewhere upon experienced cadres. This difficulty was in part overcome by the use of the most promising of the conscripts as instructors after they themselves had been trained. To counter the opposition, de Lattre even tried to project the next stage of his grand design, an Army University College, for conscripts who decided to serve on as regulars to enable them to hold their own against the more formally educated, often privileged, products of Saint Cyr. He seems to have hoped that this liberal Arts and Science

College might eventually replace Saint Cyr. The idea found supporters on the political Left and amongst academics, but not
elsewhere, where some whispered again that de Lattre was playing
politics. This was unjust. De Lattre's passion for unity derived from
his own experience, as did his on-going concern for junior leaders, in
particular lieutenants and captains.

De Lattre's personal style remained larger than life, winning ad-
mirers and alienating critics. After the extension of his responsibilities, he moved into a big house at Saint Cloud. There a steady
stream of influential visitors were welcomed and entertained, and
shown models of the light camps in the evenings. By day, an immaculate de Lattre would hasten off on inspections, whenever possible to
the light camps. *Colère* awaited those who obstructed in any way or
failed to welcome him with the ceremonial he considered his due.
Sometimes it seemed that he deliberately picked on some minor
shortcoming (on one occasion the absence of a light bulb) in order, by
an explosion of *colère*, to impose his personality. On other occasions,
no one could be more charming or considerate. Punctuality on visits
meant nothing to de Lattre and he would arrive late or without warning. He set himself, somewhat excessively, out to inspire fear, and
some cautious camp or unit commanders even went so far as to post
watchers on approach roads.

The sites of the camps were carefully selected, often by de Lattre
himself, with an eye to beauty and grandeur. The camps were laid out
as a garden estate, with little groups of buildings always including a
workshop, parade ground, basketball court and obstacle course for
each platoon, all under its own commander. Generally, feeding was
central but there were also platoon kitchens. The general aims
differed little from the Opme of 1941: to instil into the Army's cadres,
both officers and NCOs, a Lyautey concept of a wide social role as
well as one purely military, *la passion du commandement* to use de
Lattre's own words, and personal self-discipline. It was intended that
the teaching would lead students to realise these values for themselves rather than have them preached. The day to day emphasis of
training lay in personal confidence-building, initiative and
adaptability, with as the means physical fitness, drill modified to
develop alertness, assault course practice and live ammunition exercises. Weapon training suffered from the shortage of weapons and was
often limited simply to acquiring the feel of rifles and machine-guns.
Weapon training was in any case considered by de Lattre as of secondary importance. He believed that a well trained and motivated man

would acquire the techniques of any weapon quickly when necessary, a view not shared by many who argued that the light camps were producing Boy Scouts rather than soldiers. Each day's training began with ceremonial hoisting and lowering of the Tricolour; there would also be frequent evening tattoos or other spectacles watched by de Lattre with, again, a crowd of personal guests.

The light camp system was both ahead of its time and exceedingly expensive; in the end it could not be extended for all conscripts, though the camps acted as a catalyst for the reform of conscript training. De Lattre was, as before, indifferent to the expense, but the costs, together with doubts among more conservative officers about the adequacy of specific weapon and combat training, and de Lattre's own showmanship and authoritarian behaviour, all attracted growing military and political criticism. In appointments and promotions for which he was responsible, too, de Lattre often favoured either former officers of the *1ere Armée* or promising younger personnel against those who for one reason or another had not participated in the Liberation campaigns. But some of these latter were well-connected. Again there were rumourings of dark political ambitions. No serious evidence whatever exists to suggest this but de Lattre's passionate concern for the Army and his consequential passion for pleading its case to anyone and everyone had, as in 1934, gained him a bad reputation for intrigue. Much of this opposition to him was that of envy or jealousy which de Lattre found hard to understand. Forgiveness was one of his Christian virtues, it even extended to those who gave him away at Montpellier in 1942. But he became very suspicious, and at times understandably resentful.

Another important task carried out by de Lattre in 1946 was to contest and ameliorate the poor conditions of, and demobilisation arrangements made for, the North African soldiers of his former *Armée*; these conditions were a poor reward for valiant service.

In March 1947, as abruptly as July 1945 and to his fury, de Lattre was relieved of his responsibilities as Chief of Staff of the Army. He remained Inspector-General and, as a sop, was made Vice President of the *Conseil Supérieur de la Guerre*. This appointment carried with it that of Commander-in-Chief designate should there be a war, but it left de Lattre with little more than some exercise planning and ceremonial status, without any real authority over any policy of administration.

A pleasant interlude in Latin America recouped de Lattre's spirits. He was sent as head of an economic mission to visit four countries,

Argentina, Brazil, Chile and Uruguay, having been selected as additionally qualified to renew overall French prestige. Despite an unfortunate involvement in an air crash, from which he walked away shaken but still prepared to inspect a guard of honour, de Lattre greatly enjoyed his tour. Another great joy for him was the successful development of the career of his son. Having falsified his age to join the Army in 1944 Bernard had gone on to win a *Médaille Militaire*. In the course of the Liberation campaign, he had been wounded and had tried to rejoin his regiment before he had recovered, for this he had been disciplined. But in August 1945, Bernard had begun training as an officer, later being commissioned into the cavalry.

In 1948, new opportunities opened for de Lattre. Domestically he was raised to be Inspector-General of all three Services. More importantly, and following a refusal by Juin, de Lattre was appointed to serve on the new Western European Union (WEU) Chiefs of Staff Committee, formed as a result of the March 1946 Treaty of Brussels. A headquarters opened at Fontainebleau.

Western European Union Command, Fontainebleau

This appointment moved de Lattre from performing primarily on the French stage to performing on a WEU and, from late 1949, a North Atlantic Treaty Organisation (NATO) stage. The appointment came when de Lattre was perhaps at the peak of his mental powers and development. A senior British civil servant, Sir George Mallaby, wrote of him at the time

> ... de Lattre, delighting in words and figures, leaving the highway of his talk for intriguing by-paths, elaborating and refining his expressions, dwelling in irony and wit, amused with life and with people, alternating wildly between anger and compassion, rage giving place to tears, acting somewhat, enthusiastic for life and art, loving people, including those whom he most violently chastened, tender and sensitive and yet in many ways unpardonably inconsiderate and unreasonable, taking pleasure in the fleshpots, good wine, good company, good talk, uncontrolled and hopelessly unpunctual.

The description is simply an update of that of his 1908 rue Vaugirard contemporary.

But the WEU duties also brought to de Lattre an adversary worthy of his steel, Field-Marshal Lord Montgomery. Their tempestuous relationship with its ultimate happy ending dominated de Lattre's life until the summer of 1950. At the outset, the formal relationship was that of Montgomery as Chairman of the Chiefs of

Staff Committee, with de Lattre as a member. Montgomery then became Commander-in-Chief of the Western Union Forces with, from October 1948, de Lattre as Commander-in-Chief of the Land Forces. Following the establishment of the NATO command structure in 1950, General Eisenhower became Supreme Allied Commander, with Montgomery as his Deputy. De Lattre remained as Land Forces commander, a post he believed must be held by a French officer as a mark of France's return to her rightful place in Europe. He also believed that West Germany must be re-armed.

Two personalities could hardly be more different than that of de Lattre and Montgomery. The British Field-Marshal possessed the broader military experience that extended to Army Groups and a wide command of air power; he was aware that de Lattre's experience was less complete, and was at the outset reserved about the value of any continental European army. Montgomery had the more illustrious reputation but his temperament was lonely and unsociable to the point of being anti-social. His home life style remained simple, while that of de Lattre returned to the seignorial. Montgomery's speech was blunt and limited very narrowly to the matter in hand, with no enjoyment in the cut and thrust of debate on which de Lattre so thrived. De Lattre was unpunctual, and took a pride in it, Montgomery was a man of precise timekeeping; de Lattre liked to work with a team to discuss ideas at night, Montgomery preferred to work alone by day. De Lattre would reinforce his views or the interests of France with a *colère*, which in turn would make Montgomery more tenacious in his own view. De Lattre, despite a good command of English, would always speak in French; Montgomery's French was not equal to the challenge. De Lattre also profoundly distrusted Montgomery's Chief of Staff, Major General David Belchem.

But together they were supposed to work, and de Lattre remained a disciple of Foch in his belief in the importance of a general loyalty to an Alliance, even if particular national interests could, and should, be argued with Allies for whom, at the time, he did not greatly care. He found relief from controversy at headquarters in visits to French units, Allied units, colleges and schools, his devotion to the cause of youth being on-going. As before, the visits were occasions of charm or *colère* depending on reception and ceremonial. In Britain, de Lattre took an especial interest in and visited a number of public schools.

Any study of the quarrel between the two great soldiers, in particular the recriminations and the venom, leaves an impression that the differences were above all a personal struggle for power. None of the issues at stake were insuperable with goodwill, but both men were strong-willed, vain and theatrical. Both Armies, the French and the British, had found their hugely respected wartime leader difficult to live with in times of peace. To both men it seemed justifiable to talk about their perception of faults in the other; each immediately seized upon this as intrigue. Both had weighty arguments to offer, which both overplayed with inevitable reactions in the other's camp.

At the outset, in October 1948, de Lattre set out his view of their working relationship. Montgomery was Chairman of the Committee but only a collegiate co-ordinator, while he, de Lattre, was the Commander-in-Chief of the Land Forces and responsible for all operations. This determined assertion represented de Lattre's and the French Government's view that France's traditional military role in Europe must be re-established, and that a French land command would commit the British and perhaps also the Americans, so preventing any repetition of 1940. But this view was immediately rejected by Montgomery. He insisted on retaining overall ultimate control and began to question whether a separate commander for land forces was desirable. He also firmly believed that the state of the French Army, still far from recovered from the war, did not justify de Lattre's claims for power or de Lattre's preference for holding any Soviet attack on the Elbe. All this fuelled de Lattre's suspicions that the British did not believe defence of continental Europe to be practical. De Lattre next objected to Montgomery's planning directives and moved on to object, often intemperately, to almost anything Montgomery wished to plan or do that affected ground forces. His language, in a letter to President Auriol's Military Secretary, was extreme, describing Montgomery as '...undrinkable, pig-headed, senility, intellectual sclerosis, a combination of ulterior motives and actions disloyal to [the parameters of] the debate'. In turn, some of Montgomery's staff speculated on the balance of de Lattre's mind. Montgomery himself tolerated de Lattre until April 1949, when he accused him, to his face, of disloyalty and intrigue. He proposed a procedure for settling differences between them and commented on the anomaly of de Lattre still holding a national as well as a WEU appointment. De Lattre indicated agreement but suspiciously the French press and government continued to air the collegiate argument.

The peace lasted until July 1949, when the quarrel flared to a new heat. On the grounds that he had not been consulted, de Lattre refused to accept a directive that Montgomery had been able to secure from the French Defence Ministry to the effect that, in the event of war, the Supreme Commander would be supreme over the land, air and naval commanders. He pointed, with some justification, to the failure of just such a system in 1940. But the meeting grew even stormier when, on less sure ground, de Lattre first alleged that the system had failed in 1944–45 and then went on to criticise Montgomery's actions in the WEU structure. The argument then became highly personal, each alleging the other was against him. Worse followed after the meeting, with the virtual ending of social relationships and Montgomery darkly alleging that de Lattre was spreading rumours that the British were not interested in any defence of mainland Europe but only in the withdrawal of British Army of the Rhine. Certainly, at the time, the British Chiefs of Staff were thinking on these lines, but, in his defence, Montgomery was trying hard to persuade the Attlee government to accept a commitment to fight on the Rhine. On a visit to British troops in Germany, de Lattre protested sharply that he had not been received with proper ceremonial, a protest that was a little unjust as he had not understood the British military police method of arranging VIP escorts. Elsewhere, de Lattre argued that Montgomery planned too rigidly, thought too narrowly on the land battle and had not thought through the implications of new technology, in particular atomic developments. For his part, Montgomery openly expressed the hope that, if not before, when de Lattre reached the age of sixty one in February 1950, the normal retirement age for French generals, he would be replaced by Koenig.

Further differences arose, de Lattre objecting to the whole concept of a logistics exercise arranged by Montgomery in November 1949, and then, in a dispute over tank design, complaining to the British Chiefs of Staff about a very injudicious letter written by Montgomery. In December 1949, their respective British and French ministers directed that Montgomery and de Lattre should each produce an exercise that set out their different concepts of Western defence and command arrangements. These exercises, Montgomery's *Unity* and de Lattre's *Triade* were to run in the summer of 1950.

The year 1950, however, ushered in very difference circumstances. New structures for NATO were being discussed. It was becoming clear that the Americans would be willing to accept a commitment to fight in Germany, but an emerging corollary, that French forces would be concentrated in a smaller area in southern Germany, was one to which de Lattre was strongly opposed. At Fontainebleau it was known that Montgomery was trying hard to persuade the Attlee government to extend conscription largely for the defence of Europe, which served to allay some French anxieties. But they remained understandably anxious to retain the Land Command for a French officer; despite his age, de Lattre's tour was extended lest his retirement be seen as a British success.

Montgomery's *Unity* was very sharply criticised by de Lattre. The exercise had in fact strengthened de Lattre's case as his land Command had suffered harmful interference from Montgomery and his principal staff officer. But when it was over, Montgomery invited de Lattre to dinner. After a frigid start to the evening, followed by a long cataloguing of Montgomery's alleged misdoings by de Lattre, Montgomery finally broke down de Lattre's hostility. A highly emotional reconciliation followed with de Lattre, Montgomery's arm around him, in tears. Thereafter the hatchet was buried, both men working together. The new concord was cemented by the success of de Lattre's *Triade*, proving his point and securing the structure that he wanted with most of the authority he sought, all later incorporated into NATO.

One of de Lattre's senior staff officers, almost certainly Beaufre, wrote in an August 1950 paper that the defence of Continental Europe was now assured and conceived '*à la française*'. He claimed that Montgomery had, in a rapid reversal of his previous views, entirely accepted de Lattre's arguments and had agreed that the Commander-in Chief's role was that of presiding and co-ordinating, leaving the Land, Air and Naval commanders to command. The claim seems to be generally true, but the strategy which fully justified it was a consequence of the new American and British commitment. The wider significance of the events, however, left a mark. One sentence in Beaufre's paper foreshadowed the views of de Gaulle ten years later: 'France has avoided ...being absorbed in an inter-allied military structure'.

By the end of the year, Montgomery and de Lattre, assisted by their respective staffs, had created an efficient and happy headquarters. Their new personal relationship was exemplified by the occasion of Montgomery's sixty-third birthday in November 1950. The Field-Marshal invited the de Lattres to tea and, after cutting a birthday cake, gave de Lattre an extra slice for him to send to Bernard, then serving in Indochina. It appears to have been an entirely spontaneous gesture by Montgomery, but nothing could have touched de Lattre more deeply.

High Commissioner and Commander-in-Chief, Indochina

In December 1950, de Lattre set off on what was to be his last mission, High Commissioner and Commander-in-Chief in Indochina. In despair, following a succession of reverses and diasters, the French Government had turned to its most distinguished and experienced soldiers. Juin, approached first, had refused, being heavily involved in Moroccan affairs. Koenig, the government's next choice, would only accept if the government authorised the despatch of conscripts to Indochina, a condition not politically possible. De Lattre accepted, and was given a ceremonial departure from Paris. He also received a very warm letter from Montgomery offering to work with him in Indochina if it would be of help, an oblique but noteworthy tribute to his work at Fontainebleau.

In Indochina, the situation was one very different from that facing Leclerc in 1945. The Viet-minh was now an extremely efficient force which had received considerable support from across the frontier following the Chinese Revolution. It comprised some six or seven divisions, with a total of seventy battalions, of which fifty were in the north of Tonkin, as a regular force for frontal assaults. These were now well equipped with small arms together with some field artillery, and were also beginning to receive mortars and anti-aircraft weaponry. The remainder were in south Annam or Cochin-China. In addition, and equally serious, were an equal number of units of irregulars, of varying sizes and efficiency that surfaced to strike in French controlled areas. Even worse, the possibility of a full scale Chinese intervention in Tonkin had also to be considered. The frontier garrison posts had been evacuated, or been overrun disastrously. The French hold on northern Tonkin, Hanoi and the Red River Delta was precarious. Ho Chi Minh was boasting that he would be in Hanoi in a few weeks. The French Army itself, still far from recovered from the war years, was demoralised by a war that was intensely unpopular at home. The Community Party, commanding nearly a quarter of voters' loyalties, openly supported the Viet-minh; in France, the Cold War was domestic as well as international. Conscripts were not allowed to go to Indochina unless they specifically volunteered. Supplies for the Army in Indochina were sabotaged on trains and in the ports in France, citations could not be published in the *Journal Officiel*, there were almost insuperable difficulties in sending blood from French donors to Indochina, and the wounded flown back had to be landed at provincial airports for fear of demonstrations at the Paris terminals.

De Lattre's acceptance of this thankless appointment, in his sixty-second year, remains primarily a testament to his moral and physical courage. The young Minister for Overseas Territories, François Mitterand, warned him that he might lose both his health and his reputation, as had others since 1946. Further, in reorganising the Army and at WEU in Fontainebleau, de Lattre had continually found his plans frustrated by the needs of Indochina which he had tried to meet, although he had neither love nor links with the territory to motivate him. But to his courage may perhaps be added certain other characteristics. There was a touch of the gambler in de Lattre, the chance of a last throw appealed, perhaps especially so as Juin had declined to appear at the Indochina table, while many of his own *1ere Armée* followers were involved. The Korean War had begun, many French soldiers saw Indochina as another front in the same war and de Lattre had taken care to keep himself well informed on developments in Indochina. There was also no other foreseeable military appointment for him. But undoubtedly the two major contributory factors were first his concern for the youth of France, hundreds of whom were dying in Indochina, the flower of Saint Cyr being decimated each year. Second, there was Bernard, serving in Indochina as a lieutenant. Bernard was commanding a country post and, in the manner of his father, he had interested himself in every aspect of the life of the local people and had gained their confidence. But his letters home also dwelt at length on the fear psychosis, at times defeatism, of the French Army, at the louche lifestyle of a number of its officers and at the absence of firm, purposeful command. 'Tell Father we need him, without him it will go wrong' wrote Bernard to his mother on 23 October 1950.

There then followed *L'Année de Lattre*, twelve months as extraordinary and dramatic as any in de Lattre's life. In this final year of his career, de Lattre gained spectacular military triumphs, apparent political success, suffered the loss of his own son, and was stricken by terminal disease.

In Indochina, for the first time in his life, de Lattre was his own master in the field, with no Supreme Commander from his own or someone else's army to constrain him. The success of his command therefore merits study in some detail, particularly as it was set in a terrain and type of warfare totally new to him. His generalship, in command of the largest fully independent French field force since 1940, was based on four policies very much his own: command, firepower and mobility, well-engineered defensive positions, and the recruitment and training of local units.

Perhaps most important of all was command and morale. De Lattre's own personal reputation in itself served to convince soldiers that the campaign was to be fought professionally. His arrival at Saigon was stage-managed, almost royal in ceremonial. He pointedly ignored Carpentier, his predecessor, and in Hanoi he went on to inspect a mass parade of troops specially arranged despite the dangerous military situation. After this parade, he addressed a large gathering of officers at which he said that he could not promise any great improvement, reinforcements or easy victories, what he could promise was firm command; he then added that it was for the young officers, captains and lieutenants, that he had accepted his appointment. He followed this up with an important variant to his 1944–45 daily routine style; on his visits to units he spent more time with junior leaders, listening to their problems and trying to meet their needs. At the outset, to impress his authority by shock action and to show he was still the same de Lattre, there were a few violent *colères*, but his staff soon noticed that they were less frequent than before. There was less need, age was mellowing him, as perhaps also was the state of his health. As before, the inefficient and, sometimes unjustly, some who were not inefficient, were ruthlessly sent home. Morale was raised by de Lattre's energy, commitment and quick mastery of the Indochina situation. For the Vietnamese, his style was direct and clear, free from habits of Asian subtleties and ambiguities into which his predecessors had been tempted. From his arrival he reaffirmed his intention to hold Tonkin, in contrast to the views of many French officers that a concentration of effort in south Vietnam was inescapable; the decision was comparable to that of the Taza in 1925. De Lattre's first weeks in Indochina, overall, remain a classic example of the personal impact the command of a great general can bring to a deteriorating situation; once again *passion* played a lead role in that impact. American students of military history may justly compare de Lattre's arrival in Indochina with General Ridgway's arrival in Korea in the same month.

Firepower and mobility were developed versions of the traditional *Armée d'Afrique* tactics that de Lattre had learnt in Morocco in the 1920s. A constraint on mobility was the terrain: hills, forest or paddy, limiting rapid ground movement to the roads, with attendant dangers of insurgents lying up between roads and of ambush. The essentials of de Lattre's use of firepower and mobility were in the formation of *groupes mobiles* (striking groups), of an average composition of two, three or more infantry battalions carried in half-tracked armoured carriers, engineers, light armour and an artillery battalion of a dozen gun-howitzers. These moved rapidly to seek out and destroy Viet-minh units, relieve besieged outposts and clear routes; in an attack, they would adopt the *Armée d'Afrique* tactics of simultaneous assault from at least two different encircling directions. The artillery fired from the road deep into the jungle; dispersed in four-gun detachments the length of a column the artillery could not all be lost in one ambush.

Additional firepower and mobility came from an expansion of parachute forces to over 10,000, these were dropped in terrain inaccessible by road. From the air also came effective air to ground support in the form of strafing fire, light fragmentation bombs and napalm. Modern aircraft, mostly but not all American-supplied, increased the availability and accuracy of this support and the ranges at which air to ground operations could take place. Air and ground headquarters were often co-located for rapid liaison and efficient new emergency request procedures evolved; some of these were based on a concept of mobile fire control posts working with the infantry. Also supremely effective was the use of light Morane aircraft to direct sustained artillery fire, or sometimes both artillery fire and other aircraft bombing, on to Viet-minh concentrations, or to provide such fire as a screen in front of French positions under a mass attack.

Next in de Lattre's order of priorities was a pattern of mutually supporting, well-prepared blockhouses, eventually over 900, in the Delta area, particularly strong on the four main approaches from China and between Hanoi and Haiphong; this became known as the 'de Lattre Line'. These served three purposes, defence of the French military position against the Viet-minh 'human wave' assault tactics, the creation of secure bases from which the *groupes mobiles* could set forth, and the protection of the civilian population. They also reduced the large number of inadequately garrisoned small posts which de Lattre found on his arrival.

De Lattre's fourth major military policy was that of *jaunissement* (lit: yellowing), the building up and training of Vietnamese units which, at the time of his arrival, comprised eleven battalions and nine gendarmerie units. He launched a programme aimed at a further twenty-five battalions, four armoured squadrons and eight artillery batteries together with logistic units. Some of the best officers and NCOs of the French Army, among them Bernard, volunteered to provide the necessary initial cadres. All de Lattre's talents and experience in imaginative training were deployed in the training of the cadres for the Vietnam Army, trying to give them a sense of cause and mission.

De Lattre took with him many of his 1944–45 staff, including Allard, Beaufre, Salan and Cogny and attached to them others of the 1944–45 years such as de Linarès who were already in Indochina. But he also inspanned new talent that he found and recognised in Indochina. The best were appointed commanders of the *groupes mobiles*, and the *groupes* were informally named after them. De Lattre used to refer to these commanders as his 'Marshals', among the most notable were Vanuxem, de Castries, Edon, Clement, Erulin and the strange leather-nosed Thomazo, whose real face had been shot away in Italy. He used Salan as a deputy commander for northern Tonkin and de Linarès as deputy commander for the Delta area. He also reorganised the headquarters command structure to improve civil-military liaison and the field command into three divisions. His own personal mode remained that of Lindau, travel in ceremonial style, ferocious insistence on a high standard of turnout of all units in Hanoi, and the bulldozing destruction of a building that marred the view from his official residence.

De Lattre also sought troop reinforcements, which had mainly to be North African *Tirailleurs* and the *Légion Etrangère*. The total all-services strengths increased from the 145,000 of 1950 to over 180,000 by early 1952. De Lattre was, however, under no illusions. He realised that these units could at best only temporarily hold the territory until a truly national Vietnam Army was ready. They were no long-term solution. In addition to soldiers, de Lattre continually pressed the French Government to secure modern American equipment, quantities of which arrived in 1951. The detail of de Lattre's activities in these two concerns relates to military developments and is set out with them below.

In the field, de Lattre was his own master. In political policy, de Lattre had to follow directives from Paris, which continued to negate the successes of the military recovery. As in Leclerc's day, they remain the cause of France's subsequent failure in Indochina. In the unstable politics of the Fourth Republic, no non-Communist politician could afford to appear as a *bradeur d'Empire* – selling out on the empire. The most that Paris was prepared to offer in 1949 was still only autonomy to the component parts of Indochina, an autonomy misleadingly described as 'Independent Associated States within the French Union'. Above this internal autonomy, the French Union, in practice France, was to retain ultimate control of foreign affairs and defence including garrisons, and there were to be special judicial arrangements for French citizens. As a package, it compared poorly with the complete independence given to India and Pakistan. Although many Vietnamese were prepared to fight Communism, the French package was always open to criticism by militant total nationalists who were forced to move into the Viet-minh camp. The more moderate non-Communist nationalists, portrayed by the Viet-minh as creatures of the French, were impossibly placed. When they sought policies that would make independence meaningful, their requests were rejected by Paris; to survive at all, they had to be equivocal in their attitudes to the French. Their dilemma was recognised by de Lattre, who was not personally an imperialist. But he was not able to change hardline attitudes in Paris and, paradoxically, his early 1951 successes served to harden them, a linkage that was unfortunate and unexpected.

Victories at Vinh Yen, Dong Trieu and Ninh Binh; Illness and Death

The linkages between political and military developments was even closer and more complex in Indochina itself and, in any survey of events, must be set out together. De Lattre's immediate problem was how to defend Tonkin. He ordered that all the existing plans for the evacuation of civilians and withdrawal from Hanoi were to be scrapped and new plans to hold the area prepared. On 13 January 1951, Viet-minh probing attacks opened, developing on a seventy mile front north of Hanoi into a major attack focused on Vinh Yen, some twenty miles from Hanoi, two days later. This attack, directed by Giap and committing over twenty-five battalion size Viet-minh units, forced the French to give some ground despite continuous support form the French Air Force. The Viet-minh attacked in wave after wave, groups of three with ankles linked so the dead and wounded would be carried along and others deliberately blowing themselves up on reaching French positions. The French replied with napalm and almost continuous dropping of flares to expose Viet-minh night attacks.

This desperate situation brought out all the 1944–45 flair of de Lattre. He flew to Vinh Yen, despite dangerous fog and, even more dangerous, the presence of insurgents within 1,000 yards of the airstrip. His dramatic personal appearance rallied the beleaguered garrison. Colonel Vanuxem described him as having '*une volonté d'Exorcisme à ses yeux*'. Correctly assessing that the battle would decide the fate of Tonkin and perhaps all Indochina, de Lattre then ordered every available unit to be brought from as far south as Cochin China. Some were grouped to attack the Viet-minh from the rear. Once again Allard, who had been the *1ere Armée*'s chief transport officer, performed miracles in a three-day air and road movement, the former limited to fifteen elderly transports and the latter accepting the risks of mine and ambush. By the 19th, the over confident Viet-minh had been defeated at heavy cost, some 1,600 killed, 480 captured and at least 3,000 wounded. As in Alsace, de Lattre himself spent the days at the front deploying his reinforcements to best use, with in the evenings conferences, orders and press briefings. At the conferences discussion could, and often did, range very widely, de Lattre freely discussing his plans or his requests to Paris. Officers present, however, found their own wishes and views, if not strictly in accordance with those of de Lattre, were best presented in a private session rather than in open debate. De Lattre worked tirelessly, taking no midday rest despite the strain of the climate upon his health.

The victory at Vinh Yen provided both the morale boost and the breathing space that the French needed. Under close supervision in respect of siting, and constant coercion in respect of speed, from de Lattre, the concrete blockhouses were built; and requests for delay or complaints of difficulty met a furious '*inadmissible*'. The first seven *groupes mobiles* were composed; more, including some special forces *groupes* were to be formed later as the necessary personnel arrived. De Lattre often assumed personal control of their operations rather than leaving them to local divisional commanders. An important factor in their success was the skill of French Army interception and deciphering of Viet-minh signals.

At the height of the Vinh Yen battle, de Lattre called on Emperor Bao Dai, who had been restored by d'Argenlieu's successor. Bao Dai received him coolly, showing no great enthusiasm for de Lattre's plans for more Vietnamese units or for de Lattre's preference for a new Defence Minister to expedite the plans. He later offered his own list of ministerial candidates which de Lattre rejected. After Vinh Yen, however, Bao Dai did order his Prime Minister, Tran Van Huu, to dissolve his government and form a new one including de Lattre's Defence Ministry candidate, Nguyen Huu Tri. In a message to his people, Bao Dai made no mention of France or de Lattre's victory. In response, an enraged de Lattre held a victory parade. There followed several weeks of political infighting between Bao Dai, Huu, who was a southerner and Tri, a northerner. Eventually a government was formed but it soon broke down into bickering. De Lattre considered the Emperor's inertia and indifference to be the prime cause. He refused to seek an audience with him as he felt this would connote a subordinate status, but after one notable *colère* at a meeting at which, in the presence of one of the Emperor's confidantes, he threatened to advise Paris to withdraw all French troops and leave Bao Dai to face the Communists alone, he was persuaded by his officials to make no public criticism of the Emperor. This, later, enabled the Emperor to move to his support. But the events serve to illustrate the almost impossible position of non-Communist political figures, especially if they were of poor quality. In his dealings with Vietnamese personalities, de Lattre closely followed Lyautey's example of respect for local tradition and tact in personal relations. He pushed ahead the replacement of French colonial officials by Vietnamese, and concerned himself as much as time permitted with economic development.

The fighting enabled de Lattre to press his December 1950 demand for reinforcements on Paris – he sought twelve infantry battalions, five artillery groups and other units. The demand met intense political opposition. Grudgingly, he was promised nine battalions and three artillery units for eighteen months only. Paris was also unable to persuade the Americans to provide immediately the financial aid necessary to fund French military purchases, in particular those needed for the expansion of Vietnamese units; the funds only became available in the autumn. These two setbacks were to hamper de Lattre's operations considerably, though they were to some extent offset by the success of the much smaller scale operations against Viet-minh infiltration and other insurgent groupings taking place in Annam, Cochin China, Cambodia and Laos. These released a number of units for the critical Delta area, in some cases the units being replaced by newly formed Vietnamese battalions. Even so de Lattre's forces in Tonkin only totalled 86,500 (68,500 French Union and 18,000 Vietnamese) against Giap's 170,000, now including 112 battalions, each over 900 strong.

To press his case for reinforcements, de Lattre decided to visit Paris. But the difficulties of his position were well highlighted by the necessity for de Lattre twice to postpone the date of his departure, the first postponement being caused by the Vietnam Government's political crisis and the second by the fall of the Pleven government in Paris. Pleven's successor, Queuille, believed the French reinforcement of the defence of Europe to be his overriding priority, the alternative being the rearmament of Germany, at that time still unwelcome. In addition, there was growing anxiety over the situation in Morocco and Tunisia. De Lattre argued his case forcibly but with only partial success, and was then obliged to return to Hanoi to face a new Viet-minh offensive. In addition, there was personal misfortune, painful symptoms of illness in his right hip. Whether de Lattre sought advice at this point is not known. He may have done so and decided to ignore what he was told, or the gravity may not have been apparent at the time. But from March 1951 onwards, de Lattre's health began to decline. He arrived back at Hanoi tired, discouraged and feverish.

An attack had been anticipated by the French for some time as five Viet-minh brigades, or small divisions, and an enormous force of coolie labour, had been identified in the massif near Dong Trieu. The Viet-minh forces assault on the night of 23 March showed the general direction of the attack, a Viet-minh deception plan failing to mislead the French. The direction of the main thrust by three divisions was towards Haiphong but the offensive seems to have had a further aim which was as at least equally important, a combination of frontal assault with behind the French lines insurgency seeking to destabilise the whole French Delta position.

On his return, de Lattre immediately resumed personal command of the battle. He refused to be drawn into the Viet-minh trap, aimed at enticing his units along the main road and into ambushes. Instead, he correctly assessed that the small town of Mao Khe, at the exit from the massif, was the key ground at the front. He hurriedly put together a water-borne reinforcement formation, tasked to hold Mao Khe. This force arrived as the Viet-minh entered the northern part of the town but it succeeded in ejecting the insurgents and halting their advance. Night air reconnaissance, used for the first time, played a key role. On the basis of further apparently negative reconnaissance evidence, de Lattre's staff then assessed that the Viet-minh had been obliged to withdraw and abandon a planned follow-up attack. De Lattre personally decided to reject this view completely. In a clear example of a lesson learnt in Morocco in the 1920s, he asserted that all that had happened was the Viet-minh had resorted to efficient camouflage, and flatly forbade any redeployment of the force at Mao Khe. His wisdom ensured that he was well prepared to repel a human mass attack by twelve 1,000-strong units that followed the next night. The Viet-minh suffered heavy casualties, the French being able to deploy their superior fire power, some of it warship mounted.

Following this success and with a growing appreciation of the two faceted nature of his military problem, de Lattre turned to the threat in his rear, the intensified insurgency in the Delta. He ordered his first big sweep operation, *Méduse*, for mid-April. This operation, involving three *groupes mobiles* all under the local command of de Linarès, was a qualified success but a second, *Reptile*, under another general, was somewhat less successful. The difficulty in both was the well known ability of members of Viet-minh units under threat to blend into local communities, apparently as peasants or villagers, and at the same time thereby necessitating the maintenance of a considerable French force in case they resumed attacks. Sweeps could overrun Viet-minh training centres and propaganda schools, they could disturb underground organisations, but actual apprehension of guerillas was far from complete.

De Lattre, alarmed by this development, assessed, again correctly, that the only solution to this problem was, in British Army terms, that of 'hearts and minds', the recovery of loyalty and the confidence of the population. He took the Vietnam prime minister to the scene of his Vinh Yen victory and in an emotional speech reaffirmed that the role of the French Army in Vietnam was simply one of securing a true independence. Each French unit in Vietnam was ordered to form and encadre a locally recruited second battalion. One officer cadet school opened early in 1951, two more followed a little later for reserve officers. By the end of 1951, 800 Vietnamese officers were serving. For further expansion, de Lattre provided five more cadre schools under the direction of General Spillman, a highly intellectual soldier who de Lattre knew would develop his plans.

In May de Lattre attended a conference in Singapore at which British, American and French views on the Communist challenge in South East Asia were exchanged. De Lattre gain full moral support for his fight, but to his disappointment neither America nor Britain were prepared to offer military units, even in the event of a Chinese intervention.

De Lattre wished to follow this conference with a visit to the United States, where he hoped that he could accelerate American military and financial support. He was however precluded from this by a Viet-minh attack on 28 May in the Ninh Binh area. The French had expected an attack in this particularly fertile part of the Delta, with a rice crop approaching readiness for harvesting, but not one quite so soon; its ferocity caught the local commander, Colonel Gambiez, only half-prepared. The offensive repeated the pattern of Dong Trieu, a two divisional frontal assault, a third division attacking a flank and

intensified guerilla activity in the French rear. De Lattre reacted with
characteristic vigour. His road communications to the south cut, he
rushed reinforcements to the area by water and by air; in forty-eight
hours, the French were able to repel the attackers and restore a line of
defence. The frontal assault cost the Viet-minh heavy losses.

But for the ailing de Lattre the success served only to bring further
tragic personal misfortune, one that in almost any range of human
experience could hardly have been more cruel. On 30 May, he was
told by his Chief of Staff that Bernard had been killed in a skirmish
defending a rocky outcrop at Ninh Binh. At the time, Bernard had
with him in his command post a French lieutenant and two corporals,
one French and one Vietnamese, all had been killed or wounded by
mortar fire. To his father, Bernard was more than an only and much
loved son, he was in his person all that a young Frenchman should be.
He had been de Lattre's helper in the escape from prison and in 1944
he was the youngest soldier ever to win the *Médaille Militaire*; earlier
in May 1951 de Lattre had personally awarded Bernard the *Croix de
Guerre* for bravery in the Delta operations. Inevitably, the General
felt that he must carry at least part of the blame and was for a brief
period prostrated with grief. He returned to France with his son's
body, an act that attracted much ungenerous French criticism and
bitter Viet-minh broadcast propaganda sneers. De Linarès, following
de Lattre's overall plans, completed the checking and repulse of the
Viet-minh frontal assault.

After a funeral service at the Invalides, which by the special request
of Madame de Lattre was extended to be one in memory of all those
killed in Indochina, Bernard was buried at Mouilleron. To some,
such a personal tragedy might have weakened Christian beliefs. This
was not the case with de Lattre or his wife; if anything, their loss
strengthened their faith. De Lattre, who had always attached great
importance to the selection and role of chaplains in his commands,
now paid even more attention to their duties in Indochina.

Now a man with much to do, little time left in which to do it, and
much of what he had lived for gone, de Lattre threw what was left of
his volcanic energy into the campaign. In his command, his faith and
his plight appeared to give him a new serenity; *colères* were of the past.
But his physical weakening became noticeable, even if his mental
energy remained unflagging until the autumn.

The Ninh Binh operations, or the Battle of the River Day as it was
later called by the French, although successful, once again highlighted the problem of the behind-the-lines guerilla, striking by night

at small posts and lines of communication, but by day indistinguishable from the local peasantry. De Lattre's next moves, after his return from Paris, were designed to contain this threat. On 18 June, a massive six battalion sweep of an area near Hanoi took place in typhoon conditions which, unfortunately, permitted one major Viet-minh unit in the area to slip away. The dioceses of two bishoprics, which had undertaken to secure themselves but had in fact become logistic support and safe areas for Viet-minh, were occupied by French and Vietnamese troops. De Lattre considered that the use, unchecked by the local French commander, of one of these bishoprics had contributed to the death of Bernard. A little later, their autonomous status was ended. De Lattre next pushed Huu into removing members of the ambivalent Dai Viet party, and others either inefficient or inert, from the Vietnam government and administration in a further effort to consolidate the Vietnam government and population against the Viet-minh.

The death of Bernard while serving with a Vietnamese unit had aroused some measure of local sympathy which de Lattre was able to utilise. He personally launched a campaign to publicise his expanding local Vietnamese army. For this force soldier recruits were forthcoming in ample quantity from the peasantry. The educated Vietnamese however were unwilling to serve, to the irritation of de Lattre, as it was precisely this class of Frenchmen who were sacrificing their lives. He chose a prestigious school prize-giving in July to make an emotional appeal to Vietnamese school leavers.

In plain terms, he told the boys that their country was at war and that independence and freedom were not some form of celestial prize-giving in which the prizes were leisure, but were values that had to be fought for and defended. This defence, he said, was now being undertaken by France as part of her undertaking to Vietnam, but it could not be undertaken without the Vietnamese. He denied that membership of the French Union negated a genuine independence, adding that, without France, Vietnam would be dominated by China and the deceptions of Marxism. He urged the young educated to support the Emperor Bao Dai, to discharge their patriotic duty, fight to save their land and, if necessary, sacrifice their lives as the young peasants were doing as soldiers. The speech is significant, its emotion reflecting de Lattre's own hopes, fears and views.

His efforts did, in fact, meet with a measure of success. Bao Dai consented to review a large military parade of French and Vietnamese units in Hanoi, watched by thousands, and to sign a decree placing

Vietnam on a war footing. Some young educated Vietnamese volunteered for the Vietnamese Army, many of whose units were to fight
very bravely. A little later, Bao Dai visited a combat area, his initial
distrust of de Lattre now turned to open admiration. It appeared
briefly that de Lattre's spectacular military victories had been
matched by an equally successful political development, acceptance
of the French patterned concept of independence and the legitimacy
of Bao Dai. De Lattre himself was confident, to the extent that he
rejected any suggestion of negotiation with the Viet-minh with a
threat – to President Auriol himself – of resignation. His own personal brilliance and *tour de force* served, paradoxically, to dazzle
and conceal from viewers the fatal flaws in French policy.

In practice, these July events marked the apogee of de Lattre's
direct day today control of Indochina. In August, he took a month's
leave; increasingly ill, he was prone to tell friends and associates
that he was losing the will to live. That this was not the case was
proved by his energy in September, when he visited the United States
and Britain.

To de Lattre, looking ahead to the future, the Indochina war could
be, and was being, won. But the victory could be undone by a Chinese
intervention, an event he feared might follow the end of the Korean
war. The only counter to this, in de Lattre's eyes, was the support of
the Western world, in particular the United States. He believed that
he personally could contribute to overcoming traditional American
anti-colonial attitudes and accordingly he paid a hectic twelve day
visit to the United States in September. During the course of this visit
he met President Truman, Dean Acheson, members of Congress and
officials of the State Department; he gave numerous lectures and
talks to military and civilian organisations and offered himself to a
succession of press and television media interviews. Despite increasing pain, he took meticulous care in preparing himself for these
sessions and, notwithstanding the language difficulty, his personality, intellect and grasp of the complexities of the situation
made a great impression. Television in fact proved to be a media
well-suited for his style and charisma. His speeches sought to
develop two themes, that France's war was not colonial but part of a
general struggle against Communism in Asia, and that if Tonkin
were to fall, so in turn and before long would Indochina, South-East
Asia, and very probably India and the Middle East. These views may
with hindsight appear overstated, but they were sincerely held. They
served to win American political support and a very large quantity of

military aid that arrived after de Lattre's own departure from Indo-china; they did not however secure any promise of ground combat troops.

The American visit was followed by one to London, shorter but hardly less exhausting for a man now seriously ill. There followed a few days in Paris where de Lattre attended a fatiguing *Rhin et Danube* association reunion but had also to learn, and tell his wife, of the gravity of his medical condition, now diagnosed as serious cancer of the hip.

On the return journey to Indochina, he stopped briefly in Rome in order to persuade the Vatican to direct the hierarchy of the Roman Church in Vietnam to commit itself and its one and a half million followers fully to the anti Viet-minh cause. The Pope readily agreed to this. He arrived back in Saigon on 19 October to receive a rapturous popular reception. Conscious that he had very little time left, he departed from Saigon almost immediately for Hanoi. There, with a feverish energy, he summoned the Roman hierarchy to tell them of the Papal support for the war, and very abruptly summoned one of French Indochina's leading business figures to charge him with raising money for comforts for all France's soldiers, French, North and Black African, and Vietnamese at Christmas. At the same time he turned his attention to the two final military operations of his stewardship, the battles of Nghia Lo and Hoa Binh, the former nearly over by the time of his return.

While de Lattre was away, and until mid-September, the military situation had remained generally stable, with the exception of the assassination of a French general and the local governor of South Vietnam in July. These killings were followed a little later by the Viet-minh's execution of their own commander in the area who was opposed to the extremes of the local Marxism. With the end of the rainy season, two parallel sets of operations opened in Tonkin in early October. Giap, the Viet-minh commander, wished to draw French forces northwards to facilitate his infiltration into the impor-tant Delta area; his programmes of infiltration had been seriously hampered by de Lattre's line of blockhouses and *groupes mobiles*, and Giap badly needed the rice. The French assessed one key area of the Delta to have been infiltrated to an intolerable level and that it must be cleared.

To draw the French northward, Giap attacked in terrain of extreme difficulty – mountainous jungle. His objective was the town of Nghia Lo, which the French commander, Salan, could not abandon without loss of control over an important approach route to Hanoi; de Lattre had considered the garrison insufficiently strong. With constant air support, Salan was just able to hold the town in face of mass Viet-minh assaults. Two parachute unit drops served to save the town and throw the Viet-minh extended lines of communication into disarray.

In the Delta, French units encircled a vast area, some 360 villages surrounded by water or rice paddy with a population of over a quarter of a million. With great difficulty they proceeded to sweep through it in a two week long operation. The sweep achieved the usual pattern of success and failure; in the area a flag French authority was re-established, but numerous guerillas either hid, pretended they were locals, or slipped away to return later. Troops arriving in a village would be ambushed, but on the few occasions when the Viet-minh attempted to stand their ground, French firepower inflicted heavy losses. Certainly the Viet-minh regular regiment in the area was broken up, a success in itself. In sum, in the two operations, the French could justifiably claim a further victory.

De Lattre had been concerned with the strategy, but not the tactics of these two operations. With the last battle of his career, however, he was more directly involved. He was determined that French forces must not only regain the initiative, but also regain it with an offensive battle on ground of their own choosing; the ground must also be an area which the Viet-minh would have to defend, accepting a pitched battle. This, he believed, would at local level end infiltration as access and supply routes were denied. A successful offensive would also both stifle criticism of defensive battles and secure credits in Paris. At international, above all American, level it would show that France was regaining the ascendancy. And, of course, such a course of action was in accord with the teachings of Foch and de Lattre's own temperament.

The town of Hoa Binh, an important communication centre between China and Annam, was chosen, after careful study, as being a military objective likely to meet these aims and also to be within French military capabilities. It was also the chief town in the Muong people's region. The Muong had a tradition of loyalty to France. De Lattre additionally believed the town's capture would check attempts by the Viet-minh to infiltrate Annam by outflanking the de Lattre line. Hoa Binh possessed other added advantages, it lay on the Noire river, so water transport and fire power could be used; civilian casualties could also be kept low. Lastly and most attractively, if captured, the town could be the first stage in a strategy of cutting all the Viet-minh forces in two by occupying their Thanh Hoa province central bastion. For this additional troops would be necessary, but de Lattre believed that once the possibilities were seen, these reinforcements would be sent. A man who knew he was dying wanted to mark out the road others should follow.

The operation, under the local command of Salan and de Linarès, was a spectacular if not entirely substantial success. As a prelude to secure a flank, the town of Cho Ben was attacked and occupied, the Viet-minh withdrawing precipitately. This attack was partly a deception feint, but the area had economic value of its own. Some 15,000 men were then moved rapidly, in a notable logistics achievement, to the Hoa Binh front where, in a classic assault operation involving water-borne, vehicle mounted and parachute dropped units, the town was occupied late on 15 October. The Viet-minh, however, again refused battle.

On 19 November, de Lattre, concealing his physical agony with great difficulty, bade a farewell to his troops at Hoa Binh; few present knew that he would never return. At the end of the day, exhausted and feverish, he handed his command over to Salan.

What had he achieved? His critics have claimed that his strategy was already failing; certainly the military difficulties were highlighted when Hoa Binh was evacuated early in 1952. But de Lattre was a general of exceptional imagination, his generalship in 1940, 1944 and 1945 showed that he could very quickly recast plans to meet new needs or opportunities. Two claims may be made for *L'Année de Lattre*. The first is indisputable, that the entire year showed what a decisive contribution to events a truly exceptional leader can make. A second claim may reasonably be advanced, de Lattre's successes show what might have been achieved, a non-communist Vietnam, had he been given a more realistic political framework by Paris. De Lattre had converted a campaign of colonial repression into a Vietnam civil war. It was a war that the Franco-Vietnam forces could actually have won. But this was not appreciated in either Paris or Hanoi, where, after he had gone, irresolution and defeatism almost immediately returned, Hoa Binh being the first example.

On 20 November, de Lattre flew back to Paris, ostensibly for a meeting of the Grand Council of the French Union. He addressed the meeting with clarity and force despite such physical weakness that he had to be carried in a chair up and down the stairway to his Paris apartment. His return to Paris had in fact been primarily for medical reasons, and with no publicity he entered a clinic on 18 December for a major operation. this had to be followed by further surgery on 5 January. His condition steadily worsened until his death, his confirmation crucifix in his hand, on 11 January 1952. His last words, uttered on 9 January in a brief conscious period were 'Where is Bernard?'.

In his last days, he was told that he was to be created a Marshal of France. Aware that Juin was also a deserving candidate he asked if he was to be the only one. The process was not completed by the time of his death, but he was given a prolonged and theatrical State Funeral, much in accord with his own temperament. His coffin, mounted on a tank carrying the name 'Alsace', lay in state under the Arc de Triomphe. Before it paraded regiments of soldiers; groups of ex-servicemen and thousands of ordinary French men and women filed past. Dignitaries who visited included political leaders and ambassadors. The President of the Republic placed a Marshal's baton on a cushion beneath the coffin. One who arrived alone and remained standing solitary for some time before the coffin was Charles de Gaulle.

For the Invalides service, the pall-bearers included Juin, Eisenhower and Montgomery. After the service, mounted on an armoured car with its turret removed, the funeral cortege proceeded slowly from Paris to Versailles, Chartres and Saumur, and on to Mouilleron. There the coffin was placed in a grave next to that of Bernard. A nearby windmill of the Vendée, that de Lattre loved, was later converted into a memorial chapel where people might pray for a Marshal of France and a lieutenant, father and son.

8

North Africa and NATO: Marshal Juin

Juin was never to be at ease in the post-war world, and the changes which that world brought began, slowly at first, to affect his personality. He became increasingly assertive, often tactless and irascible and at times idiosyncratic. Although fond of social life and for many years still capable of dancing '*comme un sous-lieutenant*', the robust good humour, political finesse and judgement that he had displayed in Algiers and Italy began to fail him. Personal anxieties over his sons, one serving in Indochina and the other whose unstable character led to a tragic death, added to his tensions. His appearance altered as well, from stocky to slightly portly; with the removal of his greying moustache, the cheerful good-natured expression of the pre-war and war years also began to go.

It would be unjust to attribute these changes to fame and success, the causes lay deeper, a post middle-age 'decay of hope' to use a psychiatric term. Juin was a man who must have realised, perhaps only in part consciously at first, that in Italy he had achieved a renown he would never surpass. He had a soldierly contempt for the political irresolution and instability of the Fourth Republic, a contempt reinforced by the difficulties he had in securing firm decisions. In his four year tenure as Resident-General in Morocco, for example, Juin had to serve nine different administrations. Neither did he like the emerging consumer society and its technologically based values, very different from those of his up-bringing. He also distrusted its military counterpart, the highly sophisticated army with its massive logistic back-up requirements, '*un matérialisme à prétention scientifique*'. Above all, the world of French North Africa and its splendid *Armée d'Afrique*, Juin's own world, was beginning to disintegrate. The violence of the Sétif uprising in Algeria in May 1945, foreshadowing the 'coffin or suitcase' final solution of 1962, profoundly disturbed him.

Juin's reactions became similar to those of white settlers elsewhere in Africa: emotive outbursts and much confused political analysis. From his Constantine school-days, Juin had fought for the under-dog, but to his perceptions the under-dogs in North Africa now were the Berbers of Morocco and Kabyles of Algeria who had served so well as soldiers, and the small *colons* of Algeria, the society of his own origins and the bearers of French culture and achievement. Neither should be abandoned to an alien, negative, Arab nationalism seen in Juin's perspective as a small minority of gangster terrorists.

As France's most experienced *général d'Afrique*, he began to assert a right to voice his opinions on all Maghreb affairs, an assertion that became more marked when he became a Marshal. His views became increasingly reactionary as France's difficulties worsened; the events of the late 1950s and early 1960s were to tear the ageing Juin apart. We shall see how it was the affairs of the Maghreb that would dom-inate his thoughts and emotions for the rest of his life, despite the considerable importance of the military appointments he was to hold. With one exception it was the Maghreb, and Algeria in particu-lar, that would bring him into almost ceaseless, and often bitter, conflict with political authority.

A complete account of Juin's role in these years may never be written. He became a highly controversial figure and opinions and allegations concerning him range from the adulatory to the vitupera-tive. Any search for the truth is complicated both by the actions of officers and politicians who took his name in vain to support their views, and by Juin's own divided loyalties and consequential ambiguity – for example, he would make gestures appearing to sup-port those who sought to retain Algeria for France, but would not, for reasons of loyalty and personal caution, declare himself openly. He also tried to influence opinion by writing, where his impact is imposs-ible to quantify.

Chief of Defence Staff

In the immediate post-war months, however, France's difficulties seemed manageable, and Juin's careful study of problems and their analysis in his own clear logical style brought him satisfaction. He also enjoyed much travel on visits, two of them with de Gaulle. The re-building of France's armed forces went ahead despite the progress-ive ending of American re-equipment aid and, more seriously, despite the absence of any respite for a war-weary army and people. There were residual metropolitan problems arising from the war, the provision of a garrison for Germany and a border problem in the Alpes Maritimes, where de Gaulle claimed adjustments in France's favour, backing the claim by the presence of French troops and the establishment of a French administration. The Italians sought American help and President Truman threatened de Gaulle with an abrupt termination of all military aid. De Gaulle once again used Juin to defuse the crisis, Juin visiting Field-Marshal Alexander, still in command of the theatre, and reaching a compromise by which France secured most of the territory she sought.

More serious were the imperial problems. The first was a nationalist revolt in the Sétif area of Algeria almost immediately after the end of hostilities in Europe. Then followed the problems of Syria and Lebanon with, at the same time and ever increasing in difficulty, that of Indochina. With all these Juin was only concerned indirectly, as the metropolitan administrator of the Army. In the case of Indochina, he visited the territory after a brief sojourn in China in April 1946. One of his main aims, in both territories, was to support Leclerc and d'Argenlieu in securing the departure of the Chinese. He sought this by diplomatic pressures in Chunking, meeting with some success there as the Nationalist Chinese were beginning to realise their need for Western friends in view of the menace of the Communists. The Chinese Army Chief of Staff was however less sympathetic. He held expansionist views and also feared that Tonkin would become a base for Communists attacking southern China. To add to the tension there had also been a shooting affray in Hanoi, in which Chinese soldiers had killed a number of French civilians. In Hanoi itself, Juin met Ho Chi Minh, and then went on to have an altercation with the local Chinese Army commander, who protested transport difficulties, to which Juin riposted that the Chinese transport problems was one arising from their own pillage. However, on being told that Chiang Kai Shek and his Chief of Staff both agreed to the withdrawal, and given a reminder that the French possessed force and fire power, the Chinese commander agreed.

Like de Gaulle, Juin did not fully grasp the realities of Indochina, although he was courteous and not without understanding for Ho Chi Minh during the latter's visit to France for the summer 1946 Fontainebleau conference. He believed that Indochina could still be held for France, and the only change necessary was a devolution of power, leaving a smaller number of exceptionally able Frenchmen at the top. He also feared both the effect of any independence on other

French territories, particularly in North Africa, and any spread of Communism; he was therefore – with de Lattre – opposed to Leclerc's more liberal approach.

The departure of de Gaulle from office early in 1946 changed the nature of Juin's work greatly. He had achieved an excellent working relationship of mutual trust and direct access with de Gaulle, though the latter did sent Juin abroad at a time when Juin was planning to testify to Pétain's patriotism at his trial. The first new Prime Minister, Gouin, made it clear that he would only deal with defence matters through his Minister for Defence, so ending Juin's direct access. The next, Bidault, abolished altogether the Ministry of Defence. Juin was told that the economic reconstruction of the country had to take priority, and his plans for an Army of 460,000 (a total including Maghreb and other colonial units), which he thought the barest minimum for France's many commitments, would have to be scaled down. A reduction of formations, in the number of military regions, and in naval and air projects, had to be effected.

North Africa: Morocco

In January 1947, Juin was offered the post of High Commissioner in Indochina by the then Prime Minister, Ramadier, an offer he declined. He was to be criticised for this by those who fought in Indochina. But Juin was a soldier of the Maghreb, of the *Armée d'Afrique*. By his own admission he knew little of Indochina while problems with which he was anxious to be involved were looming in the Maghreb, especially Morocco. A former Military Assistant to Lyautey could hardly think otherwise, and Juin's next appointment, in May 1947, as Resident-General of Morocco fulfilled a lifetime ambition – but also one carefully publicised. However, in the end, his return to the Moroccan scene in the French Empire's most prestigious post was to prove unfortunate, as some critics of his appointment forecast at the time.

Juin's personal approach to the problems of Morocco was, in practice, the result of several strands of thinking. The first was that of the general French philosophy: an acceptable first stage goal of indigenous political activity might be internal self-government but that goal would take time to reach and in any case remain within a French Union that would retain control of foreign affairs, defence and economic strategy. Morocco, as part of French North Africa, was also seen as an important component of the defence of the free world. At this time (though less so later) Juin did also talk of full independence, but only as a remote final stage very many years distant. For the time being, there could therefore only be co-operation with moderate nationalists and not extremists, though in 1949 Juin advanced a modified concept, that of 'co-sovereignty', as an immediate goal. The second strand was the product of his own background and personal views at the time: Maghreb peoples were far from being capable of fully governing themselves, and any attempt by them to do so would mean corruption, theocracy or Arab dictatorship, together with the victimisation of his beloved Atlas Berbers. Of Tunisians, for example, Juin considered that as a people they suffered from an *'impuissance congénitale'* in respect of government. As time passed, he began also to fear the effects of Moroccan constitutional changes upon Algeria, fears strongly shared by his wife. The third component was the directive given to him on his appointment by Bidault, the Minister for Foreign Affairs, whose ministry was responsible for the Moroccan protectorate. Bidault, an old-fashioned imperialist, directed that French authority must be re-asserted, and re-asserted very firmly.

But the Morocco of 1947 had advanced considerably from the days of Lyautey. The rise of nationalism in Asia and Egypt, the ideas disseminated by the Americans in Morocco during the war, the message of the Atlantic Charter and the emerging anti-colonialism of the United Nations had all strengthened indigenous voices calling for rapid political advance. In the van were the popular 38-year old Sultan Sidi Mohammed (later to be King Mohammed V), and in an embarrassing rivalry to him, a radical nationalist party, the *Istiqlal* (Independence) Party, whose leaders threatened to turn to republicanism if they felt they lacked a royal lead. *Istiqlal* stood opposed to any gradualist approach and also to any truly democratic reform; it was an oligarchy that would talk only of independence. The Gouin government that succeeded de Gaulle had appointed an exceptionally far-sighted French official, Eirik Labonne, as Resident-General. Labonne, a liberal, appreciated that the political clock could not be turned back and favoured economic and political advance to meet nationalist aspirations. These views led to bitter opposition from the French settler community that Lyautey's successors had unwisely allowed to arrive in Morocco; a crisis arose in April 1947 when, on a visit to Tangiers, the Sultan called for Arab unity and complete independence for Morocco. Ramadier, the Prime Minister at the time, recalled Labonne. The instructions given to Juin required

him to inform the Sultan that such political demands were unaccept-
able and, if developed further, could lead to his deposition. These
instructions were drafted by Bidault and approved by Ramadier.
They were neither discussed with the rest of the Cabinet, nor with the
President of the Republic, Auriol, who learnt of them – to his fury –
only in 1950.

To make the point very plainly, Juin arrived on a cruiser to a
martial reception, large numbers of former *Tirailleurs* giving him a
tremendous welcome. On the following day, Juin called on the
Sultan. He was dressed in full uniform, riding breeches, boots, spurs
and medals, a style without precedent for such a call; photographs of
him show a very stern countenance. This start to a proconsulate indicated its style for the next four years under Juin, and beyond that
under other Residents-General in whose appointment Juin had a
powerful voice. The style was confrontational. Juin believed that,
sooner or later, the Sultan would have to be deposed. Dialogue
between them became stilted and formal, Juin speaking plainly, at
times brusquely, while the Sultan, his face masked by large dark
spectacles, became evasive or devious, slipping in controversial addi-
tions to pre-agreed speech texts. An uncertain working relationship
was maintained, however, with difficulty until the end of 1950, giving
Morocco three years of relative stability and economic development.

For much day to day advice Juin leaned on his senior officials, of
whom Francis Lacoste and Jacques Lucius were of exceptional
ability. Less fortunately, Juin also heeded advice from another, his
Director of Political Affairs and later administrator for the Casa-
blanca region, Philippe Boniface. Boniface was, like Juin, of Algerian *colon* stock; he believed that Moroccans should be so grateful
to France for her Protectorate that France had the right to pursue
almost any policy she wished. He used the traditional French policy
of protecting the Berbers as a divide and rule measure and even more
than Juin, he was out of sympathy with the new generation of young
educated Moroccans, very few of whom, in common with any progressive political figures or even progressive officials, were ever to be
seen as guests at the Residency's full social life. President Auriol
came to have ever increasing reservations over Juin's policies, which
he saw as humiliating the Sultan; he also particularly disliked
Boniface. But in Morocco, Juin was master pursuing in practice and in
the name of Lyautey a policy of extending direct French rule, ignoring that direct rule was a policy Lyautey had only used perforce and
had planned to discard. Criticised, Juin would refuse to listen to

arguments with which he disagreed, falling back on an attitude of military authority and determination, or a threat of resignation. On occasions in Rabat he would express open contempt for Paris, a recurrent characteristic of France's African generals and one to prove disastrous later in Algeria; but in Paris and in the presence of ministers, his former natural instinct for discipline would generally return. The power of Boniface, distrusted by more liberal officials and military commanders, was increased by Juin's periods of absence from Morocco on military business elsewhere.

Juin began his proconsulate with a number of liberal statements, phrased in non-commital terms; at this stage he was talking of full internal self-government in twenty to twenty-five years. But he outlined no stages of progress towards this goal, and the creation of a joint 'Council of Viziri and Directors', ten Moroccans and ten Frenchmen all nominated, to advise the government on general policy was of no comfort to the Sultan or the nationalists, particularly as Juin compelled the Sultan to dissolve his own private Cabinet. In day to day matters Juin's actions were clearly designed to bring Morocco under closer French control. He moved to bring the two not very well co-ordinated governments of the country, that of the *makhzen* controlled by the nonegenarian Grand Vizir and that of the Residency, closer together; in so doing he hoped to involve greater Moroccan participation but under French supervision. The Moroccan directorates of agriculture, finance, posts and telegrams, public works, public health, social affairs, commerce and industry were reorganised to achieve this, and also the *Conseil du Government* (a body whose functions were almost entirely consultative), for whose second Electoral College Moroccan members were to be elected on a limited franchise to represent different indigenous communities. In the elections, a number of nationalists were returned. For a joint administration of towns, Juin also devised a system of *khalifas*, which he hoped would provide experience for Moroccans judged responsible. The Sultan repeatedly argued that these measures were either insufficient or in the case of the *khalifas* the thin end of the wedge of the policy of 'co-sovereignty' which he rejected. The Sultan also, wherever he could, encouraged the teaching of Arabic in place of French and endeavoured to place either his own followers or members of *Istiqlal* in any institution, economic, sporting or social in order to oppose co-sovereignty. There were, in consequence, increasing differences of opinion between the Sultan and Juin on the appointment of particular individuals of whom he disapproved, notably the Vizir for education who had collaborated with the Axis but who was also a cousin of the Sultan, together with the pasha of Agadir and three caids. Juin also forbade certain religious gatherings, such as the opening of Koran schools, which the Sultan liked to attend but which were becoming anti-French.

Towards the end of 1947, President Auriol, in Paris, noted his dissatisfaction at the small scale of Juin's reforms and their absence of real political advance. Relations between Juin and the Elysée worsened in 1948 when a virulently anti-Sultan tract appeared in Morocco and its origins were traced to a Residency official whom Juin then tried to protect. President Auriol considered the real instigator was Juin himself.

In the autumn of 1950, the Sultan visited France, to the misgivings of Juin; in the course of this visit he made a number of criticisms of Juin to Ministers and political figures. This led Juin to defend his policies with a threat of resignation and forecasts of doom if hard line policies were weakened, and to an intensification of the 'Berber policy', a development that was to lead directly to the 1951 crisis. The Berber chieftains led by Thami El Glaoui, the Pasha of Marrakesh, had for some time been encouraged quietly, notably by Boniface, to develop an anti-Sultan political stance. El Glaoui was a man of massive wealth and political power, both built up over the years by a variety of dubious methods, a number being either extortionate or criminal. He relied on the French administration to preserve this against nationalist criticism and attempts by the Sultan to control him; he accordingly portrayed himself as remaining a loyal ally of the French. One or two other leading Atlas Berber chieftains were similarly placed and together they could influence numerous lesser chieftains, Glaoui describing the Sultan as the tool of the '*Istiqlalo*-Communists', unfit for his political and religious functions. In turn, the Sultan saw Morocco falling behind other Arab countries, particularly Tunisia, in the march to independence. In consequence, while in France, the Sultan, frustrated and piqued by the very vague commitments to political progress given him, issued a statement calling for the end of the Protectorate treaty and the establishment of Franco-Moroccan relations on a new basis.

In October 1950, slightly delayed by the Sultan's visit to Paris, Juin was asked to examine and report upon the state of France's campaign in Indochina, where the military situation was worsening rapidly. Juin was not impressed by the decisions to withdraw from the areas bordering with China, despite the fact that in the southern province of

Yunnan Mao and the Communists, triumphant in the Chinese civil war, were building up both military strength and logistic installations to support the Viet-minh. He was even more dismayed by the seemingly resigned approach of the local French commanders, whose planning centred upon a defeatist withdrawal to the Delta area; this Juin saw as fatal. In a remarkably clear and forthright summary of the situation which he gave to assembled commanders and staffs at Hanoi, Juin urged the need to regain the initiative, which he saw being achieved by grouping the French forces scattered in small garrisons in a *masse de manoeuvre* of two main components, both strong in infantry and artillery. These were to strike out at Viet-minh columns as they came down from the north. Juin envisaged this as an interim measure while air power to destroy Viet-minh logistics supply was built up and plans for the eventual reoccupation of the northern border areas completed. Pivotal to the project was the local raising of a Vietnam army, under French cadres and control, for garrison duties. In respect of air power, Juin personally secured two groups of B26 bombers from the Americans.

These views merit mention, as they were essentially those formed and carried out later by de Lattre. On his return to Rabat, Juin was once again invited to assume command in Indochina. For the second time he refused, claiming that his departure would appear a victory for the Sultan; for Juin, Morocco, or anywhere in North Africa, mattered much more to France than far off Asian possessions.

The Sultan's visit had resulted in only limited progress, the setting up of two mixed Franco-Moroccan Commissions to consider education and industrial relations respectively. Juin accepted these with reluctance but insisted on his nominating the membership; the triumphal welcome that greeted the Sultan on his return only worried him further. Events accelerated towards the end of the year. Juin personally dismissed a militant critic from the Second College of the *Conseil du Gouvernement* by peremptorily ordering him to leave the Chamber. This move led to a walk out by *Istiqlal* and other nationalist members, and a little later their official reception by the Sultan. In December, Glaoui demanded that the Sultan disavowed the *Istiqlal* who were branding the Berber chieftains as agents of the French and feudal relics. The Sultan refused, and there followed a spectacular public quarrel in which the Pasha felt himself humiliated. He launched an opposition movement which at this stage drew considerable support from other chieftains, pashas and caids who resented the tribute they were expected to give to the Sultan, his family and his court officials – venality on a considerable scale. By the end of 1950, Juin could present the Moroccan scene as one of *Istiqlal* militancy, Berber chieftains disavowing the Sultan and Glaoui talking of secession.

In January 1951, Juin formally warned the Sultan that he must disavow *Istiqlal* within a month. the disavowal was to centre on *Istiqlal's* practices rather than its ideology, and to provide for the removal of a number of *Istiqlal* supporters from the Sultan's entourage. In addition, Juin asked the Sultan to reaffirm, unequivocally, his allegiance to France. The Sultan, predictably, objected and later both he and the *Istiqlal* alleged that Juin's demands were underlined by a full threat of deposition. Juin later denied any formal threat but the message was certainly conveyed in a style more delicate.

Juin then went on a visit to Washington where he very aggressively defended his Moroccan policy both in public and in a meeting with State Department officials; he spoke dismissively of any reactions by the Arab League or the United Nations. Later in the year, in discussion with a still horrified President Auriol, Juin made it clear that he himself would have gone further, either using France's veto at the United Nations or even withdrawing from that organisation. Washington, alarmed, advised Paris that the United States could not support any such deposition of the Sultan.

On his return to Morocco, Juin re-applied his pressure upon the Sultan, adding that in his view the Sultan's life could be in danger if the Berber chieftains marched their followers on to the capital and *Istiqlal* was not disavowed. Horsed followers of the chieftains, in hundreds, began to move on Rabat and Fez to underline their threat. It was freely suggested that another royal prince was available to become Sultan in the event of a deposition. Juin was able to portray himself as the sole authority capable of holding the balance and preventing bloodshed. Faced with this situation, the Sultan appealed to President Auriol. The latter was, it seems, exceedingly angry but felt that it was politically impossible not to support Juin and accordingly advise Sidi Mohammed to concede. The Sultan gave way. Whether Juin would have preferred to force the issue to the point of deposing the Sultan or whether he felt the pressure applied was sufficient is debatable. He himself saw the outcome as a respite, not a final solution, but on the initiative of President Auriol, the sections of Bidault's 1947 instructions empowering him if necessary to depose the Sultan were revoked.

Juin's time in Morocco was running out, for he was due to return to

Paris as Inspector-General of the Armed Forces and Commander-in-Chief NATO Land Forces Central Europe. Juin took advantage of his success to coerce the Sultan into authorising the creation of local councils in all the rural areas of Morocco, a measure which had been strongly opposed by the urban based nationalists. His efforts to gain representation of elected French representatives in municipalities were however blocked by the Sultan and Juin chose not to force any further issues in order to retain maximum influence over the selection of his own successor. With *Istiqlal*'s leaders under arrest, the remaining six months of Juin's period at the Residency were again months of uneasy calm. At the time of his departure, indeed, it seemed that the *politique du sabre* had succeeded. Juin's tenure of office, too, had achieved much technical administrative reform, in particular in the supervision of urban government, civil rights for Moroccans, the provision of family allowances for Moroccan workers, the opening of a School of Administration and the initiation of studies for a reform of the judiciary together with a penal code. But the reality was, however, one of opportunity for the development of a new Franco-Moroccan partnership being wasted, with in its place resentment smouldering, later to explode.

As a final act, Juin insisted on the appointment of General Guillaume – the commander of the *goums* in the Italian campaign – as his successor, knowing that Guillaume would follow his policies. He backed his insistence by threats to resign or to refuse to serve in the NATO command structure. President Auriol at first refused to accept such dictation, accusing Juin of being a French MacArthur, but in the end he gave way.

After his departure, Juin again threatened to refuse to take up the NATO appointment unless Boniface's tour of duty was extended. Juin's hard line policies, modified only in detail, were pursued with increasingly unfortunate results both by Guillaume and others to follow. In Paris, and sometimes also in Morocco, Juin continued vigorously to support the hard-line. After serious rioting in late 1951, tension mounted throughout 1942 and early 1953. In May 1953, Juin, accompanied by Guillaume, presided over a politically-loaded mass rally of some 100,000 Berber ex-servicemen. In June Juin was installed as a member of the honoured *Académie Française* but the ceremony was marred by Juin's speech, openly attacking much respected liberal writers and academics, and by his chosen companion for the occasion, the disreputable Glaoui, whom he praised lavishly. At the end of July, matters came to a head, stage-managed in

Morocco by Boniface and, in the opinion of President Auriol, directed from afar by Juin, another march into the major cities of thousands of armed Berbers and a political crisis. Guillaume, with the approval of the Laniel government (except for one minister, François Mitterand) deposed the Sultan, replacing him with another prince, a move represented in public as a deposition by the people of Morocco and not by France. The deposition awakened, slowly at first, a new mass nationalism throughout Morocco in favour of the deposed Sultan whose reputation Juin continued to attack in Paris. The Mendès-France government returned the diplomat, Francis Lacoste, to succeed Guillaume in June 1954. But Lacoste, a qualified admirer of Juin, found himself constrained on the one hand by an alliance of French residents, the Army and the administration, an alliance strongly supported in Paris by Juin, and on the other by the outbreak of a campaign of terrorism which, in turn, threw frightened French ministers back on to the hard-line counsels of Juin, who threatened to voice open criticism. By October, however, even Juin was beginning to see that the client Sultan did not command allegiance.

Mendès-France's successor, Faure, sent a liberal Resident-General, Grandval, to try and implement a new policy but he could neither suppress the worsening violence – including the killing of forty-nine Frenchmen and women – nor win any support from the French settler community. In Paris, Grandval's policies were scorned by Juin who fiercely opposed any proposal that could open the way for a return of Sultan Sidi Mohammed. Juin's influence also secured Grandval's replacement by another *Vieux Marocain* (old Morocco hand) general, Boyer de Latour du Moulin. Even with a military force strengthened to over 100,000 men, Boyer de Latour was not able to contain the insurgency, now taking the form of a 'Liberation Army'. Paris finally accepted the inevitable in 1956; the Sultan was allowed to return and under Dubois, the last French Resident-General, the territory moved to independence.

Juin warned Dubois that independence under Sidi Mohammed would bring about a bloodbath of the European community and of the Berber pashas and caids who had opposed him. In the case of the Europeans, the killings were limited. Hundreds of Berber chieftains were killed, though Glaoui escaped death by a humiliating public appeal for pardon. French policy had been a total failure. As one of that policy's major architects, Juin, however well-meaning and devoted to the old Morocco of Lyautey he may have been, must be held in part accountable. His personal example of contempt for Paris politicians, also perpetuated an unfortunate *Armée d'Afrique* attitude which others later were to follow.

North Africa: Tunisia and Algeria

Juin was also out to influence policy elsewhere in North Africa in the time of the Fourth Republic. Much of this pressure was behind the scenes and verbal – it is therefore exceedingly difficult to assess. An indicator, perhaps, is the remark reliably attributed to Prime Minister Edgar Faure in 1955. In reply to a critic of the appointment of Boyer de Latour to Rabat, Faure replied 'I had to appoint a soldier. Juin insisted.' The instability of Fourth Republic political life, with its incessant changes of ministries creating conditions where it was dangerous to appear weak, provided Juin with a stage. The ministers themselves increasingly feared, or justified their weakness by saying that they feared, Juin as a twentieth century General Boulanger, seeking to overthrow the Republic. As the Indochina war dragged on, public restiveness grew. There were occasional crowd demonstrations in which loud voices shouted 'Vive Juin' or 'Vive le maréchal', seemingly justifying the ministerial fears.

In 1953, Juin opposed a proposal to appoint Admiral Barjot as Resident-General in Tunisia in succession to a hard liner, de Hautec-locque. He agitated successfully for another hard-liner, Voizard, whom he then told very firmly whom he was to appoint as military commander. In 1954, while on leave in Algeria, Juin was very abruptly ordered to be present when Prime Minister Mendès-France, in a progressive statement of policy known as the Declaration of Carthage, gave virtually complete internal self-government to Tunisia, but at the same time Juin's presence was meant to emphasise a continuing French presence. Juin agreed with the statement in principle but had reservations about certain terms of the statement; he understood from Mendès-France that amendments to strengthen the French position that he proposed would be included in the final version. Juin, looking stern, then stood at the Prime Minister's side supposedly as a specific reassurance to French settlers and a clear warning to Tunisian nationalists not to exceed the limits set out. At this occasion, the first after the well publicised dispute with the French government over European defence policy (examined later) which had led to his being deprived of some of his privileges as a Marshal, Juin was given a tumultuous welcome by the French colony. But an observer described his mood as *sombre et laconique*. The amendments to the Statement that he had proposed had not been included in the Prime Minister's Statement; Juin, furious, felt that he had been both used and abused. Later, when the armistice offered to Tunisian insurgents resulted in huge numbers of young men parading through Tunisian streets and towns as victors, Juin's reservations were proved correct.

The opening of the Algerian campaign inevitably deepened Juin's emotional involvement in France's North African policies. As early as May 1954, Juin had sensed that trouble was likely and had warned the government. From the start, he urged strong counter-measures on the government, arguing also that a continuing French presence in Morocco and Tunisia was essential if Algeria was not to be lost to what he saw as a carefully synchronised foreign-inspired attack upon France, French North Africa and the West. He was made a permanent member of a Ministerial Co-ordination Committee for North Africa – probably a ministerial effort to keep an eye upon him.

In June 1955 he vainly tried to intercede for the hard-line French Army commander in Algeria, Cherrière, whom Paris wished to replace. More significantly, in the same month but for no constitutional reason, Juin was present when Prime Minister Faure interviewed the Algerian nationalist leader Ferhat Abbas. Ferhat Abbas presented an apparently moderate nationalist case, but his listeners had been informed that he was in secret contact with the *Front de Libération Nationale (FLN)*. A little later, Juin resigned from the Co-ordination Committee, protesting that while his advice was sought, it was not heeded. In particular, he felt his views on the need for a special War Committee to direct the Algerian conflict and the undesirability of any return of Sultan Sidi Mohammed had not been given proper weight. In early 1956, when a group of the senior officials of the French Resident Minister in Algeria, Robert Locoste, visited Paris, some made contacts with Juin. But Juin's refusal to become openly involved was soon recognised in Algiers and later in the year, when the Algiers *colon* crowds were calling for a military strong man, the cries were for Boyer de Latour or Cogny rather than Juin.

Also in 1956, after the Algerian uprising had been in full spate for eighteen months, and when Morocco was on the verge of independence, Juin returned to an idea he had first advanced in 1951 that NATO should establish a North Africa Command, arguing that the Maghreb must remain part of the Western Alliance as otherwise NATO's southern flank would be turned. He offered to head this command which he saw ensuring a French hegemony in the theatre. The French Government did not support the proposal, clearly seeing more dangers than gains from any internationalisation of the conflict.

By the end of 1956, Juin seems to have decided to limit his efforts to influence North African affairs to writing. Certainly in late 1957, and early 1958, when General Salan, commander in Algeria was the target of fierce *colon* criticism, there was again no popular call for Juin, nor was there any call for him either in Algiers or in Paris at the time of the return to power of de Gaulle in May 1958. The real breaking points, however, were to follow as de Gaulle's policies moved towards withdrawal from Algeria.

NATO Land Forces Command

Juin's final active service appointment, however, was as successor to de Lattre in the newly-formed NATO command structure. Generals with a wartime reputation who could command the respect of the Americans and to a lesser extent the British were needed. No French officers carried 'five star' (Field-Marshal or, in American terms, General of the Army) rank. In 1948, Juin had very brusquely refused command of the Western European Union's land forces, a command offered him by President Auriol and Prime Minister Queuille at the Elysée Palace. Juin had argued that the project was ill-conceived and not in France's true interests, and that no effective defence of Europe could be organised without American participation. Behind his decision was also his view that his presence in Morocco was the more urgent priority. De Lattre's contention, that command of the land forces would be subordinate to the 'five star' Field-Marshal Montgomery, the overall chairman of the WEU Commander in Chief's Committee, was an additional reason for Juin's decision. In the next year, Juin should have retired from military service on reaching his sixtieth birthday; this requirement was waived and he was appointed French representative on the Committee of the Chiefs of Staff for Central Europe and the Western Mediterranean. This was followed in January 1951 by his appointment as Inspector-General of all three of France's Armed Services, an appointment which included within its functions Chairmanship of the Chiefs of Staff Committee, official Military Adviser to the Government and French military representative in Inter-allied councils. In turn and consequential upon de Lattre's departure for Indochina and General Eisenhower's appointment as NATO forces commander, Juin was selected in March 1951 by Eisenhower to be the Land Forces Commander of the Central European Theatre Command. By NATO thinking of the time this command had evolved to be that of the main Western land bastion, supported on the northern and southern flanks by commands held by admirals, British in the north, American in the south. Within the command were British, Belgian and Dutch forces in northern Germany with American and French troops in the centre and south. Juin's *maréchalat* with, in NATO terms, five star rank, followed in May 1952 and as the only living Marshal of France Juin enjoyed a very significant status and position.

On his actual return to France from Morocco, Juin found his dual roles served by two separate staffs, one for his purely French national duties in Paris and one for the NATO Central Europe command at Fontainebleau. He himself settled into a personal routine of a morning ride, bridge in the evening and, whenever possible, hunting weekends, often in Germany.

In respect of his French national functions, Juin tried initially to interest the Americans in a project for the shared defence of South East Asia. The Americans, still preoccupied with Korea, refused to become involved beyond the provision of aid and equipment. As 1952 progressed and France's difficulties worsened, Juin came increasingly to believe that France could not support both a massive Indochina war and her European and North African commitments, these latter, in his view, in jeopardy as a result of Indochina. He did not believe a victory was possible in Indochina and advised successive governments to seek a political solution. For the immediate situation and after a visit to Indochina in February 1953, Juin gloomily recommended that the best that could be achieved was a thorough clearing out of the Viet-minh from the Delta area so enabling French forces to consolidate in south Tonkin. From there pursuit into the mountainous north could perhaps later be mounted and the Vietnam army built up. With success, he thought French troop reductions could follow late in 1954. Above all he urged that French forces should not become bogged down in static positions in the mountain areas.

Later in 1953 a new French Commander-in-Chief for Indochina, Navarre, was selected – not by Juin. At the time of his appointment, Juin commented on the Indochina situation in a letter to the Prime Minister. He noted that the French forces in the north had lost the initiative, and withdrawn into strongpoints; he had hoped these strongpoints, involving some twenty-five battalions, would have been sally ports from which, albeit on a small scale, harassing operations against the Viet-minh could have been launched. But he had found they were not able to do so and were in danger of being encircled and trapped. He believed that further reinforcements were necessary if Navarre was to regain any initiative. This advice is of particular interest, Juin appreciating, once again, that if an army withdrew into strongpoints and manoeuvre was lost, disaster would follow, as it was to do in the next year. It is advice also that needs to be set in the context of Juin's overall views; some military success was needed to strengthen the hand of those involved in political negotiations to end the fighting.

Juin's February 1953 advice was endorsed by a Committee of National Defence, which envisaged more offensive operations being mounted northwards from a secure south Tonkin towards the end of 1954. The Committee also warned against the French Army's acceptance of any commitment to defend the mountain area of north Laos, which would require a large force. But these policies were only embodied into a directive to Navarre in November 1953; meanwhile France had undertaken to defend Laos. Navarre accordingly decided to establish a strongpoint in the Dien Bien Phu bowl to cover Luang Prabang, Laos's capital. The decision was fatal, particularly in view of a catastrophic under-estimate of the Viet-minh's artillery capacity. The finest units of the French Army in Indochina were drawn from the Delta area to one where air support was difficult to provide. Giap, the Viet-minh commander, rearranged his plans so as to destroy the French force.

The catastrophe profoundly moved Juin, who had foreseen its likelihood. His former aide, Hervouët, was killed, which reduced him to tears, and he paid an especial and emotive visit to the *Légion Étrangère* depot in Algeria. Once again, the government asked Juin to go to Indochina with full powers as High Commissioner to restore morale and also to impress upon France the necessity to despatch conscript soldiers. After several days of thought Juin again declined. In his letter to Laniel, the Prime Minister, Juin pointed out that a mere name and a Marshal's title changed nothing, except perhaps for the worse in the likely event of fresh reverses. He said if he were to go he would need a very clear statement of French government aims, which he believed he would never be given in view of the divisions between those who wanted to fight on and those who like himself believed the troops in Indochina were *dangereusement aventurées* when they were in fact badly needed in Europe and North Africa. He recommended a politician of ministerial rank supported by an able subordinate

general. In the event, the Laniel government fell a little later and
Mendès-France, the next Prime Minister, signed the Geneva agreement with the full support of Juin. In 1956, the French government
wanted to appoint a commission of enquiry into the failure of the
Indochina campaign. Juin suspected that this commission, a political
one, would seek to blame the army. He reacted very angrily. In a
letter to the Minister for National Defence, Juin placed the blame on
the nation as a whole and its political leaders, who had tasked but
failed to support the Army.

Juin also advanced views on the organisation of defence, projecting
a case for a single Defence Ministry responsible for all the Armed
Services; this Ministry would execute defence policy as laid down by
the Prime Minister after consultation with the Committee of
National Defence. He wanted to see clearer distinctions between
ministerial staff concerned with policy decisions and those concerned
with day to day administration, and also a system of policy plans to
last for a number of years, not liable to sudden change at the fall of a
government. These arrangements were not introduced in Juin's time,
though several features of them were initiated in the Fifth Republic.

In his NATO role, Juin had particular problems more practical
and less theoretical than those that faced de Lattre. Most American
and British officers saw France as in irreversible decline with national
interests that could and should be subordinated to those of the Alliance or its major members. French claims for a leading role, in some
form of directorate of three, were ignored. At a purely military level,
NATO staffs worked in English and used either American or British
concepts, exercise procedures and training programmes. A tradition
of the French voice being one of protest rather than consent was
already forming. Juin had also once again to contend with a precarious political base, successive ministers holding different views on
France's role in the alliance.

At Fontainebleau Juin's initial preoccupations were first: his belief
that the land forces commander must also command the theatre air
forces, which Eisenhower initially felt should be kept for deployment
on either NATO flank if necessary, but which were conceded to Juin's
land command in 1953, next came the complex NATO lines of communication, those supplying the British and American Armies running north to south to Bremen and Hamburg parallel with the front,
and from a French point of view more alarmingly, seeming to suggest
a line of retreat to the North Sea rather than a defence of the French
border. He persuaded the Americans to use French ports but was

unable to prevent the British selection of Antwerp. From the outset, Juin also gave attention to a problem to cause him ever deepening anxiety in the next four years, the heavy in-theatre numerical superiority of the Soviet Army and the lack of depth for defence, there being but 150 kilometres between the inner German border in Thuringia and the Rhine. The only effective check to a mass Soviet onslaught would be American atomic weaponry over which Juin had no control, the Americans not even revealing to him their plans for the use of nuclear power. The very cavalier personal style of Eisenhower's successor, Ridgway, fuelled the disharmony. Juin had however to make plans for some form of defence on the assumption that, for one reason or another, nuclear weapons would not be available. The plan that he made provided for a covering force screen of troops *in situ*, tasked to obstruct and delay a Soviet attack while stronger forces were mobilised. Predictably, this did not suit the deputy Commander at SHAPE, Montgomery. Among several points of friction, Juin held that without German troops, little more than a delaying check on any Soviet advance could be achieved, and he counselled that plans for a withdrawal west of the Rhine also be prepared. This project, realistic in the context of the contemporary force levels, was authorised in secrecy, despite strong opposition from Montgomery.

Juin saw his role at this time as including the supervision of some reorganisation of the logistic supply routes, his attendance on exercises and where possible, ensuring that the exercises corresponded with his assessment of how the Soviets (based on studies of the Soviet Army in 1944) might actually launch an attack, and the persuasion of political figures from NATO countries of the need to provide more troops and equipment. In March 1952 he attempted to persuade President Auriol of this in a stormy interview, Juin even threatening to resign. Auriol considered Juin was speaking out of turn and relations between the two men suffered another reverse. By NATO agreements in 1952, France was supposed to increase her 1951 contribution of fourteen active divisions committed to NATO to a total of twenty active and twenty reserve divisions. But with inflation running at over 25 percent, and the Indochina war engrossing over 40 percent of the defence budget, the actual contribution in 1953 was less than half of that promised. This shortfall inevitably weakened Juin's hand in the politics of NATO and Fontainebleau.

In 1953, Juin's hand was however, somewhat strengthened by the promotion of his old Italy campaign friend and fellow bridge player, General Gruenther. Gruenther had been Ridgway's Chief of Staff, he was now to succeed him. Gruenther reorganised Juin's command to provide him with a chief of staff, and air, land and naval subordinate commanders all of whom, except the airman, were French officers. At the same time General Norstad was appointed the Alliance's first Air Commander-in-Chief alongside the Supreme Commander, a judgement worthy of Solomon if somewhat overweight. In the event, Juin later recognised that the land subordinate commander was not necessary and the command structure had become top-heavy, with dangers of friction in time of stress.

By now the developments in battlefield nuclear weapons by both the United States and the Soviet Union, together with Gruenther's decision that a major Soviet attack, even if non-nuclear, might have to be met by first-use atomic weapon counter-measures were adding to Juin's worries over strategy. His first theoretical proposition, seemingly designed for conflict that was not nuclear and might not develop into a nuclear exchange, was the result of the work of a staff study cell appointed by Juin and under another colleague from the Italian campaign, General Pedron. Returning to his favourite theme, manoeuvre at tactical level, Juin advocated light mobile battle groups to complement the major NATO formations, which he believed inadequate to contain a Soviet onslaught on any firm line. Penetrations of any line, in other words Soviet forces fanning out into NATO rear areas, could be dealt with by these lighter mobile battle groups, so avoiding the necessity of withdrawing the major formations from key areas. Juin envisaged that these groups be French-equipped, and believed that such equipment would not be too costly.

At the end of 1953, Juin took his tactical argument a stage further with his Shield and Javelin, *Bouclier et Javelot* concept. The Shield would have to provide time and cover for a riposte to the first Soviet shock, and would have to make provision for dispersion, the absence of a clear front-line (*fronts discontinus*), and rear area protection. It would be composed of a number of small defensive positions, spaced well apart, and well dug in against nuclear attacks. The Javelin would have to be deployed very quickly and would take the form of light mobile strike forces equipped with rockets, nuclear weapons tasked to find and destroy Soviet communications, equipment and ability to fight. He drew a distinction between tactical and strategic nuclear weapons, believing the former could be used on the German battlefield without risk of the latter being used against France. Juin also expressed further doubts on the suitability of traditional large military formations, armies, army corps and divisions for the nuclear battlefield. He saw them as too heavy and unwieldy, with cumbersome combat procedures, and very vulnerable to napalm, rockets and armour-piercing shells, even if nuclear weapons were not used, and providing no real answer to the problem of numerical inferiority. Fire power, movement and the abandonment of any idea of a continuous front – which he saw as simply giving an enemy the initiative and choice of area in which to strike – were his solution to the tactical problem.

Similarly, he saw the German battlefield in strategic terms, as one in which there should be a number of strongly held zones sited in depth and covering vital airfields and logistic installations. In the areas between these zones an enemy would be lured, by the withdrawal of light screening forces, to points where he would be struck out by carefully prepared nuclear strikes. For this scenario Juin argued for smaller formations with lighter equipment capable of more flexible tactics. More specifically, he wanted light armoured vehicles that infantry could use. These vehicles were to be small, lightly armoured with a good cross country capability and carrying anti-tank and medium machine-gun weaponry. He repeated his belief that these could be produced inexpensively and deployed 'in swarms' in the areas between the fortified defensive positions and in the enemy's rear, in the manner of the horsed cavalry of the past. He also, without ruling out digging-in in radiation-proof hides in some cases, saw mobility as the better protection against nuclear attack and fall out.

At the time these ideas and the *engins du Maréchal* were viewed with polite scepticism or disinterest within NATO. With hindsight, however, it can be seen that Juin's views contained much that was later to emerge as NATO doctrine. He was one of the first senior commanders anywhere to think through the problem of the land tactical nuclear battle. As *engins* the French army received developments, with greater gun or anti-tank missile first power, of the already existing AMX 13 light tank and EBR eight wheeled armoured car. Experimental light mechanised divisions were also created, and were a little later emulated by the Americans.

On other Central Front problems, Juin also offered interesting views. He believed that Northern Italy should be included in his command, though accepting that peninsula Italy was a Mediterranean problem; this view did not find favour. He was generally strongly in favour of German rearmament as the only method to level up with the Soviet mass of manpower – though his particular

views on the European Defence Community project are examined
further later. He envisaged German units in the immediate couverture
role, sustaining the initial shock of a Soviet assault while other
NATO forces built up strength for the ripostes; he was totally
opposed to any reduction of French forces as a consequence of German rearmament. He believed that the increased number of soldier
available – the twelve divisions of the Bundeswehr – would serve two
useful purposes. They would reduce the likelihood of a nuclear war
by making it less necessary, and they would improve the chances of
keeping all conflict, especially any nuclear one, away from French
soil. But he was also apprehensive both for the British – with whom,
especially Field-Marshal Montgomery, he had found relations difficult – and for France over the implications of so many German
formations for NATO command appointment; he correctly foresaw
German claims. But in the NATO context, his longest lasting concern
was that France should as soon as possible fully join *'l'aristocratie des
puissances atomiques'*. For him a land command in which another
nation controlled the nuclear weapons and would not reveal its plans
for their use was an impossible situation. He was profoundly worried
also by the delay that followed the Soviet threat to use nuclear
weapons against Britain and France at the time of the Suez crisis.
Eight days elapsed before the United States promised retaliation if
the Soviets were to strike.

These activities and views, although sometimes controversial, were
all within accepted limits of controversy. Juin as a Marshal earned
his first official reprimand, from the Minister of Defence, in June 1952
when at a Verdun anniversary ceremony he praised the role and
leadership of Pétain at Verdun in the First World War; any praise
for Pétain was still seen as sympathy for Vichy. It was however Juin's
views on the proposal for a European Defence Community that were
to blow up into a major political storm.

The EDC project was first put forward by the Pleven government in
1951; a European Army was seen as the best and safest method of
allowing West German rearmament. The idea met with opposition
within France and later rejection by other NATO members, including
Britain. Juin approved, in principle, of German rearmament but had
no faith in a supra-national army. 'Coal and steel can be fused together, but one cannot fuse an Army together' he remarked.

Unwisely, successive governments did not properly consult Juin
on the project as a policy, but only on certain technical details. But, as
originally proposed, the EDC was to have an army that would be

unified down to unit level. Juin correctly believed that in such conditions the French Army would lose its identify, and above all its capacity to fulfil national out-of-theatre or other overseas commitments. In April 1953 he wrote to the Prime Minister of the time, Mayer, stating that he could not support the project and a successor for him should be considered.

Other matters at the time, however, created a lengthy political crisis and it was only in late 1953 and early 1954, under the Laniel government, that Juin could return to the charge. He argued strongly that despite the addition of protocols which were to be added to the treaty, so as to give member nations the right to use certain units for national purposes, the treaty was nevertheless wrong in principle. He put forward his own proposal, that of a community of contiguous West European sovereign states working collectively but strictly within the overall framework of NATO. He saw this community as being the sole means of ensuring that guarantees given by the 'Anglo-Saxons' would be honoured.

Laniel did not accept this view, while Juin came to feel that the government was presenting the EDC project to the nation as one that carried the support of the Army. He decided that he must, therefore, speak out in public and chose a reserve officers function on Saturday 27 March 1954 at Auxerre as the occasion. His speech covered defence generally, but in respect of the EDC he was particularly forthright. He protested openly at not having been consulted and stated that the whole treaty, even with the addition of protocols, was too inflexible, the protocols themselves being both vague and inadequate. He made clear his hope that Parliament would reject it in favour of an alternative scheme.

On the following Monday, there were major press reports, some under banner headlines on 'Marshal Opposed to EDC' themes, of his speech; the reports also carried a note that the Prime Minister was summoning him for an explanation, giving the precise time so that the press and photographers could be present. Juin first heard of this summons from a newspaper – he told his aide-de-camp that he was not prepared to be treated like a bugle boy and refused to go. He followed this up with a letter to the Prime Minister recording his displeasure at reading of the summons in the press and, while offering to give his views, declining to do so in response to a summons presented to the public as they might have been directed to a trumpeter. He went on to say that he felt he had no alternative course but to speak out in view of the *'conspiration du silence'* and reminded Laniel that post-war critics of the inter-war years senior military officers often alleged those officers had not been sufficiently outspoken.

Laniel expressed regret at the terms of Juin's letter and ordered the Marshal to report to him at 7 pm that evening, the 31st March. Juin, whose brother-in-law had just died, again refused. But he did say that he would be willing to meet Laniel on some other occasion provided that there was no publicity, and also provided that a 1939 instruction which required serving officers to seek permission before they spoke in public was not to be levelled against him. He then went to attend a cavalry reserve officers dinner at which, when asked about the EDC, he replied testily that he was not prepared to repeat a mass for the deaf.

On his return to his flat after the dinner, Juin's aide received a telephone call, this time from the Elysée, the Presidential palace, requiring Juin to accept an urgent communication. A little later this was delivered by an Elysée official, and the aide took it to Juin saying that an acknowledgement was required. Juin was never at his best when woken and replied in terms very soldierly; his tactful aide returned to tell the Elysée official that the Marshal had no comment to make. The communication was in fact a Cabinet decision depriving Juin of his French national appointments, functions and staffs, most importantly membership of the Permanent Military Committee, and the measure was publicised by a decree in the following morning's *Journal Officiel*. The reader may need reminding that this fracas was taking place at the height of the Dien Bien Phu drama. Also on the next day, 1 April 1954, Juin offered Gruenther his resignation from his NATO command, an offer which Gruenther refused, pointing out that there was no certainty that a French officer would be chosen to succeed Juin if he did go. Nevertheless, the NATO Council passed a resolution censuring Juin for his opposition to the EDC and the Italian government refused to allow him to attend a *CEF* Veteran's rally in Italy. Many Frenchmen believed the censure motion reflected British ambitions to secure Juin's post for a British officer. In fact, Juin's common sense rendered NATO and his country a very great service.

The clash occasioned excited press reports and political debate. Some argued that if Juin had chosen to speak in favour of the EDC he would not have been disciplined. Others argued Juin's tone was simply not acceptable. But massive unexpected and unqualified support both for Juin's views and his conduct came from de Gaulle – at that time generally reticent on political matters.

The affair fizzled out. In July, the newly installed Mendès-France government, which badly needed Juin to underwrite its proposed constitutional package for Tunisia, issued a decree restoring Juin to almost all his previous privileges and functions. In August, the French Assembly voted down the EDC project, some members undoubtedly influenced by Juin's views. Juin was consulted by Mendès-France on all other major military matters as if nothing had occurred. The long term significance of the event was that it was yet another example of political jobbery that the constitutional arrangements of the Fourth Republic seemed inevitably to throw up; as such it was another, albeit early, nail in the Fourth Republic's coffin. The signs of this were there to be seen. Already, before Dien Bien Phu, there was large scale dissatisfaction in France with the régime and its constant changes of government. After the EDC affair, Juin received visits from a number of people who hinted that he should take the issue further, in particular to attend a ceremony at the Arc de Triomphe on 9 May. It was remarked that the Elysée was not far distant from the Arc de Triomphe, that Juin's presence at the ceremony would draw so much obvious support that the government would fall, and that the Marshal could then offer himself as a presidential candidate. Juin flatly refused.

Last Years; Breach With de Gaulle; Death

Juin remained in his NATO command until 1 October 1956, on which date he resigned. He was then 67, nearly 68. General Gruenther was being recalled to the United States and Juin had no wish to serve under any other American general. He was increasingly irked by the restrictions on the use of atomic fire power, and even planning, being kept exclusively in American hands, leaving other NATO commanders in an anomalous position. NATO exercises had highlighted these dilemmas very clearly; recent exercises too had also shown up France's weakened military capabilities, a result of the Indochina and Algerian wars. The trend within the Alliance to subordinate, ignore or, in the case of Algeria, even oppose, French national interests had developed. Juin had sincerely and honestly tried to contribute to the Alliance, but his frustrations as a NATO commander contributed to the anti-NATO resentment forming in the mind of de Gaulle. This anti-NATO resentment was to worry Juin in the last years of his life.

Retirement was to provide the ageing Marshal with torment rather than tranquillity, as the flames of revolt spread across his beloved Algeria. In matters military he quite correctly avoided all day to day issues but his advice on wider military questions was still sought, and as a Marshal he was a member of the *Conseil Supérieur des Forces Armées*, for which he was entitled to have a small staff. Juin turned to writing, his anxieties over Algeria figuring large in his first book, *Le Maghreb en Feu*, which appeared in 1957. In this work he argued that the Maghreb was linked historically with Europe and was an essential component of the security of the *bloc Eurafrique*, but the region was being deliberately and bloodily subverted by the Soviet Union under the guise of support for Arab nationalism. Algeria at least had to remain linked to France. He hoped for a federal linkage which would accommodate a *'personalité algérienne'*. He did not see this future being achieved either by integration or universal suffrage, but he hoped constitutional experts could devise a method of representation which would nevertheless carry a legitimacy. Next followed in 1959 and 1960 two volumes of *Mémoires*. These, well documented and compiled with fastidious care covered only the years 1943 to 1956 and state Juin's position in a number of events simply and clearly. However, on a few occasions, notably concerning his time in Morocco, Juin was economic with the truth. In 1960 also appeared *Je suis Soldat*, perhaps his best book, a little autobiographical work covering his life up to 1943. This engaging account is much more subjective and revealing of his personality than the *Mémoires*. In 1962 his *La Campagne d'Italie* followed.

Juin's anguish over Algeria found literary expression in his novel *C'étaient nos Frères*, which also appeared in 1962. The plot is thin, the hero an army colonel whose career and views were modelled on those of the writer and who is killed by the Algerian insurgents. Most of the pages express Juin's anguish over the approaching abandonment of Algeria and Algerians loyal to France. Officers and officials from Algeria regularly visited him and kept him informed on developments. He anguish was clearly evidenced in political terms by periodic speeches and articles. As early as 1956, he besought de Gaulle to act to save Algeria but de Gaulle, in a letter nevertheless warm and friendly, declined. In 1957, Juin gave full support to the Mollet Socialist government when it despatched massive reinforcements to Algeria enabling Salan, the Army commander, to develop the threefold system of area defence known as *quadrillage*, heavily fortified frontier lines, and highly mobile intervention forces which came to contain and later virtually destroy, the insurgents. Juin also urged, without success, French governments to authorise 'hot pursuit' of insurgent groups seeking rest and refuge in Tunisia, and spoke out contemptuously of the Anglo-French failure to follow up the success of the Suez landing and overthrow Nasser.

In May 1958, the disorders and the seizure of power by a revolutionary committee of *colons* and Army officers in Algiers finally destroyed the Fourth Republic and on 1 June de Gaulle assumed power. Juin was initially overjoyed, particularly as de Gaulle had only a little previously hinted at a senior appointment for him connected with Algeria. In the event, to Juin's bitter disappointment, others were nominated. As a final gesture of reconciliation after the EDC affair, Juin was given a seat on the newly reconstituted Supreme Defence Council, *Conseil Supérieur de la Defense Nationale*, which he accepted. He was also offered a post as Inspector General of National Defence; this Juin evidently suspected would be one without any real power and might simply be designed to keep him quiet. He therefore declined. In practice, de Gaulle deliberately avoided consulting Juin almost from the start of his period as head of government.

As time passed and it became clearer that de Gaulle was not going to follow the right-wing *Algérie Française* path which so many soldiers and *colons* had expected of him, Juin's despair returned. Initially, he kept his anxieties to a private circle of friends; also, in a typically *colon* misjudgement, he saw the September 1958 referendum result as an expression of an all-Algerian loyalty to France. As late as May 1959, while more freely expressing his private doubts, Juin was still prepared to speak out in support of de Gaulle's Algerian policies in very traditional French Army terms – France and its Army being, as in the past, willing to develop the majority population of Algeria and protect it against any oppressive minority. Another facet of traditional French thinking was also emerging at this time, the *Cité Catholique* network of Catholic groups and cells in the Army with its own news bulletin, *Verbe*. The *Cité Catholique* philosophy was one in which Catholicism was seen as the only real defence against all forms of materialism, Marxist or consumer which liberal democracy too often abetted. In respect of Algeria, *Verbe* was strongly in favour of integration. Juin attended the 1959 Congress along with Weygand and several other senior officers.

In September 1959, however, de Gaulle spoke for the first time openly about a self-determination, even independence, option for Algeria; the other options being integration or a French supported Algeria governed by Algerians. For Juin, the self-determination option would inevitably lead to independence; he was now no longer prepared to give de Gaulle's delphic statements the benefit of any doubt. After five weeks of thought, he wrote an article in a Paris daily, *L'Aurore*; in this he claimed that de Gaulle's option would simply give comfort to the insurgents, but which only gave the greatest anxiety to him and other French Algerians. He once again urged hot pursuit or other action against insurgent bases in neighbouring territories.

De Gaulle, nettled, instructed his Prime Minister, Debré to ask Juin for an explanation, which a reluctant Debré, who had some sympathy with Juin's views carried out perfunctorily. Juin, however, followed his criticism with a confused and confusing letter to the President. In this he somewhat ingeniously claimed his letter was not a personal attack upon the President but an attempt to attract public attention to the gamble being taken by inclusion of the self-determination option. He concluded on the one hand by foreseeing a situation in which, personally torn apart, he might have to return his Marshal's baton and Grand Cross of the Legion of Honour, and on the other, by assuring de Gaulle of his continuing friendship. De Gaulle replied briefly but not unkindly to say that he would see Juin but could not do so for the moment.

The next year, 1960, saw further drama. On 24 January began 'Barricades Week', a week of protest by the Algiers *colons* against de Gaulle's transfer of the popular parachute general Massu, who had remarked that de Gaulle's policies were no longer understood. The *colons* had stockaded a large area of Algiers city. Juin learnt that de Gaulle had instructed Debré to go to Algiers and give, if necessary, an order to open fire on the rebels. Donning uniform and with his aide – who later provided Juin's biographer with an account of the extraordinary interview that followed – Juin arrived at the Elysée to see de Gaulle.

The forty-five minute interview began with the Marshal angrily demanding that no order to fire be given on Frenchmen whose sole desire was to remain French; de Gaulle equally furious replied that they were lawbreakers in revolt. Both men became excited and began to shout. Juin threatened to oppose the President publicly, a threat to which de Gaulle replied by saying that he would break Juin; in turn Juin told de Gaulle that he could do what he liked with his Marshal's baton. But, emotion soon spent, the two old soldiers, still bound by the loyalty of the 1912 Fez *promotion* of Saint Cyr then exchanged condolences on the death of de Gaulle's brother, and revived memories of the past; de Gaulle voiced gloomy fears of a Communist resurgence. On leaving the Elysée Juin encountered Debré, just back from Algiers. Debré told Juin that it had not been necessary to open fire and hinted that the President had a mission in Algeria in mind for Juin. For this Juin waited several days – in vain.

The year 1960 saw a slow, steady worsening of the Algerian situation with on-going large-scale fighting and the failure of one peace initiative; at the same time, in November, a speech by de Gaulle envisaged an Algerian Algeria, governed by Algerians, with its own institutions and laws all leading to a Republic of Algeria. A referendum on this proposal was to follow in January 1961. For Juin the agony increased; visitors and a massive post-bag from soldiers and *colons* in Algeria besought his support and help, but the policy he saw as disastrous was being pursued by his head of government who was in addition his chief in the Second World War and of the same Saint Cyr *promotion* as himself. An additional twist of pain, one especially sharp to a soldier who had commanded North African troops, was the growing anxiety of French officers in Algeria that de Gaulle's policies were going to lead to the abandonment of the many thousands of Algerians who had fought for the French cause in Algeria or elsewhere, an abandonment that would result in revenge massacres. While raising this issue with Messmer, the Defence Minister, Juin nevertheless continued until November to remain quiet in public and emphasise the importance of obedience to gatherings of Service officers. Also related to the Army was a movement to encourage young conscripts serving in Algeria to desert, the 'Manifesto of the 121' group. Juin with some 300 other political and military figures signed a public counter-manifesto.

De Gaulle's November speech, however, was for Juin the last straw. He announced, in a press communique, that he was not going to be present at the 11 November Armistice Day ceremonies. His statement bluntly stated that he was making this gesture, as the senior officer of the Army and as an Algerian, as a protest against the policy of abandonment of Algeria and its people, which he saw as a danger to France and the free world. De Gaulle replied with the issue of a decree, not however publicised, that relieved Juin of any official functions, a decree that by this time in the circumstances amounted to little.

At this time, a loose gathering of French political figures of several parties united by opposition to de Gaulle, the *'Front de l'Algérie Française'*, began to meet together. This Front drew up plans for the formation of a provisional French government in the event of an unforeseen (*inopine*) departure from office of de Gaulle. Juin does not appear to have been personally involved with the Front, but they nevertheless considered him as a Head for this administration. The plans never amounted to an actual conspiracy, but they were known to security officers and reported to de Gaulle, where they were to fuel the fires about to erupt.

The explosion occurred at the time of the referendum that de Gaulle had ordered. Juin, ever more alarmed by the reports of violence and communal hatred, asked to see de Gaulle, but he was refused an audience and told to put any views he might want to express in a letter. In a rage, Juin wrote an open letter to de Gaulle in which he protested against his being refused an audience, expressed his total opposition to the President's Algerian policy and announced he would vote 'No' in the coming referendum. Juin intended that de Gaulle should have a prior copy of the letter, but as the President was away from Paris, this prior copy never reached him and de Gaulle first saw the text in newsprint. There followed a new decree reconstituting the Supreme Defence Council so as to end the right of a Marshal to be a member. This in practice deprived Juin of almost all his small staff (though leaving him still his official apartment), and excluded him in a form of quarantine from all official correspondence and official ceremonies.

In April occurred the notorious coup attempt, led by four generals, in Algiers. The whole fabric of the Fifth Republic was shaken to its foundations and order only saved by the iron determination of de Gaulle and his brilliantly successful broadcast appeal to the French public at large, and in particular to the conscript soldiers serving in Algeria, to remain loyal. Although the conspirators saw a Eurafrican future for Algeria much as Juin had set out in *Le Maghreb en Feu*, Juin had nothing to do with the conspiracy and coup attempt which he instantly and openly condemned. The conspirators had correctly assessed that Juin's conception of loyalty and obedience would hold him loyal to de Gaulle. The younger colonels involved in the conspiracy, notably Argoud, even despised him as a man who would bluster but never act. Juin's personal anguish could however, be seen when in June he donned full uniform to visit the prison at Fresnes. There he sat silent for a while in a room into which a number of officers involved in the coup had been discreetly gathered.

No retribution followed for either this gesture, nor for a press article in which Juin appealed to France's allies, especially America, to try to intervene in support of some form of loose federal solution for France and Algeria. But there was to be one last humiliation for the old Marshal. One of the leaders of the Algiers coup attempt, General Salan, had gone underground in Algeria after the coup's failure. With the support of a number of officers, embittered soldiers from élite regular units, and *colons* he was directing the violence of a *maquis* known as *OAS, Organisation de l'Armée Secrète*. After a number of very bloody *OAS* outrages, French security forces began to close in on the cells of the movement. Seeing the end approaching, Salan sent a letter in March 1962 via an emissary, to Juin imploring his support. Juin very unwisely replied in a manuscript note of which he kept no copy; in this note he said firmly that however much he might sympathise with those torn by despair he could not act or intervene. He then wrote to de Gaulle to explain what he had done. But the *OAS* 'edited' the letter, taking phrases out of context and omitting others so as to portray Juin as being in support of their movement; they then published this version in a leaflet. Inevitably, a political storm blew up in Paris. De Gaulle's reaction was brutal. Juin was, without publicity, sentenced to thirty days of house arrest; one source claims that he was 'retired', unheard of for a Marshal of France. Except for one family sized car, his few remaining privileges and allowances were taken away and he was told he would have to pay for his official apartment, though this was later commuted to payment only of the taxes upon it. However, despite this humiliation, Juin continued to refuse any pleadings, even one from Bidault, to lead or even support any overt anti-de Gaulle movement.

Thee followed the last bitter acts of the Algerian debacle, the final appalling rounds of insurgent atrocities, *OAS* terror and killings, and savage French army reprisals, the disembarkation of the withdrawn French Army to a Marseille decorated with *FLN* and Communist flags, the evacuation in misery to France of over a million and a quarter *colons* the majority with no more luggage than a suitcase, the abandonment of thousands of loyalist Algerians, notably the *harki* irregular levy units, and the reports needing no exaggeration of the torture and massacre of these unfortunates. Juin saw these events as a monstrous betrayal. He retreated further into solitude and despair, writing, almost as an apologia for his own behaviour, his last book, *Trois Siècles d'Obéissance Militaire*. This is an overview of the French Army's history from the days of Louis XIV, stressing the theme of obedience and discipline. Of 1961, Juin drew the conclusion that when obedience broke down, fratricidal strife was the inevitable result. In an *avant propos*, Juin drew a distinction which he did not pursue, between simple military discipline and the concept of loyalty to a legitimate political authority, no matter what that authority did; he added, not entirely accurately, that he had always obeyed the government even when many thought that he should not have done so.

Not surprisingly, the events had told upon his health. In December 1963, he suffered a thrombosis and was taken to the Val de Grace hospital. He was not expected to recover and, although there had been no personal communication between them since 1960, President de Gaulle came to pay a last visit. Juin lay semi-conscious murmuring 'You see, over there, Constantine, Algeria, my country'. De Gaulle quietly replied 'Yes, I know your country is there, I do understand' and embraced him.

Always a man of strong constitution, Juin recovered in some measure, to live on another three years as a very frail old man. He had earlier been given a pleasant sinecure, *Conservateur* of the Domains of Chantilly, which included residence in an elegant country house with a fine art collection, and he divided his time between this and his Paris flat. His grandchildren gave him pleasure, as did country walks. He neither wrote any more nor commented on political events.

In November 1966, Juin's heart trouble recurred and he was again taken to the Val de Grace hospital, where after a brief rally, he died on 27 January 1967. President de Gaulle, in uniform, arrived to pay his last respects and offer his condolences to *La Marèchale*, the Marshal's widow. The Marshal's coffin then lay in state at the Invalides, guarded by officers, Saint Cyr cadets, and veterans of the Italian campaign. The presence of these veterans was a final illustration of Juin's outstanding characteristic as a battlefield general, the extraordinary devotion and loyalty he inspired, as a front-line soldier's general, amongst his soldiers.

On 1 February, Juin's coffin was taken with full military honours to Notre Dame Cathedral for the funeral service. Present at the service, some as pall-bearers, were many of Juin's surviving wartime and post-war comrades, Field-Marshal Alexander, General Ridgway, Generals Béthouart, Carpentier, Pedron and others.

Alphonse Juin was the last Marshal of France to die in the rank, and the last of three great field commanders who, after catastrophe, had fought with *passion* to liberate their country and regain its military pride. At the funeral service a solitary figure out in front of the congregation alone with his thoughts and memories, stood the President of the Fifth Republic. Charles de Gaulle, also with *passion*, had at his level re-cemented the country's political fabric; French military revival had been a vital component of this political process.

A national task was complete, a trauma had been surmounted, and the rank of Marshal of France was restored in honour.

Bibliographical Appendix

Alphonse Juin

No full biography of Juin has been written in English and indeed two important and otherwise reliable works of reference even note in brief entries that he was made a Marshal posthumously by de Gaulle. There is a useful chapter written by Colonel Alphonse Goutard in Field-Marshal Sir Michael Carver, *The War Lords*, (London, Weidenfeld, 1976), but this and both John Ellis, *Cassino, The Hollow Victory* (London, Andre Deutsch, 1984) and General Mark Clark, *Calculated Risk*, (London, Harrap, 1951) limit themselves to Juin's career to 1945.

Juin's own autobiographical writings must be a start for any French bibliography. *Je suis Soldat*, (Paris, Conquistador, 1960) covers his career to the Second World War; this is amplified and followed with his *Mémoires* in two volumes, (Paris, Fayard, 1959 and 1960). His two biographers' works should follow next, Bernard Pujo, *Juin, Maréchal de France* (Paris, Albin Michel, 1988) and General Chambe, *Le Maréchal Juin duc du Garigliano*, (Paris, Plon, 1983). Three other works written by Juin himself add to understanding; there are his *Le Maghreb en Feu* (Paris, Plon, 1957), his novel, *C'étaient nos Frères*, (Paris, Presses de la Cité, 1962) and his *Trois Siècles d'Obéissance Militaire*, (Paris, Plon, 1964). Also useful are two booklets, *Hommage au Maréchal Juin, Numéro Spécial du Bulletin de Liaison des Anciens du CEFI, Juin 1967, No. 49* and *Alphonse Juin, Maréchal de France*, (Musée de l'Armée, 1988).

In respect of particular phases of Juin's career General Beaufre, *Mémoires 1920–1940–1945*, (Paris, Presses de la Cité, 1965) and Armand Leoni and Marcel Spivak, *1942/43, La Campagne de Tunisie*, (Vincennes, S.H.A.T., 1985) are all useful on the war years.

A long paper written by Juin after the May 1945 violence in Algeria is published in part in *La Guerre d'Algérie I, L'Avertissement 1943–46*, (Vincennes, SHAT 1990): this document reflects his acute anxiety over the future of the territory.

For Juin's period as Resident-General in Morocco and his wider influence on North African affairs Pujo's *Juin* is weighted too heavily in favour of the Marshal to be satisfactory. Two useful basic texts are General Spillman's *Du Protectorat à l'Indépendance, Maroc 1912–1955*, (Paris, Plon, 1967) and Charles-Andre Julien's *Le Maroc Face aux Impérialismes, 1915–1956*, (Paris, Editions J.A., 1978). Spillman, a fastidiously scholarly general, writes critically but not without sympathy about Juin's policies. Julien's work is supported by massive footnoting but is marred by an obsessive animosity towards Juin that is revealed in *ad hominem* and spiteful comments. The footnoting is, however, important as the sources are documents, records of meetings or correspondence. President Auriol's memoirs and opinions of Juin were taken by Julien from the volumes of his *Journal du Septennat 1947–1954*. Julien also draws on the memoirs of Prime Minister Joseph Laniel, *Jours de Gloire et Jours Cruels, 1908–1958*, (Paris, Presses de la Cité, 1971) and on the memoirs of soldiers, including Commandant Antoine Argoud, *La Decadence, l'Imposture et la Tragédie*, (Paris, Fayard, 1974) and General Augustin Guillaume, *Hommes de Guerre*, (Paris, France-Empire, 1977). Finally Julien makes use of other works whose authors in one capacity or another have had access to official papers from which he quotes. These include Claude Paillat, *Vingt Ans qui déchirent la France, I, Le Guêpier*, (Paris, Laffont, 1969); J. R. Tournoux, *Secrets d'État*, (Paris, Plon, 1960), Romnauld Landau, *Moroccan Drama, 1900–1955*, (London, R. Hale, 1956); Roger Letourneau, *Evolution politique de l'Afrique du Nord musulmane, 1920–1961*, (Paris, Colin, 1962); Jean Lacouture, *Cinq Hommes et la France*, (Paris, Seuil, 1961); Stephane Bernard, *Le Conflit Franco-Marocaine 1945–56, I*, (Brussels, Univ. Libre. 1963); Georgette Elgey, *Histoire de la Quatrième Republique, I*, (Paris, Fayard, 1965) and Robert Barrat, *Justice Pour Le Maroc*, (Paris, Seuil, 1953).

Three of the four volumes of Yves Courrière's history of the Algerian conflict are useful. The second and third volumes, *Le Temps des Léopards*, and *L'Heure des Colonels*, (both Paris, Fayard, 1970) note Juin's actions early in the Algerian war and his apparent inactivity in the middle years 1956–1959. The last volume, *Les Feux du Désespoir* (Paris, Fayard, 1971) notes Juin's name on the list of a possible successor government to de Gaulle. Alastair Horne's *A Savage War of Peace*, (London, Macmillan, 1977), records Juin's name on the October 1960 counter-manifesto.

Nigel Hamilton's *Monty, The Field Marshal 1944–1976*, (London, Hamish Hamilton, 1986) notes Juin's objection to serving under Montgomery; this work also records Juin's belief in the need of a plan for a withdrawal west of the Rhine. Also useful on the early years of NATO is Michael M Harrison, *The Reluctant Ally, France and Atlantic Security*, (Baltimore, Johns Hopkins University, 1981).

The Times, 28 January 1967, published a somewhat ungenerous obituary of Juin. A general introduction to the *Armée d'Afrique*, setting out its especial allure, appears in Anthony Clayton, *France, Soldiers and Africa*, (London, Brasseys, 1988).

Jean de Lattre de Tassigny

A mass of material concerning de Lattre exists. For purely English readers there is one biography, Major General Sir Guy Salisbury-Jones, *So Full a Glory, a Life of Marshal de Lattre de Tassigny*, (London, Weidenfeld, 1954); much has however come to light since this book appeared. In French, perhaps the best biography is that of Jean-Luc Barré, *De Lattre*, (Paris, Perrin, 1990). Barré's work includes the photograph of de Lattre, *éperdu*, at the Vichy military parade described in Chapter 1. Also useful are Bernard Simiot, *De Lattre*, (Paris, Flammarion, 1953); Louis Chaigne, *Jean de Lattre, Maréchal de France*, (Paris, Lanore, n.d.); René Thomasset, *La Vie Exultante de Jean de Lattre de Tassigny*, (Paris, Baudiniere, n.d.); Jean d'Esme, *De Lattre*, (Paris, Hachette, n.d.); Jacques d'Infreville, *Le Roi Jean*, (Paris, La Table Ronde, 1964); Pierre Davcourt, *De Lattre en Vietnam, Une Armée de Victoires*, (Paris, La Table Ronde, 1965); (General) Vanuxem, *Le Général Vainqueur, Le Destin Exemplaire du General de Lattre en Indochine*, (Paris, SPL, 1971); Simonne de Lattre, *Jean de Lattre, Mon Mari*, (Paris, Presses de la Cité, 1986) and *Jean de Lattre, Ma Raison de Vivre*, (Paris, Presses de la Cité, 1978).

De Lattre himself wrote *Histoire de la Première Armée Française*, (Paris, Plon, 1949); this has been translated into English under the title of *The History of the French First Army*, (London, Allen and Unwin, 1952). More important are three volumes of De Lattre's papers collected and published under his name as the author.

These are Maréchal Jean de Lattre, *Ne Pas Subir, Ecrits 1914–1952*, (Paris, Plon, 1984), *Reconquérir, Ecrits 1944–1945*, (Paris, Plon, 1985) and *La Ferveur et le Sacrifice, Indochine 1951*, (Paris, Plon, 1988).

A useful folder of documents, *Jean de Lattre, Maréchal de France* edited by the Institut Jean Moulin is published by the Ministère de l'Education Nationale Académie de Bordeaux. Also informative is Volume 3, 1989 issue of the *Revue Historique des Armées* which contains four biographical articles under the collective title of 'Dossier de Lattre'.

Other works not primarily concerned with de Lattre add to knowledge of his activities at different stages of his career. Bernard Destremau, *Weygand*, (Paris, Perrin, 1989) suggests that Weygand was the real target of the Left after the events of February 1934. Much detail on de Lattre's style of command in the Liberation campaign appears in General Beaufre, *Mémoires, 1920–1940–1945*, (Paris, Presses de la Cité, 1965).

De Lattre's period at Fontainebleau is additionally described from two British points of view in Nigel Hamilton, *Monty, The Field-Marshal 1944–1976*, (London, Hamish Hamilton, 1986) and with rather more understanding in George Mallaby, *From My Level*, (London, Hutchinson, 1965). Philippe Heduy, *La Guerre d'Indochine 1945 – 54*, (Paris, SPL, 1981), contains interesting first-hand accounts of de Lattre at work in the field by Generals Allard and Vanuxem, and at political levels by Georges Gautier.

Phillipe Leclerc de Hauteclocque

Several biographies of Leclerc de Hauteclocque exist. One is in English, Henry Maule, *Out of the Sand*, (London, Odhams, 1966) but this is very sketchy. The best biography is written by a close associate of Leclerc, General Vézinet, *Le Général Leclerc*, (Paris, Editions J'ai Lu, 1982). Also useful are Andre Martel and Pierre Goumen, *Leclerc, Un Homme, Un Chef, Une Epopée*, (Paris, Charles Lavauzelle, 1987) and Adren Dansette, *Leclerc*, (Paris, Flammarion, 1952).

The Fondation Maréchal Leclerc de Hauteclocque held two *colloques*, in 1987 and 1990 respectively, on aspects of the Marshal's life. Very interesting papers from the first have been published as *Le Général Leclerc et l'Afrique Française Libre*, (Paris, Fondation Maréchal Leclerc de Hauteclocque, 1990). General P Duplay, of the Fondation, kindly sent me three of the papers of the 1990 *colloque*, the subject of which was Leclerc's post-war service in Indochina, his own and those of General Crepin and M. de Valence.

For Leclerc's period in Indochina, several additional works are helpful. The best general background introduction in English is J Davidson, *Indochina: Signposts in the Storm*, (Kuala Lumpur, Longman Malaysia, 1979), and the best full history of the war, as noted earlier, is General Yves Gras, *Histoire de la Guerre d'Indochine*, (Paris, Plon, 1979). *La Guerre d'Indochine, I, Le Retour de la France en Indochine, 1945–1946*, (Vincennes, SHAT 1987) provides the text of documents and other useful detail. Giap, in an interview published in Section 6 of the *New York Times Magazine* of 24 June 1990 confirms Ho Chi Minh's initial willingness to retain a French affiliation. Also particularly informative on Leclerc's role is René Pleven's contribution 'Leclerc, le Hoche de l'Indochine' in Philippe Heduy, *Histoire de l'Indochine, 1624–1954*, (Paris, SPL, 1983). Leclerc's remark to Schumann about the passing of colonial empires appears in the 1990 *colloque* volume *Le General Leclerc et l'Afrique Française Libre*.

Index

(Ranks and Honours are those held at the time of mention in the work).